America's
Immigrant Women

America's Immigrant Women

By CECYLE S. NEIDLE

HIPPOCRENE
BOOKS, INC.

First Paperback Edition Published 1976 by

HIPPOCRENE BOOKS, INC.
171 Madison Avenue
New York, N. Y. 10016

Library of Congress Catalog Card Number 75-37110
ISBN 0-88254-369-5

MANUFACTURED IN THE UNITED STATES OF AMERICA

Contents

About the Author

Cecyle S. Neidle is editor of Twayne's Immigrant Heritage of America Series. She received her Ph.D. from the Department of American Civilization at New York University and has had a life-long interest in the immigrant and particularly in the human element, the lives and personalities of those who have created the America we live in today. Her previous contributions to the Immigrant Heritage of America Series have included *Great Immigrants* (1973) and *The New Americans* (1967), wherein more than sixty immigrants recount the experience of America as they lived it.

Preface

It is agreed that the United States is a nation of immigrants, but there is some disagreement about who should be excluded from this designation. There is no objection to labeling true immigrants those who began to venture forth across the ocean after the Revolution, and the "huddled masses" of the late nineteenth and early twentieth century immigrants. But the first settlers?

Those who were the first to enter the wilderness of a new continent can also be considered immigrants in the sense that they left their homelands to take up life in a new setting, even though most of these newcomers were moving to colonies of what were their mother countries—Great Britain, Holland, Sweden. The immigrant label does not negate the legitimate claim that they were colonists. The bulk of the early settlers came to America with the intention of remaining, but some returned to their natal countries. These, too, can be said to be immigrants, if only transiently so. The necessity of adjusting to a new mode of existence and accepting alterations in life-style is what basically distinguishes the immigrant from the visitor. It is this broad meaning of the term "immigrant" that is being used in this book about one particular group of such newcomers—women.

Hence this book begins with the wives and daughters of the earliest immigrants—the seventeenth and eighteenth century settlers—proceeds to representatives of the early and late nineteenth century, and concludes with some twentieth century figures, many of whom are still living.

The facts are that immigrants as a group made contributions of incalculable import to the development of the nation, and that the term "immigrant" relates to both men and women. Most discussions of the immigrant contribution are confined to the achievements of males. But women? The general assumption is that mature women immigrants functioned predominantly as wives and mothers, and their young daughters as domestics and factory workers of some kind until they, too, joined the ranks of wives and mothers.

This is true enough, but it is not the whole truth. If it were, it could be summed up in one sentence and nothing more would need to be said. There would be no excuse for a book on this subject. But all immigrant women were *not* just wives and mothers.

Many possessed valuable skills which some at least used to good advantage. There were also among the newcomers educated women who had received a classical education, or had been interrupted in the pursuit of one, even in Russia and in Poland, where education was severely restricted and to Jews almost unavailable. They needed only an opportunity to make use of their abilities and/or training, and not infrequently they found it, though not without considerable perseverance. Also there were among them professionally trained women, some of whom were forced in the beginning to work as "hands" (at various kinds of factory work, including sewing). There is at least one of them in the book, and she was an experienced physician. For those who were young and ambitious and had received some educational preparation in their places of birth there were no barriers to returning to American schools and fitting themselves for positions that offered broad scope for social and professional advancement, or starting from scratch. But even domestic and factory workers possessed abilities which the frustrations of being an immigrant brought to the surface. One who had begun as a domestic was invited to meet the King and Queen of England when they visited the White House. Clearly President Roosevelt and his wife considered her an American woman to be proud of. Her story is also in the book.

Not even the wives and daughters of the first settlers in the British colonies can be dismissed as *just* wives and mothers. Anne Hutchinson, who was wife and mother, was a leading figure in the Massachusetts Bay Colony, and was both famous and infamous. Anne Bradstreet was also a most devoted consort and mother, but at the same time the first woman poet on American soil, and her poems were good enough to be hailed in England where there was never a dearth of good poets.

As for Hannah Callowhill Penn, the wife of William Penn, proprietor of "Pennsylvania," she possessed high business acumen and her abilities were invaluable to her financially inexperienced husband. But it was precisely as wives of the first settlers and mothers of the first native generation that these women were so magnificent. Can the possibility be denied that had these women been less brave, less willing to endure hardships to which they were totally unaccustomed, less supportive of their husbands, the growth of the first settlements would have been set back, if not foiled? Also can the claim be easily set aside that the reason why the northern colonies flourished more rapidly and more luxuriantly than the southern ones, may lie in the presence of wives, who were much scarcer, if not absent, in the southern plantations?

Because this book was envisaged in a historical perspective, it had to keep pace with national development. In what way did women newcomers contribute to national progress? In the same way as men though with understandable modifications. They did not work as seamen, or on canals and the first arteries of communication to the West, as wilderness guides, or on railroads, but they worked on farms, in stores, as tavern and boardinghouse keepers and in other occupations, either alongside their husbands or alone. They started schools, not only "Dame schools"; they participated in the reform movement of the nineteenth century and not only helped in giving reform a big push forward, but initiated specific reforms. Yes, several of them were the leaders and native women their followers. This is in the book too. In the twentieth century when millionaires seemed to grow on trees, some women of foreign birth also reached "millionairedom," as Andrew Carnegie smugly put it. Among those of strong religious convictions there were nurses, administrators of hospitals and orphanages. Others labored in promoting social goals.

During the postbellum decades when the labor movement kept pace with accelerated immigration and women began to enter the labor market in droves, a new class of working women was formed, and out of their midst arose an extraordinary able group of foreign-born women—union organizers and labor leaders —some of them very young and untutored, whose latent abilities were sharpened by the competitive struggle around them. Their lives in Europe had not prepared them for their new role, for, with the exception of Emma Goldman, most young women were kept at home carefully sheltered. Their teacher was America itself. Some of their achievements were astounding.

In the mid-nineteenth century three immigrant women were the first women in the world to force open the medical profession to women. There were no trained women physicians in the United States or Europe until an English immigrant of the 1830s, Elizabeth Blackwell, earned the first medical certificate ever awarded to a woman. One hundred years later women emigrés began significantly to augment the roster of physicians, especially in a new branch of medicine, psychiatry and psychoanalysis. There were also outstanding foreign-born women scientists. Two of them are Nobel Prize winners.

A most significant contribution was made by women in the musical fields as singers, performers on musical instruments, and teachers. Even though many, but by no means all, returned to their places of birth, we are indebted to singers and instrumentalists for the pleasures they brought to American audiences and to music teachers for creating a large group of superbly trained American musicians, judged to be the equal of any trained in Europe.

Some categories of women immigrants—teachers, lawyers, judges, creators of the visual arts—had to be omitted for reasons of space, but the female tycoons could not be passed over.

These then are the women in the book. With the submission of the evidence the author rests her claim that foreign-born women, no less than men, played distinctive roles in American society from the beginnings of the American experience.

CECYLE S. NEIDLE

Acknowledgments

I gratefully acknowledge the help given me by Gay Wilson Allen, Professor of English at the Graduate School of New York University, who read the entire manuscript, and that of Mr. Jacob Steinberg, president of Twayne Publishers, who not only went over the whole manuscript with a careful editorial pen, but whose enthusiasm for the project was a constant encouragement.

I am also indebted to the following: Professor Bayrd Still, head of history at New York University, who made his counsel available to me, Professor Kenneth O. Bjork of Saint Olaf College, Professor Barbara Miller Solomon of Harvard University, Professor Sheila Tobias of Wesleyan University, Professor Sally Miller of the University of the Pacific, Professor Babette Inglehart of Chicago State University, Professor George J. Prpic of John Carroll University, Professor Henry L. Feingold of Baruch College, the City University of New York, Mr. Leon Stein, editor of *Justice*, all of whom read parts of the manuscript and contributed their time and their valuable insights to this endeavor.

My debt extends also to the librarians with whom I came into contact, those patient, knowledgeable scholars who can do so much to ease one's path through the mazes of research. I want to thank particularly Ms. Judith Schiff of Yale University, Mrs. Dorothy Swanson at the Tamiment Library of New York University, an unnamed, but most kind and courteous librarian at Union Theological Seminary, the librarian of the Medical College of Pennsylvania, the library staff of the New York Academy of Medicine, Mrs. Eleanor R. Clise, archivist of the Geneva Historical Society, the ever willing staff at the Forty-Second Street Public Library, those of my friends in academe who made some of their records available to me, and all those who by their interest helped me to finish this undertaking.

Despite the help I received, errors will be found. I acknowledge them as wholly mine.

Photo Credits

The author thanks the many institutions, organizations and individuals who made available the photographs appearing in this book.

Mother Jones, Eleanor Roosevelt and Rose Schneiderman, Rose Pastor Stokes and *Mary Anderson*: courtesy of the Tamiment Library of New York University.

Evangeline Booth: courtesy of The Salvation Army.

Needle Trades Workers' Demonstration: courtesy of *Justice*, newspaper of the International Ladies Garment Workers' Union.

Dr. Elizabeth Blackwell: courtesy of the Demarest Library, Hobart and William Smith Colleges.

Drs. Gerty Cori and Carl Cori: courtesy of Washington University School of Medicine.

Rosina Lhevinne: courtesy of the Juilliard School.

Bessie Abramowitz Hillman and Sidney Hillman: courtesy of Mrs. Philoine Hillman Fried.

Dr. Valentina Suntzeff: courtesy of Dr. Suntzeff.

Clara Mannes and David Mannes: courtesy of Marya Mannes.

Nadia Reisenberg: courtesy of Mme Reisenberg.

Suzanne Bloch: courtesy of Miss Bloch.

Anzia Yezierska: courtesy of Mrs. Willy Pogany.

Jennie Grossinger: courtesy of the Grossinger family.

Pauline Trigère: courtesy of Pauline Trigère.

CHAPTER 1

Virtuous Gentlewomen, Godly and Sober— Not Always Prudent

MOST IMMIGRANTS WHO LEFT ENGLAND FOR THE NORTHERN plantations of the North American continent embarked for the New World with their families. Their intention was to create permanent homes for themselves and their progeny. By disposing of their homes in England and such possessions as they did not take with them, they made the break irreversible. Occasionally wives and children remained behind, but they soon followed, albeit fearfully, like Mrs. John Winthrop, or after some coaxing. One who remained hesitant was Mrs. Wilson, wife of the eminent clergyman John Wilson. Mrs. Winthrop remarked of her in a letter to her stepson, John Winthrop, Junior: "I marvel what mettle she's made of."[1] However, when the Reverend Wilson went back to fetch her, she allowed herself to be persuaded. For most women the departure from their native land meant goodbye to "deare England" for good. Officials, ministers, sea captains returned to England periodically to attend to business or to matters of state, but for most women the separation was permanent. The request to be buried in the direction facing England that we occasionally read may be taken as a sign of homesickness.

By contrast, the great majority of early Virginians who preceded the settlers of Plymouth and Massachusetts by thirteen and twenty years, respectively,[2] were unattached males, adventurers, debtors, ne'er-do-wells. Emigration was for them one more adventure in their lives, no more hazardous than volunteering to fight for foreign princes. They were drawn to the colony not to find permanent homes but, according to the Virginia historian Robert Beverley, "to fetch away the Treasure

1

from thence." The young woman who elected to go "across the seas" was a rarity. One was a young Norfolk woman of knightly family whose name was Temperance Flowerdew. She left for Virginia in 1608; there met and married George Yardley, a professional soldier under Sir Thomas Gates. Temperance Flowerdew endured that awful period known as "starving time," when sixty famished colonists, decimated by disease and lack of food, admittedly practiced cannibalism."[3] If Lord Delaware had not arrived with food and reinforcements they would have quit Virginia. George Yardley would not have become Sir George Yardley and Governor of Virginia,[4] and Temperance Flowerdew would not have become the progenetrix of one of the earliest American families. She had three children, all of whom remained in Virginia.

The scarcity of women proved a serious drawback to the viability of the Jamestown colony; unattached males were more likely than married men to chuck their tobacco acres when loneliness and the lack of civilized amenities bore down too heavily.

In 1620, thirteen years after the planting of the Jamestown colony, ninety maids were dispatched to Virginia for purchase as wives at the price of one hundred and twenty pounds of leaf tobacco each, worth about eighty dollars.[5] They were snatched up. Other shiploads of women—respectable women—followed, and none languished for want of a purchaser.

This practice was also followed in the French province of Louisiana. In 1706 a group of young girls was dispatched to the colony and quickly spoken for. Later, shiploads of girls were likely to come from houses of correction and were known as "correction girls."[6]

Though women were no rarities in the northern colonies, there was at no time a superfluity of them. For instance, when the first church covenant was signed in Charlestown, the subscribers were said to have numbered sixty-four men and half as many women.[7] The Puritans assigned lots to spinsters, "Maid's lotts," as they were called, but the presence of single women was not encouraged.[8] At first women paid poll taxes, but the practice was soon discontinued. The number of young women was further reduced by the high incidence of death in childbirth.[9] That made the scramble for wives keener, for Puritan males refused to remain widowers.

Puritan families were large, but frequently half or more of their children failed to grow to maturity. The extent of this affliction is evident in the diary of Samuel Sewall, Massachusetts Bay Colony's eminent jurist, who mentions "carrying" one child after another to its grave.[10] He had fourteen children by his first wife, was married three times, and after the death of each wife was occupied in shopping around for a successor. Men did not stop marrying until they were on their deathbeds.

The tendency toward quick consolation was encouraged because immoderate grief on a death of a spouse was frowned upon as an indication that he or she had not kept earthly love within bounds.[11] The popularity of widows made them literally the "queens of society," particularly when they had inherited property. Both men and women were adept at chaffering about marriage portions, money arrangements, and so on. Such highly esteemed individuals as Benjamin Franklin, Thomas Jefferson, George Washington, and James Madison, to cite some examples, married widows. The "reign of the widow" was still absolute at the time of the Revolution.

The wives of the first settlers seem to have had no less difficult a time than their husbands. Women were not permitted to be slothful. They bore child after child, cooked, baked bread, took care of the children, oversaw the work of servants, tended the sick, had charge of the kitchen garden, brewed ale and cider, spun, made candles and soap, and were expected to present themselves at the meeting houses, there to be exhorted and threatened with hellfire if they disregarded the preachments of the ministers.

Colonial women knew better than to seek to lead or to influence. English women of that time generally did not assert themselves or try to compete with men. They were expected to "guid the house and not guid the husband."[12] Any woman who attempted to make herself conspicuous would have been censured. The sensible ones performed their tasks as best they could. That some lost their wits was admitted, as when one threw her child into a well. Governor Winthrop, in mentioning it in his "History," did not expatiate on the reason why a heretofore sane woman lost her mind. It was easy to explain that women were "the weaker vessels." Like men they were supposed to live by the dictum—and in this men and women were equal— "God's will be done," no matter what they had to endure. For a meekly religious woman, of whom Margaret Winthrop, the third wife of the governor of the Massachusetts Bay Colony, was a good example, it was outwardly not too hard to accept an existence God had supposedly decreed. Milton, the great Puritan poet whose own married life had been stormy, explained it very simply: "He for God, she for God in him."

Of course, they had to be possessed of Brobdingnagian courage from the beginning of the hazardous journey, which lasted from eight to twelve weeks, during which fear of death was their constant companion, and no less so after they had reached their Zion in the wilderness. There was the constant menace of illness, fear of attack by Indians and by wild animals—wolves were no imaginary threat. Yet Governor Winthrop asserted that among the English women "there appeared no fear or dismayedness among them."[13]

The truth of the claim that women defended themselves against Indians by throwing boiling soap at them, or live coals, or that they put them to flight with a stout ax, is not to be doubted. Goodwife Hannah Dustin during King William's War slew, with the help of a captured youth, ten Indians, then scalped them in order to be able to prove her claim.[14] She received twenty-five pounds from the General Court, and her helper ten.

However, many women were taken captive by Indians. One of them was Mary Rowlandson, who was found and ransomed for twenty pounds.[15] Another, Eunice Williams, the daughter of the minister at Deerfield, the scene of a terrible massacre, was carried off by Indians, but she grew to like her life among her captors so much that after being restored to her family, she is said to have preferred to return to the Indians. In the words of Cotton Mather, the great virtues of women were to be "pious, prudent and sober, to be good consourts," which meant they were expected to be Godfearing, courageous, uncomplaining, and respectful of male authority. When survival

was so difficult, disturbed relations between men and their wives
would have complicated their lives immeasurably.

The qualifications for being a "good consourt" were filled
to perfection by Margaret Winthrop, the aforementioned third
wife of John Winthrop, who was appointed governor of the
projected Massachusetts Bay Colony before the group of settlers
left England. Evidence about her is understandably scant, but
her character can be reconstructed from what is known about
her. In her serene acceptance of her husband's authority she
represented the highest ideals of wifehood for that time and
an example for others. When he departed on the *Arbella,* one
of the four ships[16] conveying the first large contingents of emi-
grants to New England, she was left behind until her fifth
child was born and the Winthrop manor house sold. Her baby
died on the way to New England and was buried at sea.

Margaret Tyndall, spelled variously Tyndal, Tyndale and Tyndall, was the daughter of a noble family in East Anglia, strong-
hold of religious nonconformism. She was said to have been a
very gracious woman with exquisite manners and a compas-
sionate heart. By her husband's description she had a "lovely
countenance." John Winthrop's first two wives had died young.
He had married for the first time when he was less than
eighteen and still a student at Trinity College, Cambridge.
When his first wife died, leaving three sons and a daughter, he
took for his second wife a young girl of whom he was said
to have been very fond. She did not survive the birth of her
first child, and within a year he was a widower again. When
Winthrop fell in love with Margaret Tyndall, he was thirty-one
and she twenty-seven, and he had already begun to turn in-
ward, to eschew smoking and all drink but water. In 1618
Margaret Tyndall became his "loving faithfull yokefellow," and
made herself beloved by the four children of his first marriage
and his two orphaned nieces for whom he was responsible.

Though Margaret Winthrop feared the trip and the unknown
existence awaiting her, there was never any doubt that she
would join her husband as soon as he sent word he was ready
to receive her and his family. By the time she was about to
leave England, her husband's third son, who had been destined
for the ministry, died suddenly, a few weeks before his twenty-

first birthday. John Winthrop's second son, Henry, a daredevil whose wife was awaiting the birth of a child in England, accompanied his father to America, but on one of the other ships, and drowned in Salem just as he was about to tread the soil of the New World. The news of his death was a blow to the governor. Henry had spent some time on Barbados and the governor expected that his experiences there would be of value to the new colony. With the death of the child born during his absence John Winthrop lost three children before his wife joined him.

It was to be taken for granted that a pious, etiquette-conscious man like John Winthrop would expect his wife to properly fulfill the role which in the Puritan ethos God had assigned her. He seemed to have responded with considerable gratification to the privileges of his rank, which permitted him to be accompanied by fife and drum and a detachment of halberdiers whenever he conducted official business. He fancied wearing the elaborately pleated and starched ruff, a piece of raiment that some may have considered unfitting for a Puritan who advocated plain living and high ideals.

Margaret Winthrop was the ideal wife for a man who never doubted that he had been called to turn dream into reality. His dream was to build a "Citty upon a hill" where the "God of Israell" would dwell among them if only the settlers would live in righteousness and follow the admonition of His viceregent. The virtues she possessed: bravery, dignity, good manners, were exactly those needed to reinforce respect for her husband's authority. In addition to fulfilling all the responsibilities of the colonial housekeeper, except that she probably did not brew ale because her husband forbade its use at home, she was his hostess, for the governor held court in his home,[17] entertained deputies and official visitors. Undoubtedly her demeanor made him proud of her.

In money matters John Winthrop was distinctly an imprudent man. For many years he refused a salary and often used his own funds for public business.[18] In addition he allowed himself to be cheated by dishonest men to whom he had entrusted the management of his property. At the end of her life Margaret Winthrop bore with her husband the loss of his fortune.[19]

By the time the colony reimbursed him for his services, she was dead at fifty-six after an illness of one day. The man who had addressed her as "My dearest wife, my chiefest love, mine own, mine onely," and had written to her, "And now my sweet love, let me a while solace myself in the remembrance of our love,"[20] solaced himself quickly with a wealthy widow, Martha Coytmore. He survived Margaret by only two years, dying at sixty-two, which was then considered a long life.

Margaret Winthrop was the recipient of extraordinary love letters from her husband. As a young lawyer in England and as justice of the peace he had often been absent from home and he tried to make up for it with affectionate letters. Before he departed for New England, they had arranged between themselves that "in order to bring some ease to us both" they would devote an hour after five o'clock on "Mundays and Frydays to commune with one another." One of his letters contains the following summation of what they meant to each other:

... love was their banqueting house, love was their wine; love was their ensigne; love was his invitinges; love was her fayntinges; love was his apples; love was hir comforts; love made her seeke him; love made her follow him; love made him her saviour; love makes hir his servant.[21]

She wrote to him: "I wish that I may be allwayes pleasing to thee and those comforts we have in each other may be daily increased as far as they be pleasing to God."[22]

Also: "And now I shall longe for that houre when I shall see you and enjoy my sweete and deare husband..."

His appreciation for his wife notwithstanding, the governor was thoroughly old-fashioned in his opinion of women. They were to be honored as wives, yes, but only when they did not make nuisances of themselves. What he thought of Anne Bradstreet, who became known as a poet even during his lifetime, is not revealed in his journal. But his opinion of another woman who obviously aspired to being more than just wife and mother is known. She was the wife of Governor Hopkins of Hartford, and she had a "mental breakdown" in his words, after indulging in "reading and writing of books." His explanation:

If she had attended to her household affairs and such things as belong to women and not gone out of her way and calling to meddle in such things as are proper to men whose minds are stronger, she would have kept her wits and might have improved them usefully and honourably in the place God had set her.[23]

He was an awesome bigot who saw God's hand in everything. It was God who had "set" the women in New England and not their husbands, who were acting as instruments of God. Women were assigned their places in the Great Chain of Being and their place was not to write books. Complaints could serve no other purpose than to become known as shrews and malcontents. The governor was not the only one to believe that it was better for women to confine themselves to "such things as are proper to women." When the sister of Thomas Parker wrote a book she received the following communication from her brother: "Your printing of a Book beyond the custom of your Sex doth rankly smell."[24] Anne Bradstreet, the first poetess of New England, was aware of what she might expect from some people, for she wrote:

> I am obnoxious to every carping tongue,
> Who say my hand a needle better fits,
> If what I can do prove well, it won't advance,
> They'll say it's stolen, or else it was by chance.[25]

But there were women in the colonies who, in addition to fulfilling their roles as wives and mothers, demonstrated a variety of abilities. In New Haven, for instance, during the decade following the first settlement, the wife of the minister John Davenport was said to have been a very capable manager. According to her husband she "could set all wheeles going." She helped newcomers in getting started and carried out very capably many tasks assigned to her by Governor John Winthrop, Junior, son of the governor of Massachusetts Bay, and after 1635, governor of the new plantation of Connecticut.[26]

A woman who possessed uncommon business sense was Margaret Brent of Maryland (1607–1671).[27] She arrived with her sister in 1638, six years after the founding of Maryland. Margaret Brent and her sister were kinswomen of the proprietor,

Cecilius Calvert, second Lord Baltimore, who received a grant of a hereditary estate from King Charles I. Margaret is supposed to have acted for the governor, Leonard Calvert, who made her his executrix. For him she conducted litigation, disposed of property, and in 1647 requested an unheard-of privilege for a woman—two votes in the Assembly—one for herself and one as the proprietor's attorney.[28] A very important achievement, in which she played a part, was the passage in 1649 of the Toleration Act of Maryland, intended to safeguard Catholics as well as Protestants. Later in her life she removed to Virginia, where she became equally respected.

In the colony of New York, the Dutch wife of Frederick Philipse, Margaret Hardenbroeck Philipse (1659–1690),[29] is said to have helped make him the richest man in the colony of New Netherland. She was considered an astute businesswoman even before she became his wife. In her marriage to Philipse, who was her second husband, she continued her business activities, which included the shipping of furs to Holland in exchange for merchandise she then sold to the burghers of New Netherland. Other hardy Dutch women were Anneke Jans, who secured a considerable portion of Manhattan real estate, and her daughter Sarah Roelofse, who became an expert linguist and acted as official interpreter in dealing with Indians.

In the Carolinas there was an extraordinary young woman, Eliza Lucas Pinckney (1722–1793),[30] whose most important contribution before the Revolution was the cultivation of indigo. By distributing the seed of a particularly successful crop to other planters, she helped them produce a harvest of 100,000 pounds in 1747.[31]

Eliza Lucas was the daughter of Lieutenant Colonel George Lucas, who purchased land in the Carolinas and, when he was appointed governor of Antigua, left the farm to be managed by his seventeen-year-old daughter. She was a very independent young woman. When her father proposed a man for her to marry she told him that "the riches of Chile and Peru put together if he had them could not purchase a sufficient esteem for him to make him my husband."[32] The man she married, Charles C. Pinckney, was a cultured man who was a native of the Carolinas. Eliza Pinckney planted all manner of new trees in her new home and encouraged the work of the botanist Dr. Gardner, after whom the gardenia was named, while at the same time supervising her husband's and her father's plantations.[33] She has the additional distinction of having been the mother of two eminent Southern statesmen who served in the Revolutionary War and in several diplomatic missions to England, France, and Spain. One, Charles Cotesworth Pinckney, was a presidential candidate of the Federalist Party in 1804. When she died, President Washington by his own request was one of the pallbearers.

A woman who was clever enough to found a town and to assume its direction was Elizabeth Haddon Estaugh (1680–1762), a Quaker.[34] Her father had purchased a five-hundred-acre tract in New Jersey, which attracted many English Quakers, but when he found it impossible to leave his business in England, she went in his place. She was nineteen when she arrived in New Jersey in 1701 and started to build the town of New Haddonfield on her father's property. Her marriage to the Quaker minister John Estaugh turned out to be a happy one. Her story so impressed Maria Child, one of the early women writers of the nineteenth century, that she made it a part of her book, *The Youthful Emigrant*.

In spite of the strictures imposed on women by the standards of their time and society, the colonies did not lack for women who stood out among the rest by indulging in what Cotton Mather referred to in his magnum opus, *Magnalia Christi Americana*, as "seditious or mutinous practices," or in John Winthrop's words, "those nourishing contentions." In that category would be included meddlers, malcontents like Quakers, and those who stirred up trouble by being suspected of practicing witchcraft; in short, all who did not content themselves by playing the role of inconspicuous "consourts."

In comparison to England, Scotland, Germany, and Scandinavia, where thousands were burned as witches, the period of witch-hunting in Massachusetts was mercifully short, and though there were mutterings against witches in Connecticut and in Virginia as well, they were accompanied by relatively mild punishments. Massachusetts, where the fear of Satan's interference was more real than anywhere else, proved most susceptible to rumors that Satan was gaining ascendancy in their godly land. "No one is exempted from molestation by the Devil and His Instruments," warned the Reverend Jonathan Mitchell.[35]

It was an opinion Cotton Mather fully endorsed and to which even the down-to-earth jurist Samuel Sewall proved susceptible. Sewall was born in England, but was graduated from Harvard College, and then entered his long career in politics, ending up as chief justice, despite his lack of formal legal training. Sewall was the judge appointed by Governor Phipps to the special court in Salem which tried a group of supposed witches in 1692. He concurred in the judgment that put nineteen people to death,[36] among them Martha Covey and Rebecca Nourse. Five years later, however, he acknowledged his error at the end of a church service in the Old South Church—the only official to recant publicly. Cotton Mather, who must by then have had serious doubts about witchcraft, set to writing his *Magnalia*, that paean to the Christian spirit of New England and what it had accomplished. Published in London in 1702, the *Magnalia* was seen as an attempt to gloss over his concurrence in the witch-hunt and, instead, to call attention to himself as the chronicler of that godly crew of ministers and lawmakers who had caused the colony to become "like a hive overstocked with bees,"[37] rather than as a hunter of witches.

Cotton Mather's condemnation of "seditious and mutinous practices" may be applied especially to the religious dissenter Anne Hutchinson, the leader of the Antinomians in the colony, and to Quakers as well. All the ministers in the Plymouth and the Massachusetts Bay colonies (which were merged in 1691) maintained that any religious creed other than the special brand of Calvinism adopted by the New England churches, was inimical not only to individual salvation, but to the welfare of the state as well. Quakers were mercilessly persecuted. One of them was Mary Dyer, a supporter of Anne Hutchinson (of whom more will be said later). Mistress Dyer was at first banished, but Massachusetts had for her the attraction of the flame for the moth. When she returned, she was condemned to death, but was reprieved on condition that she never show herself in

Massachusetts again. When she reappeared in 1660 she was hanged.

That it was possible for a woman "nourishing contentions" to achieve something that would prove of lasting significance to the colony, was proved in a litigation involving Goody Sherman and Captain Keayne. She was a humble woman who had the temerity to sue one of her "betters" and this stirred up a great to-do. Winthrop reports it in his *Journal* as "a great business upon a very small occasion."[38]

In 1636 one Captain Keayne, a rich merchant of "ill report" for overcharging (for which he had been rebuked by the authorities), acquired a stray sow. Though the town crier announced it, no one claimed it. Later, Goody Sherman, who had lost a pig, entered a claim, but did not come to identify the animal until after the sow had been slaughtered. She admitted the remaining animal was not hers, but held that the one killed, was. The case was brought before the elders of the church, who cleared the captain.

Dissatisfied with the decision, Goody Sherman allowed herself to be persuaded to bring her claim before an inferior court in Boston, where the captain was again exonerated. But it did not end there. She discovered a witness who admitted he had sworn falsely, which enabled her to bring the case to the General Court, the colony's supreme judicial and legislative body. There the court divided on class lines; the less aristocratic deputies favoring Mistress Sherman, and the Court of Assistants upholding the captain. However, two of the magistrates voted in favor of Mistress Sherman and thus against their class. What made this case significant is that it led to an important constitutional change which in 1644 brought about the establishment of a bicameral system—a House of Deputies to sit by themselves and a House of Assistants to sit separately. To Samuel Eliot Morison Goody Sherman's sow deserved a monument as "the mother of senates."[39]

The Sherman-Keayne incident might have seemed "a very small occasion," but the Antinomian[40] controversy of 1636–1637 precipitated by Anne Hutchinson was most assuredly not. It shook the colony to its foundations.

Governor Winthrop described Anne Hutchinson, who was

a cousin of the poet Dryden, as a woman of "ready wit and bold spirit." Others saw in her "Satan's fit instrument." Before becoming a self-appointed interpreter of religious doctrine she had dabbled in midwifery.[41] Her great and dangerous error was that she believed in direct communication with the Holy Ghost, which she claimed was the only evidence of salvation, whereas the ministers considered it their prerogative to judge whether or not an individual had indeed been sanctified and thus belonged to the Elect. It was a matter of gravest concern because only the Elect could become church members, and only church members were permitted to exercise political rights.

Had she not flaunted her views, she might have been ignored. But, far from being a retiring woman, she continued to inflame her supporters. Her husband William is supposed to have been an unassertive man who took direction from her. She also had several children. Many of her friends were influential people: her brother-in-law, the minister John Wheelwright, Sir Henry Vane, the newly elected governor, even John Cotton, the respected minister whose staunch friend was Governor Winthrop.

Her influence was so disturbing that a synod of ministers was convoked to deal with the crisis. Their first action was to threaten Reverend Wheelwright with banishment if he continued his dissentious practices. Mistress Hutchinson was known to hold meetings in her home which were attended by sixty to eighty women who discussed theological doctrines and the latest sermons. She was forbidden to hold "disorderly meetings of female church members." But neither Wheelwright nor she was swayed by the threat against them and both persisted in their "schismatic conduct."

Finally it became a matter for the Great and General Court to decide. Governor Vane was promptly voted out and the more reliable Winthrop was reinstated as governor. It was he who presided over the trial. During the proceedings Anne boasted of her direct revelations. This was heresy, and it proved she had been seduced by Satan. Even the minister John Cotton, who had upheld her, retracted his support of her. She was told: "Yow have stept out of yo' place, yow have rather bine a Husband than a Wife, & a Preacher than a Hearer & a Magistrate than a Subject . . . & have not bine humbled for this."[42]

They proceeded to humble her and to punish her by banishing her to Rhode Island, where Roger Williams, another nonconformist, had settled two years earlier, proclaiming religious freedom to all dissenters. She founded a settlement in Portsmouth, but in 1642, after the death of her husband, she removed to New Rochelle, then under the Dutch. There within a year she met a grisly death at the hands of the Indians, which many interpreted as "Divine Providence." John Wheelwright and his family withdrew to Narragansett Bay and were also slain by Indians. Perry Miller attributed her banishment and that of Roger Williams to their being "altogether too gifted with imagination."[43] A statue of her in the State House in Boston depicts her as a tall woman, her head raised defiantly toward heaven, holding her Bible over her heart and the other arm protectively around a child huddling under her cape. In her martyrdom, which she did not avoid and may actually have sought, she resembles the early Quakers.[44] Among her spiritual descendants —women who fought for their religious convictions and suffered persecution—the Shaker Anne Lee for example, or the Mormon women, as well as the early fighters for abolition and suffrage, none outdid her in courage and determination.

Though the authorities managed to extinguish her heresy by purging the colony of her presence, religious dissent kept cropping up anew in the manner of epidemics that erupted periodically and died down, but could not be rooted out altogether. Many men and women kept claiming they had visitations, if not from the Holy Ghost, then from the Son, John the Baptist, the Angel Moroni, or other messengers of the Lord. This was the way in which several new sects were born, and persecutions suffered by religious nonconformists were in many cases more severe than those visited on Anne Hutchinson, who was merely expelled, but otherwise not harmed. Later religious reformers found their homes burned, themselves stoned and even murdered.

There was one woman of the first generation who combined in herself the virtues expected of a daughter and wife of Puritans with the distinction of becoming the first poet of her sex in the English colonies. She was Anne Bradstreet (1612–1672), daughter of Thomas Dudley and wife of Simon Bradstreet. Both her father and husband served as governors of Massachusetts Bay Colony. Two years after her marriage Anne accompanied her father and husband on the *Arbella* on that first great voyage to New England.

Though she was consumptive and prone to fainting fits, by 1650 she had given birth to eight children and written enough poems for her admiring brother-in-law, John Woodbridge, to take to England without her knowledge and to have them published with a dedicatory preface by Nathaniel Ward, her minister at Ipswich. Ward, too, had been touched by the muse of poetry. The author was designated as "The Tenth Muse Lately Sprung Up In America."

It was lucky for her that Puritans, who rejected music and the musical arts, loved poetry. They saw poetry as "the handmaid to divinity." Many of the divines wrote verse, although most of it limped and lacked the grace and feeling associated with the lyricists and sonneteers of the sixteenth and seventeenth centuries. An example of an appreciated Puritan poem, published in England in 1662, which proved no less popular in the mother country than in the colonies, was Michael Wigglesworth's "Day of Doom." This metrical account of the Last Judgment has nothing to recommend it except its graphic descriptions of the gory punishments that await the unregenerate.

Anne Bradstreet's poems are reminiscent of the Puritan style which disdained unnecessary embellishments, yet her verses have a freshness and directness that produce a telling effect. While some of her earlier poetry was imitative of English and French models, her best work is personal. One of the most widely quoted is surprisingly outspoken for that era. It is titled "To My Dear and Loving Husband":

> If ever two were one, then surely we,
> If ever man were loved by wife, then thee.
> If ever wife was happy in a man,
> Compare with me ye women if you can.
>
> I prize thy love more than whole mines of gold,
> Or all the riches that the East doth hold.
> My love is such that rivers cannot quench,
> Nor aught but love from thee give recompense.

> Thy love is such I can no way repay.
> The Heavens reward thee manifold I pray.
> Then while we live, in love let so persever,
> Then when we live no more, we may live ever.[45]

Another poem leads us to suspect that she was not indifferent to the lowly regard in which women were held by the male element of her time.

> Let Greeks be Greeks, and women what they are
> Men have precedence and still excell;
> It is but vain unjustly to wage warre;
> Men can do best and women know it well.
> Preheminence in all and each is yours;
> Yet grant some small acknowledgement of ours.

Even Cotton Mather, that glorifier of the leaders of Christian America, whose *Magnalia* makes mention of so few women that one would be justified in wondering whether the colony was entirely male, heaps fulsome praise on Anne Bradstreet. His eulogy sounds more euphuistic than Puritan. Says he:

> ... if the rare learning of a daughter was not the least of those bright things that adorned no less a judge of English than Sir Thomas More; it must now be said that a judge of New-England, namely Thomas Dudley, Esquire, had a daughter (besides other children) to be a crown unto him. Reader, America justly admires the learned women of the other hemisphere. But she now says that ... there may be a room now given unto Madam Ann Bradstreet, the daughter of our Governor Dudley, and the consort of our Governor Bradstreet, whose poems diverse times printed, have afforded a grateful entertainment unto the ingenious, and a monument for her memory beyond the stateliest marbles. It was upon these poems that an ingenuous person bestowed this epigram:

> Now I believe *tradition* which doth call
> The Muses, Virtues, Graces, Females all,
> Only they are *nine, eleven* or *three*;
> Our auth'ress proves them but one unity;

> Mankind, take up some blushes on that score;
> Monopolize perfection hence no more.[46]

A young woman who came to Boston as an "unfree" immigrant was Phillis Wheatley (1753–1784).[47]

Precisely at what age she was brought to Boston on a slaveship is not known, but she is guessed to have been seven or eight years old. John Wheatley, a wealthy merchant tailor, purchased her to be trained as a personal maid to his wife.

The Wheatley family, who owned other slaves, took a liking to her because she was so unlike the rest. She had pleasing ways and seemed to be conspicuously intelligent. The older Wheatley children undertook to teach her and she learned so quickly that within sixteen months she could read fluently.

She was in her teens when she began to write poetry in the manner of Alexander Pope. As a member of the Wheatley family she was sponsored by them for membership in Boston's Old South Meeting House. She was such an unusual example of Negro progress that abolitionists used her as proof of what people of her race could achieve if given the opportunity for education.

The family thought so much of her that when their physician recommended a change of climate for her, she was sent to England in company of the son of the family. There she found a ready welcome, and the Countess of Huntingdon became her patroness. It was she who is supposed to have arranged for the publication of Phillis Wheatley's only book of poetry, *Poems on Various Subjects, Religious and Moral.* Evidently she was not a prolific writer. Like Pocahontas, wife of John Rolfe, one hundred and fifty years before her, she was received by English high society and would have been presented at court had she stayed longer. But after receiving news that Mrs. Wheatley was ill, she hastened home, returning just before the outbreak of the Revolutionary War. In 1776 she wrote a poem on George Washington which was published. It brought her an invitation from the general to visit him at his headquarters.

After the death of the elder Wheatleys, the family broke up. Phillis married someone who proved unworthy of her. He left her frequently to fend for herself and her child. Her husband's inconstancy forced her to seek work in a cheap lodging house. Both she and her child died in Boston in 1784. In 1834 the last edition of her poetry was reissued. Interest in her as a poet has become almost entirely extinguished.

CHAPTER 2

In the Quaker Colony of Pennsylvania

TOWARD THE END OF THE SEVENTEENTH CENTURY (1681) WILLIAM Penn, a young Quaker of Welsh descent, received a grant of land for a claim of sixteen thousand pounds, which his father, Admiral William Penn, held against the Crown. Thus he became the proprietor of the province of Pennsylvania. A year later, the Duke of York transferred Delaware to him through a legally dubious transaction, but in 1703 Delaware received a separate government.

The young proprietor had been persecuted in England for his Quaker views and had even been imprisoned. His intention was to make his colony a haven for Quakers and other religious dissenters. He began by buying land from the Indians, instead of appropriating it, and making agreements with them which he respected. After publicizing his plans for the colony in the British Isles, Holland, and the Germanies, thus becoming the first advertiser on the new continent, he received English Quakers, German religious dissidents, and a large number of individuals who were members of various Pietist sects. Among them were agriculturists as well as artisans.

After the end of the Stuart rule and the accession of the Protestants William and Mary to the throne of England in 1688, William Penn's loyalty to the new sovereigns was questioned and he lost his colony temporarily. Despite his good intentions toward the settlers and the Indians, he was not a good manager. The agents he chose proved incapable, and some were suspected of peculation. He had spent a large fortune on the colony, but his affairs became so tangled that he was imprisoned for debt.

William Penn had an able second wife in Hannah Callowhill

Penn (1671–1726).[1] She, too, was a Quaker and had been reared by her father, a prosperous tradesman, to understand business. While she resided in the colonies with her husband and family, she managed the farm in Pennsbury in Bucks County. Penn's financial difficulties finally caused him to turn over the government of his province to the Crown, but he retained title to the land.

After 1712 he suffered a series of strokes which made him unable to take care of his affairs and his wife took over. At the same time she managed the estate of her parents, who had died. Upon her husband's death she was his executrix and she and her children inherited most of his lands.

Though at fifty she became largely incapacitated, she continued for the last five years of her life to supervise her business interests. She settled the Pennsylvania-Maryland boundary, which was one of the problems William Penn had never been able to adjust satisfactorily, and she conducted protracted litigation over his lands in adversary relationships with the sons of William Penn's first marriage. She lived long enough to see her husband's will establishing her children as his heirs, upheld.

Another Quaker woman who deserves to be remembered for her contribution to the development of Pennsylvania is Susanna Wright (1697–1784),[2] daughter of Quakers who came to Pennsylvania in 1714 as part of the last wave of Scotch-Irish to settle in Western Pennsylvania. Her father, who had studied medicine and was a Quaker minister, became a representative of Lancaster County in the provincial Assembly.

Susanna became a very capable manager. After their mother's death, she brought up her younger brothers and sisters and ran the farm. There she raised her own silkworms, producing silk from her own cocoons. She was so knowledgeable that she was called upon to write documents and draw wills and deeds for her neighbors. She befriended the Indians and made it her responsibility to make travelers comfortable, and she put her knowledge of medicine and herbs at the service of her neighbors.

In addition to being an unusually versatile pioneer woman, she also had intellectual interests, read a great deal, and accumulated a large library.

Her life and activities illustrate the strengths and accomplishments of some women colonists, as well as their diversity of interests.

A graphic example of the way small beginnings developed can be found in a little school for the children of newcomers which the daughter of Count Zinzendorf began in the 1740s.

Count Zinzendorf was the head of, and an ordained bishop of, the Moravian Church, also called United Brethren or Unitas Fratrum. The Moravian Church was an outgrowth of the Protestant group which was formed by the followers of John Hus. Hounded from one place to another, this persecuted sect gratefully accepted asylum on Count Zinzendorf's estate in Saxony. His punishment for befriending religious malcontents was banishment.

The first attempt to transplant the group was to Georgia, where he hoped they would be permitted to do missionary work among the Indians and the Negroes. But their pacifist beliefs involved them in such difficulties that they were forced to remove to Pennsylvania, where they settled in Nazareth and Bethlehem. Upon coming to America in 1741, Count Zinzendorf took his sixteen-year-old daughter Henrietta Justine Benigna (1725-1789) with him and gave her the assignment to open a school for girls in Bethlehem.

This she did. After her return to Europe with her father, she married a minister of the Moravian Church, Baron Johann von Watteville, who was her father's assistant.

In 1748 she returned once more to America with her husband. By then other Moravian schools had come into existence. What she did was to consolidate the school she had begun with the others which had been founded in the meantime. After one year she returned to Europe.

Thirty years later she was back in Bethlehem, this time remaining three years. Again the school she had founded claimed her attention. At the end of the eighteenth century it was renamed the Bethlehem Female Seminary. More than a hundred years later—in 1913—it became the Moravian Seminary for Young Ladies. This was not the final metamorphosis. In 1953 the little school where a sixteen-year-old had taught the rudi-

ments of reading and writing to little children was absorbed
into the coeducational Moravian College in Bethlehem.

A different kind of heroine in Pennsylvania's early history
was a daughter of a German family, the Hartmanns, who had
come from the Palatinate in 1744 with four children. They
settled in an area that bristled with hostile Indians, Lebanon
County at the foot of the Blue Mountains. One day when
Mrs. Hartmann and one of the sons left for the mill to get
some flour ground, the two girls, Barbara, eleven, and Regina,
nine, were left alone at home. The father and another boy
were working in a nearby field. Suddenly some Indians burst
in after having killed the father and the boy. They dragged
the girls off and burned their home to the ground.

Despite a diligent search by the army, nothing could be
discovered about Mrs. Hartmann's two daughters.

In 1754, during the French and Indian Wars, a group of
German recruits under the command of the Swiss-born Colonel
Boquet won a victory over the Pontiacs in Cumberland County.
They demanded the surrender of all whites whom the Indians
held captive. Four hundred were brought back and taken to
Carlisle for identification. Mrs. Hartmann was one of those
waiting.

Though she scanned the group of girls, who looked more
Indian than European, she could not identify her daughters.
In her anguish she began to sing a German hymn: *"Allein und
doch nicht allein bin ich"* (Alone and yet not alone am I),
when a girl rushed out and attempted to continue the song.
She had forgotten everything but the hymn her mother had
taught her.

No one knew what had become of the other girl, but it
was believed she had succumbed during the trek and had
been killed by the Indians.

The story was such an appealing bit of folklore that as late
as 1905 investigators kept trying to determine the site where
the event had occurred, for the reason that several townships
were vying for the privilege of having a monument erected
to Regina Hartmann.[3]

Though during the eighteenth century the number of English immigrants declined, the large outpouring of Scotch-Irish during the fifty years preceding the Revolution added a quarter of a million to the existing population.[4] A completely non-English group were the Germans, consisting of pietists and "regular church" people (Lutherans) who augmented the population of Pennsylvania by 110,000 to 150,000. Many of the Germans came as "redemptioners," "bound labor," who became servants in order to repay their passage. After a specified time each was entitled to a grant of land, tools, seed, and a suit of clothes. During the eighteenth century, also, perhaps as many as 200,000 redemptioners were unloaded in America, nine-tenths of them in the southern colonies.

By the mid-nineteenth century many of the native families in the seaboard cities and on plantations were living in well-appointed commodious homes, staffed by servants and filled with all the appurtenances of good living. This happy state was not easily achieved by immigrant families, except possibly by the most fortunate of them. The great majority consisted of hewers of wood and drawers of water whose wives worked the land with them, or kept their small acres going while their husbands worked as day laborers.

In this their lives were not different from what they would have been in any of the European countries, except for this important difference: they lived in hope and in freedom. They were building for a better future for themselves and their progeny.

CHAPTER 3

Social Progress

NEVER WERE THE EXPECTATIONS OF THE AMERICAN PEOPLE
higher than at the beginning of the nineteenth century; never
were Americans more optimistic. The atmosphere was filled
with hope and expectation. Had not the citizen army won the
Revolutionary War which had welded thirteen colonies into
a new and independent nation? Furthermore, had the country
not won another victory over the British in 1812, as Americans
chose to believe? Even though several public buildings in
Washington had been put to the torch and (according to
legend) President Madison forced to make a hasty exit as
he was about to sit down to dinner, the American people
were in no mood to accept the War of 1812 as anything less
than a victory, particularly after the frontiersman Andrew
Jackson had inflicted a stunning defeat on the British in New
Orleans, killing General Sir Edward Pakenham in addition.
Americans were convinced that their great Constitution had
made them politically secure and was bound to keep the
country stable.

Above all, it was felt that the war had eliminated the Indian
menace and that the country now lay wide open to settlement.
Those who hoped for industrial expansion had the opportunity
to replace British imports with articles of native manufacture.
When in the 1840s the jingoist editor of the *Democratic Review*,
John L. O'Sullivan, declared it was the "manifest destiny" of
the United States to make the whole continent their own (also
hopefully some neighboring areas), he was providing a new
slogan, not an idea strange to American ambitions. Said Emerson, America's soothsayer, in a lecture in Boston in 1844:

. . . it seems so easy for America to inspire and express the most
expansive and human spirit; newborn, free, healthful, strong, the

24

land of the laborer, of the democrat, of the philanthropist, of the believer, of the saint, she should speak for the human race. It is the country of the Future.[1]

Emerson had a very benevolent attitude to immigrants, which was not universally shared. By the 1840s many Americans were suspicious of the Germans and the Irish, the former because of fears of "Germanization," the latter because of their Catholicism and their intemperate habits. In 1727 the distrust toward the Germans of Pennsylvania had been so pervasive that German immigrants had to take an oath of fidelity to the king, the proprietors, and the constitution of the province.

Though immigration had fallen off at the end of the eighteenth century, after 1812 the situation began to reverse itself, and from then on the increase of foreign peoples continued on a steadily ascending course. Most newcomers arriving at the beginning of the nineteenth century were largely English-speaking, the Scotch-Irish still predominating. The outpouring from the German states in the seventeenth and eighteenth centuries to Pennsylvania (and other pockets) had tapered off and would not resume until the 1830s, 40s, and 50s when much of Middle Europe would reverberate with revolutionary thunder. Whereas heretofore the influx of the Irish had been predominantly (but not exclusively) from the North of Ireland—the Scotch-Irish were Presbyterians—after the War of 1812 there began a constantly increasing trickle of Irish from the South of Ireland, who were Catholics.

This new Catholic immigration was the result of economic distress and political oppression. Unlike the Scotch-Irish, who had preferred the backcountry of Pennsylvania and the Carolinas, the Irish from the South of Ireland, who had largely been tied to the soil, showed a preference for town life. The spectacular increase in Irish immigration did not occur until mid-century. Its cause was hunger on such an unprecedented scale that thousands upon thousands expired of starvation before they could reach Canada or the United States.

Though the towns were growing, at the turn of the eighteenth century there were only six cities—New York, Boston, Salem, Philadelphia, Baltimore, and Charleston. America was still pre-

ponderantly agricultural. Employment opportunities were limited. Commerce and manufacturing were showing steady growth,
but the ideal mode of existence was believed to be on the
farm, where one could grow one's food and be assured of
shelter. But the credo of Thomas Jefferson that the existence
of the yeoman farmer was the most virtuous, so beloved of
the Agrarians, was on the decline. Jefferson himself became
aware of it before his death in 1825. City life would prove
increasingly the magnet that would draw natives and foreigners alike.

Women were mostly homebodies. Dolly Madison, representing
the gracious woman, was the national ideal. The cultivation of
the female mind was still a matter of the utmost indifference.
A generation before, Abigail Adams, wife of the second President of the newly formed United States, admitted that it was
"fashionable to ridicule feminine learning."[2] That superior speci-
men of American womanhood, whose letters bespeak a keen and
cultivated mind, had not even attended school outside of home.
For the upper-class woman there was nothing to do outside
the home, except to concern herself with the church, or to fulfill
such tasks as bringing food baskets to the needy, or flowers
(beginning to wilt) to the sick.

For the wives of laboring men, native or foreign, the first
concern was that of stretching the wages of the breadwinner
to provide the essentials of life. The opportunity for women to
augment the family income by working at home was very
limited, although some women found work as spinners or weavers
even during the early years of the Republic. The fact that in
1695 some single women paid a poll tax suggests that even
then some women were self-supporting.[3]

However, one kind of work that had little appeal for native
girls, as the Englishwoman Frances Trollope discovered in the
1820s, was housework. "The whole class of young women," she
remarked, not sympathetically, "are taught to believe that the
most abject poverty is preferable to domestic service. . . . they
think their equality is compromised by the latter."[4] The French
liberal journalist Alexis de Tocqueville, in discussing the American people in general, not the American woman in particular,
provided an explanation for Mrs. Trollope's observation. Said

he: "... equality is their idol ... nothing can satisfy them without equality, and they would rather perish than lose it."[5] His visit occurred during the 1830s, when the presence of Andrew Jackson in the White House encouraged anyone to feel and frequently to assert, "I am as good as you."

There were undoubtedly some women even before the end of the Revolution who were not as contented as they appeared to be, because as soon as the nineteenth century got under way, a whole crop of them came out of hiding, as it were. One suspects the doughty Abigail Adams of having been an incipient feminist, because her letters to her husband, though they were models of wifely concern and solicitude, indicate that she was not indifferent to the limited role which was allotted to women. For instance, in a letter to her husband, dated May 1776, while he was attending the Continental Congress in Philadelphia, she wrote:

I cannot say that I think you are very generous to the ladies; for whilst you are proclaiming peace and goodwill to men, emancipating all nations, you insist upon retaining an absolute power over wives. But you must remember, that arbitrary power is like most other things which are very hard, very liable to be broken; and notwithstanding all your wise laws and maxims, we have it in our power, not only to free ourselves, but to subdue our masters, and, without violence throw both your natural and legal authority at our feet;
Charm by accepting, by submitting sway
Yet have our humor most when we obey.[6]

If any year can be called the year of awakening to the urgent need for social and political reform, it was the year 1820. The burning issue then and for the next four decades was, of course, slavery, and it involved men as well as women. All thoughtful people were aware that the Compromise of 1820, which had permitted Maine to come into the Union as a free state and Missouri as a slave state, thus maintaining the desired balance between North and South, represented only a temporary settlement. What would happen when new western territories were ready for statehood? What compromises then? The issue of slavery soon became the umbrella under which gathered reformers advocating other urgently needed improvements, such as universal public education, extended education for women, social and economic amelioration, greater legal rights for women. Before the middle of the nineteenth century, women had become sufficiently emboldened to demand the right to being considered "legal" persons. The term "suffragette," which began to come into use after the Women's Rights Convention of 1848, called at Seneca Falls, New York, by Lucretia Mott, Elizabeth Cady Stanton, and others, was a term of condescension mixed with derision.

It was the propaganda of several foreign-born women who had begun to voice the heretical demand of giving women increased legal rights that induced native women to start such a crusade in earnest. Undoubtedly American women leaders would have come to that point of militancy by themselves, but it is indisputable that several nonnative women prepared the ground for native reformers to take over.

The first woman whose influence was seminal was English; she was Mary Wollstonecraft Godwin, the wife of the philosophical anarchist William Godwin and the mother of Mary Shelley, at whose birth she died. She never came to America, but in 1792 she got a book into print which she called *Vindication of the Rights of Women*. One cannot tell to what extent it was read in America, but says Mary Wollstonecraft Godwin's recent biographer, Eleanor Flexner, "it nourished Frances Wright and Margaret Fuller, Lucretia Mott and Elizabeth Cady Stanton. . . ."[7] "The woman's rights movement," continues Eleanor Flexner, "was often unaware of the existence of the woman who had originally sparked it. . . ."[8]

Because native women determined the intellectual climate, it seems desirable to stop for a closer look at the first steps taken by them as they responded to the challenges of their day. The burning issues of the early nineteenth century were slavery and abolition, general reform, and women's rights, which were nonexistent.

The early antislavery leaders were, of course, males, but they not only accepted female allies, they sometimes married them. Theodore Weld, a Massachusetts reformer, for instance, married Angelina Grimké, who with her sister Sarah Moore Grimké had freed their slaves after their father's death and had come North.

As liberals and intellectuals increased their agitation for general reform, the issue of legal rights for women became more sharply drawn.

During the first decades of the nineteenth century, very few women were bold enough to step out of their protected environments. One of the first to do so was Margaret Fuller (1810–1859). Like Sir Thomas More, who had taught his daughter enough Latin to impress Henry VIII, Margaret's father, a New England lawyer, had given her a thorough grounding in the classics. She was in her twenties when she began to hold conversational classes for women at the home of Elizabeth Peabody, a socially prominent spinster of advanced views, whose sister Mary married the educator Horace Mann, and whose other sister, Sophia, was soon to become the wife of Nathaniel Hawthorne. Women, whose husbands were the intellectual and political leaders of Boston, were glad to have Margaret Fuller lecture them on art, politics, philosophy, literature, and science. These parlor conversations, as they were called, took place in Boston and were reminiscent of Anne Hutchinson's gatherings in her home, where the emphasis was on theological topics.

Margaret Fuller became a friend of Emerson, by whom she was entrusted to edit the transcendental journal, *The Dial.* She was also the author of *Summer on the Lakes,* an account of a trip to Illinois in 1844. A year later, *Woman in the Nineteenth Century* (1845), made her a forerunner of the feminist movement. After that she was ready for a job with the New York *Tribune,* where she remained two years. Thus she became one of the first women journalists. But her career came to a premature end when, on her return trip from Italy, where she had actively encouraged the Italian revolution, she drowned with her Italian husband and baby off the coast of Fire Island.

A woman who was primarily a crusader for the alleviation of purely social problems was Dorothea Dix (1802–1887). Born in Maine, she was eight years older than Margaret Fuller. After first conducting a school for girls, her interest was caught by the need for prison reform, for almshouses, and for insane asylums. In 1845 she went before the legislators in Harrisburg and pleaded for a hospital instead of a prison for the insane. During the Civil War, when she was fifty-nine, she served as "Matron General" (Superintendent of Nurses) and was greatly respected by President Lincoln.

The first leaders of the woman's rights movement were Elizabeth Cady Stanton (1815–1902) and Lucretia Mott (1793–1880), both of whom had begun by working for Negro freedom. They were the two militants who called the first feminist meeting in Seneca Falls, New York, in 1848. There the first mention of the vote for women was made. From the Seneca Falls Convention emerged a Declaration of Rights for women which was modeled after the Declaration of Independence. It even included the exact number of grievances contained in the older document. Mrs. Stanton and Mrs. Mott were later joined by Susan B. Anthony (1829–1906), who had started out as an ardent supporter of abolition and temperance.

By 1848 the demand for greater legal rights for women, which marked the starting point of the women's crusade, was no longer a topic startling in its newness. The Scottish-born Frances Wright had been the first to bring this issue before the American public in the 1820s. She was followed by Mrs. Ernestine Rose, of Polish birth, throughout the 30s and 40s. These "pretensions," as they were referred to by newspapers and in the pulpits, had served for almost twenty years as the means for abusing and ridiculing the ambitions of women. Even in the beginning of the twentieth century, when the passage of the Nineteenth Amendment was on the near horizon, the printed comments on women as voters were condescending and quasi-tolerant. An example is the remark of the newspaperman, Peter Finley Dunne, who let his fictional Irish bartender and alter ego state: "Th' pollin' places [for women] won't be in th' office or a livery stable or a barbershop, but in a pleasant boodwar."

Among native reformers advocating higher education for women, top places belong to Emma Willard (1787–1870) and Mary Lyon (1797–1845). Emma Willard first opened a seminary for women in Middlebury, Vermont, where girls were taught mathematics, philosophy, history and science. Later she started a school in Troy, New York, which offered the equivalent of a college education for women. Mary Lyon was the founder of Mount Holyoke,, the oldest woman's college in the United States.

The idea that a school for girls would be both useful and profitable occurred to the British-born Susanna Haswell Rowson (1757–1824) before the end of the eighteenth century. Mrs. Rowson has the distinction of having been exposed twice to the Americanizing process, the first time as a child and the second time as a married woman and author of a popular tale that had found a wide reading audience in England, in America, and on the continent.

When Susanna Haswell was brought to the colonies in 1762 she was five years old. Her father was a captain of the British navy at the very time when British rule in North America was beginning to weaken. The captain was thus a witness to all the upheavals prior to the outbreak of the Revolution: the Townshend Acts of 1767, the Boston Massacre of 1770, the Boston Tea Party of 1773, the battle of Concord and Lexington in 1775, the battle of Bunker Hill in 1775, and the open outbreak of war. No doubt as a British captain he was frequently exposed to the anger of the people toward those charged with enforcing the unpopular Navigation Acts. Intended specifically to halt smuggling and to punish those engaged in evading the payment of customs duties, the Navigation Acts were the most despised of all statutes and the most consistently flouted. He could not have failed to realize the extent of the hatred colonial America harbored for the British government.

He asked permission to return to England in 1775, but it was denied to him. As an Englishman he was declared a Loyalist by the patriots and his property was confiscated. He could not go back to England until 1777. His daughter Susanna was then considered old enough to follow the example of Mary Wollstonecraft (and others) in finding a position as a governess. At twenty-four she married William Rowson, a friend of her father's, who was a hardware merchant and a trumpet player in the Royal Horse Guards. In America he was judged competent enough to perform in the Handel & Haydn Society presentation of the *Messiah*.

After her marriage Susanna Rowson began to write with the avowed intention of improving "the morals of the female sex."[9] Within less than a decade she wrote and published six volumes, four of which were fiction. In 1791 she produced her best-known novel, *Charlotte Temple*. The heroine is a feckless female and the story hinges on her seduction and the retribution she incurs.

The locale of Mrs. Rowson's story is colonial America, and the plot was supposed to have been based on an actual incident of a British colonel persuading an English girl, daughter of a clergyman, to leave her home and to accompany him to the New World, where he abandons her to die. One suspects, however, that the author was also influenced by Samuel Richardson's *Pamela*, published in England in 1741. Richardson's story is about a poor and virtuous serving girl who was seduced by an aristocratic gentleman. *Pamela* made a considerable splash, not only in England but on the continent as well, and was widely imitated. So popular was the seduction story that *Charlotte Temple* sold 25,000 copies in England and in America.[10]

In 1793 Mr. Rowson went bankrupt and the couple decided to come to the United States. They turned to the stage, to act and she to write comic operas, one of which was *Slaves in Algiers*, and social comedies. That Mrs. Rowson found postrevolutionary America very much to her liking can be gleaned from this statement:

Is it then wonderful that accustomed from the days of childhood to think of America and its inhabitants with affection, linked to me by many near connections and sincerely attached to them from principles and gratitude . . . I should offer the most ardent prayers for a continuation of their prosperity, or that feeling the benign influence of the blessings of peace and liberty, here so eminently enjoyed, I should wish that influence extended throughout every nation under heaven.[11]

Though they were successful on the stage, they abandoned the theater and she began a career as a schoolteacher in Boston. The special attraction of her school was that in addition to the usual classical subjects the pupils were taught to play the piano. Still, teaching was not sufficient to absorb all of Mrs. Rowson's attention. Though her school had sixty pupils, thirty of whom were boarding students, she still found the time to continue writing historical novels as well as supplementary teaching material. She also contributed articles on education, music, and books to the *Boston Weekly*.

After twenty-five years as schoolmistress she turned the school over to an adopted daughter and a niece. After her retirement she started a sequel to *Charlotte Temple*, which she called *Charlotte's Daughter*, a tale no less lachrymose and superficial than *Charlotte Temple*, or than the romances of native women writers whom Hawthorne was contemptuously to call "those scribbling damned women."

Frances Wright (1795–1852), the dynamic Scotswoman, came to America in 1818; it was she who imported one of the most acerb critics America would ever have, Frances Trollope. After one hundred and fifty years, her criticism is still being quoted. But Miss Wright, who was fascinated with America, is almost entirely forgotten. Between her early twenties and the time she died at fifty-seven in Cincinnati, she shuttled back and forth between Europe and America, and made five crossings during the 1840s alone. Mrs. Trollope, however, after her initial stay of three years and nine months, never returned to America.

Both women made a large imprint on the new nation, Miss Wright through the reforms she advocated for the United States, Mrs. Trollope through the book she wrote, *The Domestic Manners of the Americans*. It not only regained for her the money she had lost in her American business venture, but made her a tidy fortune. It was said she made between $130,000 and $140,000.[12]

When Frances Wright came for the first time it was to see her play produced and to have a look at the new society. Though she was critical of slavery, the book she wrote about America, *Views of Society and Manners in America*, was enthusiastic, though rather bland.[13] It lacked the bite Mrs. Trollope would put into her book.

Frances Wright was an extremely bright, persuasive, enthusiastic, and personable young Scotswoman of aristocratic background, who had lost her parents at the age of two and had been brought up in an unorthodox fashion by relatives in London. At eighteen she was on her own, an emancipated and independently wealthy young woman who held advanced views on religion, marriage, and the status of women. To judge by the subject of her play *Altorf*, she had imbibed deeply of the ideas the French Revolution had loosed all over Europe. She seemed also to have thoroughly absorbed the views of Mary Wollstonecraft Godwin, who had had a child out of wedlock before she married the philosopher William Godwin. Her daughter was the offspring of the American Gilbert Imlay. Miss Wright also did not enter into legal marriage until after her first child was born and she was in her thirties.

When she and her sister took their first trip across the ocean to witness the production of her play (which was a failure), she was twenty-three. She remained two years, then returned to Europe, this time to France. There she developed such an attachment for the elderly General Lafayette that it gave rise to considerable gossip. When he decided to visit the United States, she accompanied him. It turned out to be a triumphal tour for him as well as for her. She met ex-Presidents Jefferson and Madison and in Washington, Robert Owen, the Scottish philanthropist and social planner who had just embarked on the communitarian experiment in New Harmony, Indiana.

The utopian ideals which underlay the establishment of New Harmony could not fail to fire Miss Wright's enthusiasm. The possibilities for learning under conditions such as New Harmony provided seemed to her limitless. She was thrilled at the thought that all colonists would share work and profits, be educated together, and enjoy the bucolic pleasures of a benevolent nature. It was a vision that was shared by many idealists and reformers. Although a rash of such communitarian experiments was started during the early decades of the nineteenth century practically all of them collapsed. New Harmony lasted only three years, from 1825 to 1828.

Miss Wright visited New Harmony and met Robert Dale Owen, who had come to the colony to join his father. She was impressed by his advanced views, which an education in Switzerland had fostered, and from then on they worked for the same goals. She was especially interested in the *New Harmony Gazette* which he edited for the colony. After it disbanded, she helped him in turning the paper into a radical periodical. It became the mouthpiece for her reform ideas.

But she also wanted to do something on her own. What she had seen of slavery convinced her that it was the most serious problem besetting the new nation. By 1825 she had made the decision to buy a tract of land, and purchase some slaves who by their labor would earn the money with which eventually to secure their freedom and be transported to South America. The idea came from Lafayette's experiment in French Guiana. She planned to maintain a school for the slaves and their off-spring, and it was her hope to bring Europeans into the colony and white children into the school. That was her blueprint for the Nashoba experiment, which was to be located on a three-hundred-acre tract in Nashoba, Tennessee.

It was a spot where malaria was prevalent, and Europeans were particularly susceptible. Bouts of fever with chills and sweating, if it did not kill them quickly, reduced their vitality and turned them into skeletons. Miss Wright herself became ill, and in 1827 was forced to return to England to recover and to gather new members for the Nashoba community.

One who succumbed to Miss Wright's enthusiasm was Frances Trollope, whose husband, a barrister, was considered "undependable both as to earning capacity and temper."[14] Mrs. Trollope and three of her five children accompanied Miss Wright on her return trip to America, but when they reached Nashoba, Mrs. Trollope was so appalled that she soon departed for Cincinnati, where more disillusionment was in store for her. The fashionable "bazaar" she had envisioned did not materialize; all the money that had been invested in it was lost, and when she left America for home after three years and nine months in the New World, only one hope was left to her, that of being able to write a book about America, a course followed by many English visitors to America. While *The Domestic Manners of the Americans* made a tidy fortune for her, it also created a host of enemies in America who labeled her a liar and a libeler.

As Mrs. Trollope had been shrewd enough to foresee, the Nashoba experiment failed. Miss Wright freed her slaves, accompanied them to Haiti,[15] and settled a sum of money on each to help them to a new start. She had lost half her fortune. Having become convinced that a change in people's thinking could be brought about only through education, she made ready for the task of educating the American people.[16] Supported by Robert Dale Owen, she entered on a two-pronged approach. The *New Harmony Gazette* was converted into a radical paper called the *Free Enquirer*. Through this mouthpiece they began to condemn wage slavery, capital punishment, and to call for such reforms as the ten-hour day, workmen's compensation, the abandonment of imprisonment for debt, and other measures in tune with the Jacksonian spirit. Another radical paper, *The Working Men's Advocate*, which was being edited by the British-born George Henry Evans, went her one better by including in its demands "free homesteads" for anyone willing to move West, thus anticipating the Homestead Act of 1862.

She also decided she could reach out to people directly through speechmaking and lecturing. Purchasing an old abandoned church[17] near the Bowery, she called it "Hall of Science," turned it into a lecture hall, and there addressed large audiences who flocked to hear a rarity in those days—an emancipated woman. She also went on speaking tours, where she repeated her most radical demands: the need for property rights for women, easy divorce, birth control and full sexual freedom for women. Even a half-century later, when Emma Goldman advocated some of these principles, they were considered shocking. Miss Wright also urged a system whereby the state would take over the education of children from the age of two until they were grown, an idea she had taken over from Robert Dale Owen.[18]

The condemnation leveled at her for daring to take to the rostrum and, in addition, for expressing such radical views, drove her back to Europe. But tranquillity was evidently not what Frances Wright wanted, because within five years she was back in time to campaign for the 1836 election for the Democratic party. In the meantime she had married a Frenchman, Guillaume Phiquepal d'Arusmont, a French physician and reformer whom she had met in New Harmony. The marriage took place after her child, a girl, was born. The baby died soon thereafter. She had a second daughter who was reared in a totally antifeminist fashion by her father after he divorced Frances Wright.

By the time of Frances Wright's death many of the reforms for which she had agitated—shorter working hours, free public education, the abolition of imprisonment for debt—had been enacted. But the issue of slavery was more heated than ever and the fight for women's rights was still in its beginnings. In the late 1840s a married women's property bill would be passed in New York State, an accomplishment of Ernestine Rose, who had worked with Miss Wright and would continue to exert herself alongside native women leaders for the next two decades.

Frances Wright and Ernestine Rose (1810–1892) had many traits in common. Both were rebels; both turned heretical at an early age; both were endowed with hardihood, forcefulness, tenacity, and striking good looks. Both possessed that special quality that drew people and held them in thrall.

Ernestine Rose was the daughter of a rabbi in Poland. Her mother had died early and she was an only child. Because she had studied the Torah and the Talmud since the age of five, a course of instruction generally given to boys only, she was told she had a boy's mind. The questions she put to her father surprised him, and he answered them up to a point, often replying that such things should be of no concern to a female.

She had grown up with the idea that to be a woman was to be inferior to males. Her father brooked no arguments. At fourteen, after having earnestly pursued biblical studies, she turned heretic.[19] When she was sixteen her father decided it was time she were married and he betrothed her to an older man who, hopefully, would be able to control her more easily than her disconcerted father. It was not unusual in rabbinical circles of that time to choose a husband for a daughter.

She was outraged. Let her father determine who would be her husband? That could never be, she told him. She went to her betrothed, argued, and pleaded with him to release her. He refused. A considerable dowry had been promised him, which she had inherited from her mother and which he would not relinquish. According to Jewish custom a betrothal could not be broken without good reason. If it were, the dowry would revert to the rejected bridegroom.

She decided to take the matter to a secular court. With a courage unheard-of in a sheltered girl of sixteen, she traveled by herself to the nearest town where the Polish court sat and, acting as her own attorney, laid her complaint before the magistrate. Her father was ordered to restore her inheritance to her. But when she found herself freed from the obligation to marry the man, she promptly turned the money back to her father.

But living in her father's household became so difficult that she decided to leave home. Her first stop was Berlin. There she worked out a process by which chemically treated paper, when burned, dispelled cooking odors. Years later in New York she would open a perfumery shop in which she would sell her own concoction of Cologne water.

After traveling on the continent, she landed in England, where she discovered a pantheon of heroes, among whom were Robert Owen and Tom Paine. Trying to support herself as a teacher of Hebrew and German, she sought out Robert Owen, then sixty, who had just returned from his unsuccessful experiment in New Harmony, Indiana, and was in great demand as a speaker. He invited her to speak in the huge hall he had built for himself, and she rewarded his confidence by making a conspicuous hit with his audiences.

In England she met William Rose, whose work as a jeweler and silversmith is judged to have been unusually artistic. She married him in a civil ceremony. Together they left for the United States in 1836, when she was twenty-six. Mr. Rose not only encouraged her in her ideas, but also provided her with the means to travel at his personal expense all over the country, to hire halls where she could hold forth on behalf of the causes to which he was as devoted as she.

In the 1830s the women of America still had no legal rights. What property they owned or inherited was their husbands', to do with as they wished. Women could never sue or be sued. If they worked, their husbands could collect their wages and appropriate them. In cases of divorce, children were placed in the custody of their fathers. Men could appoint guardians for their children without having to take the wishes of their wives into consideration. Before the law, women were minors who were under the protection (or exploitation) of fathers and husbands.

In 1836 Judge Thomas Herttel introduced a Married Women's Property Bill into the legislature of the State of New York. Those favoring it were aware that it would require unrelenting effort and unwavering patience for an indeterminate amount of time before such a bill could become law. To Mrs. Rose the prospect of such a victory seemed worth every expenditure of time and effort. She drew up a petition in support of the bill and undertook to gather signatures, going from door to door, in town after town, ringing doorbells, often rebuffed, sometimes insulted. Women have more than enough rights and privileges, men told her. (Often the women agreed with them, particularly in their husbands' hearing.) The lawmakers were deluged with lists of petitions that grew longer every year. After twelve years of unremitting perseverance by Judge Herttel, Mrs. Rose, and others, among whom was Elizabeth Cady Stanton, soon to be identified as a suffragist, the bill was passed in 1848.

It was not the kind of victory that benefited all women, because it affected only those who had brought property to their husbands when they married or received it after their marriage. But it was a crack in the wall of prejudice against women, and it was a victory to which Mrs. Rose could feel she had significantly contributed.[20]

Encouraged by the example of New York State, at least six other states introduced and eventually enacted such laws. In Indiana Robert Dale Owen, then a member of the state legislature, introduced a similar bill during the 1836–37 session. In Indiana it also took thirteen years before the bill became law.[21]

While agitating for the passage of the Women's Property Bill, Mrs. Rose was also active as a platform speaker and as a writer for radical magazines. She was the first woman of non-English background to appear before American audiences. She was described as looking "queenly," as having a slight lisp and a foreign accent, which the brilliance of her remarks rendered inconspicuous. At first she spoke on subjects not likely to arouse violent opposition, but she soon plunged into such controversial topics—abolition of slavery, race relations, women's rights, easier divorce laws—that her addresses were regarded as revolutionary. At times she came close to being tarred and feathered, but she was absolutely fearless. Once in Charleston, South Carolina, where she had spoken on black and white relations, her audience became so hostile that it required considerable maneuvering to whisk her away. But she would not truckle to public opinion, because she viewed that as "moral cowardice."

Her method was to rely on wit, humor, and impeccable logic. One of her biographers commented that she "handled her logic as deftly as her needle."[22] The *Herald Tribune*, which was hostile to her, had to admit that "Mrs. Rose spun a long yarn, composed of wit, philosophy and satire."[23] At other times she could be disarmingly whimsical without abandoning logic. For instance:

It were indeed well if a woman could be what she ought to be, man what he ought to be, and marriage what it ought to be. . . . But, alas, it is not yet . . . I therefore ask for a divorce law. . . . I believe in true marriages and I ask for a law to free men and women from false ones.[24]

Many prominent people admired her, among them Wendell Phillips, Boston clergyman and abolitionist, and Moncure D. Conway, Virginia clergyman and liberal leader. To William Lloyd Garrison she was "one of the most remarkable women of our age." She often shared the platform with Garrison, Phillips, Frederick Douglass, and other antislavery leaders.

Like Frances Wright, whose path often crossed hers, she was called an "atheist," "an infidel," and an advocate of free love. But unlike Miss Wright, her radicalism would often be attributed to her Jewish background.[25]

Soon after the Women's Rights Convention at Seneca Falls, New York, Ernestine Rose began to participate regularly in feminist conventions. As chairman of one of the leading committees, she was depended upon to give the kind of impassioned speech of which the following is a sample:

But it will be said that the husband provides for the wife, or in other words, he feeds, clothes and shelters her. I wish I had the power to make everyone before me fully realize the degradation contained in that idea. Yes! he *keeps* her and so he does a favorite horse; by law they are both considered his property.... I know that some endeavor to throw the mantle of romance over the subject, and treat women like some ideal existence, not liable to the ills of life. Let those deal in fancy, that have nothing better to deal in; we have to deal with sober, sad realities, with stubborn facts.[26]

In 1869 when she was close to sixty, ill health caused her to return to England. Before she left she sought American citizenship, fifteen years after her husband had become an American citizen. The explanation her biographer suggests was that she considered citizenship unimportant when women could not vote, and that it was her way of protesting for full equality.[27]

When the territory of Wyoming enfranchised women in 1859, it was the beginning toward which Frances Wright and Ernestine Rose had worked. Susan Anthony, the suffrage leader, recognized the importance of their contribution to the goal of securing the vote for women, for she recommended that the first place in the Honor Roll of suffrage workers be given to Mary Wollstonecraft Godwin, the second to Frances Wright, and the third to Ernestine Rose.

During the last decade of the nineteenth century a number of western states gave women the right to vote, but Mrs. Rose was no longer alive. She missed the enfranchisement of women in Colorado in 1893 by one year. By then a reincarnation of her had appeared. She was Emma Goldman, the anarchist, who came from Russia. Emma Goldman had in common with Mrs. Rose great courage and remarkable oratorical quality. But Mrs. Rose was no anarchist. Miss Goldman's life and activities will be presented later.

The third in the quartet of foreign-born women to dedicate themselves to the cause of feminism in the United States was Mathilde Franziska Giesler-Anneke (1817–1884). Her activities fall into three spheres: publishing her own newspapers in Germany and in America; public lecturing; finally, teaching. One suspects that she had more of a language problem than Mrs. Rose, for Mrs. Rose's biographer speaks of her standing by during the Women's Rights Convention of 1853—four years after Mrs. Anneke's arrival in the United States—to translate Mrs. Anneke's speech from German into English, a speech which an unruly mob prevented her from delivering.

Mathilde Franziska Giesler-Anneke was the daughter of a government councillor and had received a superior education. Though she was raised as a Catholic and Mrs. Rose as a Jewess, their backgrounds parallel one another in several ways. Both had received a thorough grounding in their respective religions, Mrs. Rose by studying Hebrew, Mrs. Anneke in Catholic teachings. In the years when Mrs. Anneke was an Orthodox believer, she wrote and published several devotional books. Both became freethinkers in their youth and militant feminists because of parental and social repression.

Mathilde Giesler had experienced the opprobrium connected with a demand for divorce. On the eve of the 1848 Revolution she married her second husband, a Prussian military officer who had been dismissed from the army because of supposedly communist views and had received a jail sentence. While he was in jail she made her first attempt at publishing a newspaper, *Die Kölnische Zeitung*. It was soon suppressed. She began anew, this time calling the paper *Die Frauenzeitung*, in which she stressed equal rights for women. Again the censor stepped in and halted her activities.

The Revolution of 1848 found her husband released from jail and on the side of the revolutionary forces. Like the legendary Molly Pitcher in the American Revolution, Mrs. Anneke rode along with her husband, mounted on a horse. Carl Schurz, who served under Lieutenant Colonel Fritz Anneke, describes her as "a young woman of noble character, beauty, vivacity and fiery patriotism who accompanied her husband on this march."[28]

After the fiasco of the Revolution of 1848, both fled to the United States. She attempted to revive her newspaper in the manner of some of the Forty-Eighter refugees who hoped to maintain themselves as journalists. For most it proved a vain hope, and those who managed to stay afloat barely eked out a scanty living. Mathilde and Fritz Anneke lectured in German, on political and economic issues, and she, on women's rights. It proved especially difficult for him to find a proper niche.

During the Civil War he received a commission in the Union Army, but was dismissed in 1863 because of differences with one of his superior officers. By then Mrs. Anneke was separated from her husband, but they were never divorced.

The following portion of a speech she gave in 1869 reveals by its insistence on reason that the ideas of the Enlightenment had deeply impressed her, and by its passionate tone that she was captivated by the spirit of romanticism. In Mrs. Anneke's words:

There does not exist a man-made doctrine fabricated expressly for us and which we must learn by heart, that shall henceforth be our law. Nor shall the authority of old traditions be a standard for us— be this authority called Veda, Talmud, Koran or Bible. No. Reason which we recognize as our highest and only law-giver, commands us to be free.... Therefore, don't exclude women, don't exclude the whole half of the human family. Receive us—begin the work in which a new era shall dawn. In all great events we find that woman has a guiding hand—let us stay near you now, when humanity is concerned.... Honor us as your equals and allow us to use the rights which belong to us and which reason commands us to use.[29]

She finally opened a school in Milwaukee for young women, *die Töchterschule*, and devoted the rest of her life to teaching. Offering an advanced curriculum, the school acquired such a high reputation that her coworker Cäcilie Kapp was offered a post at Vassar College. She accepted, and Mrs. Anneke continued alone until her death in 1884. Of the four foreign-born fighters for the advancement of women—Frances Wright, Ernestine Rose, Anna Howard Shaw, whose story follows, and herself— she was the only one who raised a family in America.

It was given to another woman of English background to be among those who finished what Frances Wright had begun. She was Anna Howard Shaw (1847–1919),[30] who began as a minister, became a physician, and ended her life as a suffragette. Like many women reformers, native and foreign-born, she had been interested in abolition and temperance before she committed herself fully to the crusade to win the vote for women. Her place was not among the pioneers, but among those who

fought in the last battles before the Nineteenth Amendment
was passed.

Well accustomed to struggling against obstacles since her
youth, hers was no privileged childhood. Born in England of
Scottish parents, she was brought to the United States at three.
After living in New England for several years, her father took
up a 360-acre tract in Michigan, but soon after clearing the
land and erecting a log cabin, he enlisted in the Civil War.
When her oldest brother became ill, the whole responsibility
fell on her and a younger brother. Both were compelled to do
the heaviest physical labor. She was thirteen when she finally
began to attend school three miles from home.

Her desire to enter the ministry manifested itself after she
heard a Universalist woman minister speak. She was also influenced by the woman principal of the school she attended,
who was a Methodist. The latter introduced her to one of the
Methodist Elders, who asked her to preach a sermon at the
quarterly meeting; afterward Miss Shaw was invited to preach
in all the thirty-six churches which formed his circuit.

When she entered theological school in Boston, she was the
only woman among forty-two men. She had a very difficult
time because as a woman she was excluded from receiving
financial help which was available to men. During her vacations
she substituted at local pulpits and worked during revivals.
Though she was an eloquent speaker and had held several
pastorates, she was refused ordination by the Methodist Epis-
copal Church. The reason was not even glossed over; one of
the bishops frankly advised her to leave the church. After a
five-year struggle she was finally ordained by the Methodist
Protestant Church. While attending to her parish duties she
studied medicine, receiving the M.D. degree in 1880, at the
age of thirty-three. But while she attended patients in the slums,
she had no interest in practicing medicine.

It is easy to understand why her experience as a minister
and physician to the poor brought her first into the temperance
movement and then into the campaign for the emancipation of
women. Drunkenness and the mistreatment of wives was something with which she was familiar. When she finally committed
herself to full-time work for women's suffrage, she had to find

some means to support herself. She joined the then famous Redpath Lecture Bureau, which booked the "greats" of New England, and faithfully followed the lecture circuit despite blizzards, flood-swollen rivers and other hazards. Once she realized she was being pursued by wolves.

Susan B. Anthony was a very close friend. In 1900 Miss Anthony gave up the presidency of the National American Woman's Suffrage Association (NAWSA) and was succeeded by Carrie Chapman Catt. When the latter was elected president of the International Woman's Suffrage Association, Anna Howard Shaw was asked to head the American Suffrage Association. She retained her post until President Wilson drafted her as chairman of the Women's Committee of the National Council of Defense.

She threw herself into the new job with the zeal she had shown for all her work. But she died soon afterward, just as the struggle of almost one hundred years was coming to an end, for in June, 1919, the Nineteenth Amendment to the Constitution was passed. It was not ratified until August, 1920, but Anna Howard Shaw lived long enough to know that the fight was won.

While Anna Howard Shaw turned from temperance to the suffrage movement, Mrs. Matilda Bradley Carse (1835–1917)[31] abandoned the suffrage movement to become a temperance leader. An executive type, she was responsible for establishing the first day nursery for working mothers in Chicago, the first kindergartens, a mission for erring girls, a dispensary for the poor, an industrial school, Sunday schools, and an employment bureau. Furthermore, she raised the money with which to support these charities. Her initial brilliant success and her subsequent failure are reminiscent of Robert Burns's words: "The best laid schemes o' mice and men /Gang aft agley...."

Though born in Ireland, she was a Presbyterian of Scottish descent. She came to Chicago at twenty-three and a few years later married a Scotsman. He died within ten years, leaving her in comfortable circumstances.

The death of her youngest son, who was run over by a drunken driver, drove her into the temperance movement, and she threw herself into it with such singlemindedness that within a few years she was elected president of the Chicago Central Women's Christian Temperance Union, a job she filled until her death.

As a resourceful businesswoman, she organized two business projects intended to enrich the coffers and the prestige of the WCTU. One was a women's Temperance Publishing Association, a stock company composed only of women, which published the weekly journal of the Illinois WCTU, tracts on temperance, and undertook commercial printing as well. This enterprise went along splendidly until the Panic of 1893. The depression that followed had a cataclysmic effect on business conditions throughout the nation. The printing establishment was ruined.

An even more ambitious program was the plan to create an office building of thirteen stories to be called "The Women's Temple." It was to be the headquarters of the WCTU and was also intended to provide the organization with an income through the renting of space. She sold $600,000 worth of stock and $300,000 in bonds to the members of the WCTU with the blessing of Frances Willard, national president of the WCTU. The building was barely completed when the Panic of 1893 struck, and destroyed its prospects of becoming a profitable undertaking. The "Women's Temple" was finally taken over by Marshall Field, on whose property it had been built.

She also raised money for other charities. One of them was the Children's Foundling Home and Society, of which she was president. She was also the first woman to serve on the Cook County Board of Education.

A leader in the field of child welfare was Sophie Irene Loeb Simon (1876–1929).[32] The Child Welfare Board is her creation. No agency existed that was dedicated to aiding dependent children and their mothers until her long and painstaking efforts bore fruit. Death at the age of fifty-two cut her off at the high point of her career.

Born in Russia on America's hundredth anniversary, July 4, 1876, she was brought to McKeesport, Pennsylvania, at the age of six. When her father died, her mother underwent a difficult struggle to keep the family together. Only through tremendous effort by the older children, who worked at various occupations, were the younger children kept out of orphanages. It made such an impression on the mind of the young girl that she never forgot it.

But she was able to finish high school and to become first a teacher and then a newspaper reporter. She married, but was soon divorced. In 1910 she became a reporter and feature writer for the *Evening World*. Through her work she came in contact with destitute widows, who revived her recollections and made her realize anew the dangers inhering in the breaking up of homes. During the early years of the twentieth century no "home relief" was available; charities and private agencies which were supported by the state were opposed to direct state aid to destitute mothers.

She searched for allies and found one in Mrs. Hannah Bachman Einstein, a native American of German parentage who was socially prominent and had a strong sense of social commitment. Together they began to agitate—she through her writings in the *Evening World*, Mrs. Einstein as president of the Widowed Mothers' Fund Association. In 1913 she and Mrs. Einstein were appointed by the legislature of the State of New York to study the problem. Miss Loeb traveled through Europe to examine the welfare policies of other countries. After an initial defeat a bill was enacted for the support of needy mothers, and child welfare boards were established throughout New York State. Miss Loeb became a member of the Child Welfare Board in New York City, and eventually its president and administrator.

She also sponsored other social legislation, such as school lunches for children, slum clearance, and better housing.

Miss Loeb would never accept compensation for her work on behalf of needy children and their mothers, but supported herself through newspaper work and radio appearances.

Her dedication to mothers and children requiring help was undoubtedly due to her experiences as an immigrant. When she died at fifty-two, August Heckscher donated the funds for a children's fountain in marble in Central Park to her memory.

Two foreign-born women of totally different backgrounds were able to promote social goals through private philanthropy. One was Anna Uhl Ottendorfer (1815–1884), born in Germany, who came to the United States at twenty-two. Through her participation in business she helped her first husband to succeed. By continuing her business activities during her second marriage she became a wealthy woman.

The other was Pauline Agassiz Shaw (1841–1917) of Swiss birth. She was brought to the United States as a young girl. Reared in an intellectual home but in modest circumstances, she married a New Englander of distinguished social background, who acquired a large fortune through copper mining.

Anna Uhl Ottendorfer deserves to be held in high regard, not only for her public benefactions, but also for her business acumen. With her first husband she established and built up the most successful German language newspaper in the United States. The continued success of the paper under the editorship of her second husband, Oswald Ottendorfer, enabled her to become one of the outstanding women philanthropists of foreign birth. Furthermore, she passed on her humanitarian inclinations to her daughter, Mrs. Anna Woerishoffer, the wife of one of the railroad builders of the post-Civil War era, and to her granddaughter, Emma Carola Woerishoffer. When the latter was killed in an automobile accident in 1911 at the age of twenty-six, she was already known as a patron of working women.

Mrs. Ottendorfer was born in Würzburg, Germany. A year after her emigration she married Jacob Uhl, a printer. After eight years of struggle they had saved enough to purchase *Die New Yorker Staatszeitung,* then a weekly, but shortly thereafter a daily. With his wife installed in the business office, Jacob Uhl also began to publish the writings of Germans in America. She was said to have been a very genial and kindly woman whose presence promoted goodwill among employees and clients. Their establishment thrived.

In 1852 Mr. Uhl died suddenly and the paper became his wife's responsibility. She refused to sell it, though she had six young children to care for. She decided to carry on alone.

The highpoint of the German influx in the United States which was to reach five million by the end of the nineteenth century,[33] coincided with the growth of the *Staatszeitung*. Forging steadily ahead, it became the most powerful of all foreign newspapers in America. By offering a "skillful balance of general news with a thorough and personal coverage of personalities and activities in the numerous clubs and societies that made up the German-speaking community,"[34] the purpose of propping up the self-confidence of the German community was achieved. The reading public of the paper extended as far West as Ohio.

In 1859 Anna Uhl married Oswald Ottendorfer, the chief editor of the paper. He was of the ilk of the Forty-Eighters, having shared their hopes and ideals. He was opposed to slavery (later to prohibition as well) and became a supporter of reform and liberal causes. After the Civil War he joined the Reform Democrats in fighting the Tammany regime.[35]

The extent of the paper's financial success can be gauged by the charitable contributions made by Anna and Oswald Ottendorfer separately. While she favored hospitals, homes for the aged, and promoted an interest in German education, his main contribution went to the Ottendorfer branch of the public library.[36] In 1875 she built a home for aged women in Astoria, Long Island, in memory of her daughter Isabella Uhl, spending more than $150,000 on it.[37] When her son Herman Uhl died tragically, she contributed $40,000 to a memorial fund that eventually grew into several hundred thousands. A year later she gave $66,000 to the Women's Pavilion, now Lenox Hill Hospital, and another $150,000 to the German dispensary, and also contributed to a Newark hospital. When she died she left a quarter of a million to various causes, and $25,000 to be divided among the employees of the *Staatszeitung*. It was estimated that she distributed three quarters of a million during her lifetime.[38]

That her commitment to enriching the lives of the old and the unfortunates of society extended beyond sectarian boundaries was disclosed in a letter of condolence from the Board of Governors of the Home for the Aged and Infirm of the Independent Order of B'nai Brith, a Jewish organization. In their letter they acknowledged her "lively interest in the comfort of its inmates."[39]

She was also a life member of the Free Kindergarten and

Workingmen's School of the Ethical Culture Society, helped the Children's Aid Association, and contributed to the needs of women and orphans through the New York Women's Club. During a serious flood in Germany in 1882-83 her aid brought her a medal from the German Empress.[40]

At her death Carl Schurz offered a peroration at her grave. He did not exaggerate when he said:

Wenn unser Volk seine Wohlthäter aufzählt, wenn die Deutschen Amerika's Diejenigen nennen auf die sie mit dem höchsten Stolz hinweisen, so wird sicherlich der Name Anna Ottendorfer im erster Reise stehen.[41]

Author's translation: When our people count their benefactors, when America's Germans come to mention those to whom they can point with the greatest pride, then surely the name of Anna Ottendorfer will occupy front rank.

The benefactions of Pauline Agassiz Shaw (1841–1917) were of much greater magnitude than those of Anna Ottendorfer. Mrs. Shaw was enabled to become a philanthropist through her marriage to Quincy Adams Shaw, a prominent Bostonian. On the advice of Mrs. Shaw's brother, Alexander Agassiz, who was an engineer, Quincy Adams Shaw took over and developed the Calumet Hecla copper mines in Michigan. Eventually he became one of New England's wealthiest men.

Pauline Agassiz was the younger daughter of Jean Louis Agassiz, the Swiss-born scientist, who made his reputation as a geologist and paleontologist, teacher at Harvard, and an opponent of the Darwinian theory of natural selection.

After the death of Jean Louis Agassiz's first wife, who had been left in Europe with their children when her husband came to America, he married Elizabeth Cabot Cary of Boston. Although the family lived in modest circumstances, all three Agassiz children were raised according to the precepts of upper-class Boston. Mrs. Agassiz was interested in education and conducted a private school which Elizabeth and her older sister attended.

Pauline, who was said to have been a beautiful, delicate, and sensitive girl, married at nineteen. She had absorbed an interest in education from her father's wife, whose work on behalf of higher education for girls culminated in becoming one of the founders of Radcliffe college, and its president from 1894–1902.[42]

Long before that, Pauline Agassiz Shaw had become known as an "educational philanthropist." Her first interest was in kindergarten education, in which Boston's Elizabeth Peabody had pioneered. In the 1870s Mrs. Shaw, then in her late thirties and the mother of five children, opened the first two kindergartens. Within six years she supported thirty-one.[43] Though some of them were located in public schools, she supplied the funds for staff and equipment and even paid for food and clothing for the children. It was said that she "gave herself as well as money."[44] She became the "fairy godmother" of the children, bringing baskets of flowers to the schools and participating in the activities. In 1888 she persuaded the city of Boston to take over fourteen of her schools.

Her interest spread to day nurseries, where children of working mothers were cared for. In the evening instruction was offered to women in hygiene and sewing, and related subjects. Also these centers which became known as the Cambridge Street and the Ruggles Street Neighborhood Houses, offered library service, recreational facilities, and instruction in various crafts.[45] She also supported an industrial school where such skills as cooking, printing, metalwork, and woodworking were taught.

Mrs. Shaw was not oblivious to the problems of the foreign-born. With the help of several educators she started a center where vocational training and educational opportunities as well as guidance were provided to foreign-born wage earners. Eventually this program became Boston's Vocation Bureau.[46]

She came to the cause of woman suffrage in the 1890s and gave it financial support as well as her personal participation, subsidizing suffrage campaigns and peace organizations.

A philanthropist on the grand scale, she was Boston's major woman benefactress.

A very different type of social reformer was the militant Rosika Schwimmer (1877–1948).[47] Her special interest was the peace movement. A native of Hungary, she led a turbulent life in Europe as well as in the United States. She has the unusual distinction of being immortalized in a case reviewed by the Supreme Court, in which three Supreme Court Justices, whose spokesman was Oliver Wendell Holmes, registered their dissent from a decision adverse to her.

At first she dedicated herself to the cause of women workers, and in order to acquaint herself with working conditions for women, she worked as a bobbin girl in a factory. But between 1904 and 1914 she switched to pacifist organizations and to the International Woman's Suffrage Alliance. After settling in London she acted as foreign correspondent for several large European newspapers.

The outbreak of World War I in 1914 changed the direction of her life. Her first step was to betake herself to the United States to promote a mediated peace which President Wilson was known to favor. She secured interviews with the then Secretary of State William Jennings Bryan and with President Wilson. But she received little encouragement from the President and decided therefore to appeal directly to the American people. She was fluent in English, having lived in England. During 1914 and 1915 she toured the United States to make sensational speeches against the war. Indefatigable and very persuasive, she was at the same time a contentious woman who would not run away from any fight. Soon she could count on a large following.

By 1915 she had marshaled enough support to create a Woman's Peace Party, of which she was elected international secretary. The purpose was to press for mediation by neutrals. She enlisted the foremost women leaders in Europe and America in a crusade to interview various statesmen of the world, and was able to persuade Henry Ford to include one hundred and sixty reformers on the liner *Oscar II* he had chartered. But on board ship her influence with Ford evaporated. In Norway Ford left for home and the rest dispersed.

When Hungary collapsed in 1918, she became one of the fifteen who in effect governed Hungary. She was appointed Hungarian minister to Sweden. But the government of Count Karolyi did not survive and she refused to serve the communist Bela Kun. After leaving Hungary in 1921, she showed up a year later in the United States to find herself referred to as a spy and a Bolshevik agent. She sued Henry Ford for calling her a swindler, and obtained a judgment of $17,000 against him.

When she applied for American citizenship, the American Legion and other patriotic organizations opposed her application, and citizenship was denied her. The case reached the Supreme Court which decided against her. Justice Holmes declared for his colleagues, the Justices Brandeis and Sanford, that the principle of "free thought was the one most worthy of adherence . . . not free thought for those who agree with us, but freedom for the thought we hate."

The rest of her life was devoted to advocating world government and the establishment of a Federation of Nations. When she died in New York City in 1948, her ashes were dropped over Lake Michigan.

The post-Civil War decades saw a huge growth in immigration. During the decades of the eighties alone the increase was at the rate of more than a half-million a year.[48] A high point was reached between 1901 and 1905, when more than three million Europeans swarmed into the United States.[49] Between 1905 and 1914 the million mark was exceeded in six separate years.[50] For the first time in American history, fewer Northern than Southern and Eastern Europeans sought admission, forming what has been designated as the "New Immigration." This new breed—Italians, Slavs, Jews and others—appeared to many incapable of assimilation to the American way of life and hence undesirable. Some of the Russian and Polish Jews who were making their appearance in such overwhelming numbers were, according to Nathan Glazer, "a frightening apparition" even to their German brethren, who had by then become thoroughly Americanized. Abysmally poor, ignorant, and bewildered by the tempo of American life, these later immigrants were in desperate need of help.

The response to that avalanche—"the huddled masses" of Emma Lazarus (an American of several generations)—was a proliferation of settlement houses in slum areas, whose leaders were likely to be, like Jane Addams and Ellen Gates Starr of Hull House, Chicago, old-line Americans, or natives like Lillian

D. Wald, the daughter of Germans, in New York, and Mrs. Simon Kander in Milwaukee. Miss Wald had begun by studying medicine, then nursing and social work, to become "the guardian angel" of the new immigrants thronging the Henry Street Settlement of New York. Mrs. Kander of Milwaukee, also a first generation American, taught settlement girls to cook and at the same time built up an enduring reputation (and a fortune for herself and her heirs) as the author of the *Settlement House Cook Book*, after a hundred years still a best seller.

By the end of the century nearly one hundred settlement houses[51] had sprung up. Enormously significant help came from individuals whose impulse to aid the poor and helpless sprang from religious motives and associations. Unbelievable feats were performed by dedicated individuals, many of whom took baskets to beg for the needy under their care in orphanages, schools, and hospitals. A large number of these benefactors were foreign-born women.

CHAPTER 4

The Religious Impulse

FROM THE INCEPTION OF THE AMERICAN EXPERIMENT THE religious impulse was a strongly motivating force. The settlers of the North differed in their religious convictions from those in the South; nevertheless, Puritans, Anglicans, and adherents of other religious sects were determined to establish governments under God. Though the colonies considered themselves separate states, most of them claimed England as their "deare mother" and were united in their resolution to establish a "godly nation" across the sea.

America has always had a greater diversity of religious sects than any European country. Individualism in religion was brought over in the first ships, and it was inevitable that both religion and individualism should become reinforced by the conditions encountered by the newcomers—solitariness, danger, fear, and insecurity. Also a new land encouraged the hope that a greater degree of perfection might be achieved, and in that way earth be brought closer to heaven.

Until the Revolution, the predominant church in Virginia was the Anglican Church, and it was state supported. In Massachusetts the religious uniformity introduced by the Puritans was imposed by the colonists themselves, in spite, rather than because of, English policy.[1] The more tolerant attitude of the English government (attempts to restrain religious exclusion were made on several occasions) is explained on the basis that economic activity, the primary concern of the home state, would be furthered by a policy of toleration.

The first crack in the Puritan wall appeared when Roger Williams, banished from the Massachusetts Bay Colony, removed to Rhode Island and there proclaimed religious liberty for all. The crack became irreparable when in 1684 the Massachusetts

55

Bay Colony was forced by royal edict to accept Quakers and
Anglicans. Before that, in 1661, Charles II had intervened to
put an end to the execution of Quakers.[2] In Virginia a major
break had occurred when Quaker missionaries were successful
in establishing several communities of followers. In Maryland,
planted initially as a haven for Catholics, Protestants were soon
accepted and given the same privileges as Catholics. The
Carolinas, though nominally composed of a majority of Anglicans, soon acquired a population of varying religious backgrounds, of whom a large bloc were Scotch-Irish militant
Presbyterians.

The greatest number of differing religious sects was to be
found in the middle colonies of New York, New Jersey, and
Pennsylvania. In Nieuw Amsterdam Peter Stuyvesant would
have excluded newcomers who were not of the Dutch Reformed
Church, if he had not been ordered by the Dutch West India
Company to desist. The "holy experiment" in Pennsylvania alone
included half a dozen religious sects, including Anabaptists,
Dunkers, Moravians, Schwenkfelders, and German Lutherans.
In addition Pennsylvania received Anglicans, Swedish Lutherans
who removed there after "New Sweden" was taken over by the
Dutch; also Scotch Presbyterians and before very long, Jews.
When trouble arose during the mid-eighteenth century, it was
attributable not to religious but to political reasons, specifically
the refusal of the Quakers to take oaths and to agree on
measures of defense against the Indians.

The Revolution strengthened religious freedom by disestablish-
ing the Anglican Church in Virginia (which had harbored many
Tories) and in several other places where it had taken hold.
The Virginia Bill for Establishing Religious Freedom was the
work of Thomas Jefferson, who was so proud of having it
brought about that he ordered it inscribed on his tombstone as
one of the three most significant achievements of his life.

The Constitution spurred the spread of religious freedom
and the proliferation of religious sects in two ways: by not
requiring religious qualifications for office holding, and by stating in Article VI that no religious tests shall ever be applied
to any office. Also, the First Amendment forbids Congress to
make any law respecting the establishment of religion or pro-

hibiting the free exercise thereof. However, this did not inhibit
the state constitutions from stipulating religious limitations on
office holding and on the right to vote. In several states Catholics and Jews were specifically excluded.[3]

The Quaker proselytizer and founder of the Quaker sect, John
Fox, visited America in 1672, accompanied by twelve followers.
A Presbyterian preacher of the eighteenth century was the
Irish-born William Tennent, who established a "log college" in
Pennsylvania in 1736. Some of his followers founded the College of New Jersey, chartered in 1746, which was renamed
Princeton in 1896 after the town in which it was situated. Another religious key figure was George Whitefield, a young man
and a powerful orator who came to Georgia purportedly to
establish an orphan asylum. A friend of the Wesley brothers,
he first preached Methodism, then Calvinism. His spellbinding
powers impressed even the cool Deist, Benjamin Franklin. In
his wry manner Franklin commented:

It was wonderful to see the change soon made in the manners
of our inhabitants. From being thoughtless or indifferent about
religion, it seemed as if all the world were growing religious, so
that one could not walk through the town in an evening without
hearing psalms sung by different families of every street.[4]

Franklin went back to attend another of Mr. Whitefield's
sermons, but was resolved to contribute no money. Then:

As he [Whitefield] proceeded I began to soften, and concluded
to give the coppers [in his pocket]. Another stroke of his oratory
made me ashamed of that, and determined me to give the silver;
and he finished so admirably that I emptied my pocket wholly into
the collector's dish, gold and all.[5]

The Wesley brothers, founders of Methodism, were also
charismatic preachers. When they arrived in the colonies in
the 1770s, they provided a powerful impetus to their followers.
In the early nineteenth century the Scottish-educated Thomas
Campbell (1763–1854) who came from Ireland, settled in western Pennsylvania and became the leader of the western Christians, or the "Disciples of Christ" as they called themselves.

Religion was a most serious matter in the West, where the isolation was more pronounced than in the more developed parts of the country.

Clergymen themselves made rapid switches from one sect to another, as had Campbell when he had abandoned the Baptists, or as the Campbellite Sidney Rigdon did when he joined Joseph Smith and the Mormons to become the first counselor in the church presidency (later to be sacrificed by Brigham Young). Joseph Meacham, originally a Baptist, was another who changed his religious affiliation when he came into the Shaker fold, followed by his whole congregation. Sometimes it was only necessary to announce a new interpretation of the Scriptures as did William Miller, a New York farmer, when he proclaimed that Christ "would come about 1843."[6] Many of his followers were so convinced that they disposed of their earthly goods, donned their ascension robes, and took to the hills to await the Second Coming. Anyone who claimed to have been visited by a heavenly personage (as Joseph Smith did) or offered a new interpretation of the Bible was sure to attract followers.

What is more surprising than that males dominated America's religious life, is that some religious leaders were women, several of whom were foreign-born. The very first one was, of course, the redoubtable Anne Hutchinson, who rammed her head against the brick wall of Puritanism. Had she lived a hundred years later she might have succeeded in becoming the founder of a new religious fellowship. Another foreign-born religious leader was Ann Lee, who founded the Shaker sect, and a third who wielded great influence among the "True Inspirationists" was Barbara Heinemann. More of them later.

Long before the Revolution, religious groups had begun to multiply by the splitting off of dissidents from parent organizations and through the continuous exhortations of proselytizing clergy from England. The number of Quakers, Baptists, Methodists, and Presbyterians increased enormously even before the Revolution. One reason for the growth of religious fervor in the colonies is attributed to a series of religious revivals called "The Great Awakening." Beginning with the 1730s it raged through the colonies with the force of an epidemic. Manifesting itself in emotional prayer meetings, the result was a rapid increase in church membership. The hurricane force with which these revival meetings raged has been attributed to their emotional content, which is judged to have appealed to the heart rather than the head. The religious ardor that was generated through these camp meetings made people susceptible to new creeds, which were sometimes propounded by backwoodsmen who had never read any other book but the Bible and claimed no other instruction was necessary.

It is not surprising that many people were willing to follow a self-styled prophet when he claimed a direct revelation from the Father, the Son, Saint John the Baptist, or any other heavenly messenger. But these supposedly divinely guided individuals were not free from persecution in England, the German states, or in America, as we can see from the stories of the Shakers, the "True Inspirationalists" in Southern Germany, and the Mormons in America. Of these three only Joseph Smith, the founder of the Mormon Church, was a native American; the leaders of the other two were immigrants.

Two of the earliest women proselytizers in the colonies, both English-born, were the two Quakers, Mary Fisher and Ann Austin. Nothing is known of Ann Austin, except that she was the older of the two.[7] Mary Fisher (1623-1698)[8] came from Yorkshire, where she had been a servant. When she started preaching in England she was persecuted as a vagrant. In 1656 both came to Boston from Barbados. Before the two Quaker women could disembark, Deputy Governor Bellingham of the Massachusetts Bay Colony boarded the vessel, seized their pamphlets, imprisoned the two women, and later sent them back to Barbados. After returning to England, Mary Fisher traveled to Turkey, where she interviewed the Sultan. She did not convert him, but he received her more courteously than had Bellingham. In 1682 she returned to the colonies, this time to Charleston. After her death her family remained in South Carolina. One of her descendants became a well-known Quaker preacher.

Two years before the Declaration of Independence, Ann Lee (1736–1784), who could neither read nor write, took herself with eight followers to the colonies after claiming to have received a vision of Jesus, who revealed to her that the "second Christian Church" would be established in America and that the colonies would gain their independence.

Hers was not the first chiliastic prediction that America, especially New England, was to be the center of the New Jerusalem. Puritan divines had predicted it in the seventeenth and eighteenth centuries, specifically Michael Wigglesworth (1631–1705) in his *Day of Doom* and later Timothy Dwight (1752–1817), grandson of Jonathan Edwards. To this day the Seventh Day Adventists, who are descendants of the Millerites, await a Second Coming.

As the second of eight children in a poverty-stricken home in Manchester—her father was a blacksmith—she was sent to work in a cotton factory when she was still a child. Later she worked as a cook in a Manchester infirmary. At eighteen she married a blacksmith; in the words of one of her biographers, "notwithstanding her repugnance to the married state."[9] She had four children, all of whom died in infancy. Another biographer suggests that her attitude toward sex may have caused her to dedicate herself to celibacy.[10] She is said to have been short, rather stout, with a fair complexion, blue eyes, and light chestnut-brown hair. Many called her beautiful. At the age of twenty-two she joined a religious group to which her parents belonged and which had been formed as a result of a religious revival in 1747. The followers were laborers, mill hands, servants, who worked during the day and worshipped at night. An offshoot of the Quakers, the group began their meetings in Quaker fashion with silent meditation, suddenly to break out in shaking, dancing, singing, or prophesying that the second appearing of Christ was at hand. According to a chronicler of the Shakers:

They were often exercised with singing, shouting and leaping for joy at the near prospect of salvation. . . . These experiences so strange in the eyes of the beholders, brought upon them the appellation of "Shakers."[11]

In 1770 she experienced her first revelation, and when she communicated it to her fellowship she was acknowledged as "mother in Christ" and called "Mother Ann." Her followers looked upon her as the "feminine embodiment of the divine spirit in human flesh."[12] Before she left England she was imprisoned for heretical behavior and blasphemy and was even accused of witchcraft. Church authorities wanted to brand her cheek with a hot iron, but were made to desist.

During her imprisonment in the Manchester House of Correction she had a vision of Christ commanding her to preach the gospel of a celibate life. From then on she felt Christ residing within her, speaking through her. She was his special instrument. She became convinced that she was being protected by an invisible power, because when she went fourteen days without food in prison, she looked as well upon being released as when she had entered. Also, when people attempted to stone her, they did not seem to be able to hit her. During the three months' trip to America when the boat was in danger of sinking, she told the captain she had seen two angels standing at the mast who had given her the promise of a safe landing.[13] For this vision she suffered no punishment. A theosophist suggests that these revelations could be interpreted as "direct messages from the spirit world."[14]

When Ann Lee left with her eight followers for America in 1774, she considered herself to be, and was acknowledged among her disciples as, the messenger of the Second Appearing of Christ. The money for passage had been supplied by John Hocknell, the only well-to-do member, a bricklayer of Manchester, who would also purchase the first settlement in Watervliet, New York, seven miles from Albany. But until the site was found and made habitable, the members of the group supported themselves, she as a servant and the others by working at their respective trades. Ann Lee did not dissolve her marriage to her husband until they moved to Watervliet. The move marked the commencement of the "Kingdom of Christ Upon Earth." But it was several years before they had a church or followers. This did not worry the foundress. She said Christ had prepared her for it.

Shakerism was rooted in two principles: celibacy and a form of communitarianism. Evil was represented by the sex act.[15] Shakers felt that marriage was not a Christian institution and that marriage and private property had been introduced by the "Gentile Christian Church." Sex was considered the "root and foundation of all human depravity and of the very act of transgression committed by Adam and Eve in the Garden of Eden."[16]

According to a contemporary interpretation:

The Shakers did not condemn marriage as a sin among "the world's people" but they considered those who practiced it to be on a lower spiritual plane than themselves.[17]

Before being accepted into the fold, one had to make an oral confession of sins to God in the presence of one or two witnesses; all just debts had to be paid; all wrongs done to anyone erased. No transfer of property was required for admission. No believing husband or wife was allowed to separate from an unbelieving husband or wife, except legally or by mutual agreement. If they separated, each got his just and righteous share.[18] Parents could not divide their property unevenly among their offspring. Children were not accepted to be brought up according to Shaker doctrines, except by free and lawful consent of parents or guardians. They were taught manual skills and were treated with the greatest gentleness.

Shaker society was divided into three classes: novitiate, junior, and senior. Only those of the senior class turned their property over to "the service of God." If they decided to withdraw peaceably, they were never sent away "empty."[19] In seventy years there was never a legal claim against the society.

The novitiate class lived with their own families, managed their own affairs, were not controlled by the society, but accepted the faith.[20] The junior class could give part or all of their property to be used for the mutual benefit of all, but retained the right to reclaim their property without receiving interest or wages of any kind.[21]

They practiced simplicity in dress and food and avoided overindulgence; they believed in extending hospitality and charity to the poor and needy. They abjured oaths, alcohol, and pork. They accepted the Bible as the word of God as far as it went, but they did not believe it was God's final revelation to man.[22]

They did not expect resurrection to come as a sudden event. Shakers who confessed their sins were considered personally saved and resurrected. The world had come to an end for them.

Thus the small band of people settled down at Watervliet to await Christ's Second Coming. Men and women worked at manual labor. The women cooked, sewed, nursed, gathered medicinal herbs, garden seeds, fruits for preserving, and the men made furniture (an occupation at which they became particularly adept), tools, straw objects. Agriculture became a later activity.

In 1779 there was a revival among "New Light" Baptists in New York, Massachusetts, and adjacent areas, making people apprehensive about redemption and the Day of Judgment, and thus receptive to Shaker doctrines. Some Baptist elders met with Ann Lee, were impressed with her demeanor, and became her first converts.

One of them was Joseph Meacham, who laid the basis for communal living and brought system and organization to the group. Other converts joined the Shakers as a result of missionary tours undertaken between 1781 and 1783 by Ann Lee and other leaders. Though they frequently experienced mistreatment, their efforts led to the opening of new communities in Connecticut, New Hampshire, Massachusetts and Maine. Eventually eighteen Shaker communities were formed, the largest in Ohio and Kentucky, all holding property in common. All Shaker communities were considered essentially religious institutions.

The only time Ann Lee and other Shakers were imprisoned in America was in 1780, at the height of the Revolutionary War. Her English birth and the pacifism professed by the group aroused suspicion. After six months in prison they were released on the order of Governor Clinton. But mob violence toward Shakers continued past the first quarter of the nineteenth century.[23]

The reason why Shakers encountered dislike, if not hatred, was that some people felt that they were sowing dissension among families and appropriating people's property. While some considered Ann Lee a witch, to Shakers she was virtue personified. She was a little over forty-eight when she died, but it was claimed that she continued to appear to her followers in visions and "to speak through the instrument of others." She was succeeded by the zealot James Whittaker, and he in 1787 by Joseph Meacham.

The period of the greatest Shaker influence was between 1830 and the Civil War with a membership of six thousand distributed in eighteen communities.[24] By then the Shaker men were celebrated as excellent furniture makers, weavers, printers, and craftsmen of all sorts. The women were recognized for their cooking, their herbs, preserves, breads, and for many other foodstuffs of superior quality.

After the Civil War membership fell off as a result of their celibate way of life and the lack of new converts. One by one Shaker colonies were discontinued and by 1903 there were only ninety believers left.[25]

At present two communities are still extant—one at Sabbath Day Lake, Maine, and one at Canterbury, New Hampshire. There are fifteen sisters "in all the world," eight in Maine and seven in New Hampshire. The oldest sister is ninety-four, the youngest is forty-three, having become a convert twenty-five years ago.[26] All that remains is the Shaker Museum in Old Chatham, New York.

There was much that the Shakers and the True Inspirationists had in common. Both sects believed in revelation; both were communitarian. Both were directed to America by heavenly messages. The members of neither group would serve as soldiers or take oaths. Last but not least, both sects had women leaders, though Barbara Heinemann (1795–1883) shared her authority with a male member of the sect, Christian Metz.

They differed in that celibacy was not imposed on the True Inspirationists. But though they did not forbid marriage, they considered living in wedlock "a spiritual fall from Grace." When Barbara Heinemann married, she was judged to have lost her "divine calling."[27] But she regained it eventually.

A most significant distinction between the two sects is that the membership of the Shakers numbered at its highest point only six thousand. Today they have only historic significance, whereas the Amana community in Iowa, to which the True

Inspirationists emigrated, continues to flourish, probably because of its altered organizational form which has turned it into a secular society. That society was able to adapt to changing conditions.

The Community of the True Inspirationists was an outgrowth of the German Mystics and Pietists of the sixteenth and seventeenth centuries. The name "Inspirationists" became attached to them because they "prophesied like the prophets of old." The members considered themselves instruments in the hands of the Lord and His children and therefore maintained that He spoke directly to them. Those to whom He communicated were called "Werkzeuge," and their prophesies, which were imparted to the membership, were called "Zeugnisse" or "Bezeugnunge." Barbara Heinemann was the last "Werkzeug."[28] Since her death none other has appeared.

Like other religious groups, they suffered a great deal of persecution. They were frequently uprooted; forced to move from one German state to another. One of the reasons for the antagonism to them was that they would not recognize the Lutheran Church and would not send their children to schools conducted by the Lutheran clergy.

Barbara Heinemann came into the fellowship almost a century after it was formed. Born in Alsace in extreme poverty, she was sent to work as a spinner at the age of eight. Later she became a servant, like Ann Lee and many early converts to Quakerism. When she joined the group she was twenty-three and completely untutored. An "inner voice" had propelled her to join the community in the Palatinate. Though she was looked upon as *"eine geringe und ungelehrte Magd"* (an insignificant and ignorant serving maid), she was accepted as "the Lord's special instrument." She taught herself to read, but never learned to write. After her marriage, judged "a fall from Grace," she lived for twenty-six years as an ordinary member of the group. She had no appreciation for learning, for she said in one of her testimonies, "knowledge puffeth up."[29]

Many leaders of religious sects found it no handicap to be totally untutored. Two examples are Joseph Smith and Brigham Young, both Mormons and native Americans. It seems ironic that the Puritan ministers who began to agitate for a college

within six years of the founding of the Massachusetts Bay
Colony so that their progeny would not be consigned to the
care of an ignorant ministry, should not have been able to
establish a tradition that would automatically have disqualified
clergymen who were ignorant backwoodsmen.

In 1826 it was revealed to the True Inspirationists, though
not through Barbara Heinemann who was then not prophesying,
that the Lord intended to lead them into a new land. The first
exodus took place in 1842 and deposited the first group of eight
hundred on an Indian reservation that had belonged to the
Senecas. It was near Buffalo and it was called Ebenezer. But
their troubles were not at an end. In 1854 communal living was
adopted, after receiving the announcement that it was God's
Holy Will that they were to remove further West[30] and live
as communitarians. A tract of eighteen thousand acres was purchased in Iowa, and seven villages were formed. The settlement
was called "Amana," a word that comes from the Song of Solomon and means *"Glaub Treu"* (Believe Truly).[31]

After the death of Christian Metz, Barbara remained as the
only transmitter of messages, retaining her gift until her death
at eighty-eight. Since then no heavenly directives have been
transmitted.

Though the prophetess seemed always to have had difficulty
in getting along, she wielded a great deal of influence. She
chose schoolmasters, denounced "godless marriages," rebuked
and condemned erring Brothers and Sisters, thereby causing
withdrawals from the Society during her later years.[32]

Amana was one of the last and most enduring communitarian
settlements. Most of the others—Fourier's philansteries, Etienne
Cabet's Icarian colony and others—had waned by the time the
True Inspirationists came upon the scene. There was much
less dissent among them than in some of the other colonies.
Perhaps it was because they had retained the customs of primitive Christianity and were used to accepting authority, to
obedience, and to living in fraternal relationships. Their constitution stated specifically that the foundation of their government "is and shall be forever God . . . and the faith he worked
in us."[33] Chief power was wielded by Elders and Trustees
from among whom the Elders were selected. While they did

not encourage marriage, people generally did marry.[34] Too large
a growth of population was apparently not desired.

Their main occupations were agriculture and the raising of
cattle and other livestock. They were also very competent
spinners and weavers and produced a superior quality of wool-
ens. They had no unemployment problem, no conflict between
labor and capital. Everyone received his private dwelling and
garden, where anything could be grown for his own consump-
tion, and an annual allowance in the form of credit at the
store.[35] Children were sent to school and physicians were educated at the society's expense.

The Amana Society retained the old pattern until 1932; then
they became more secular. "The communitarian system as such
is no longer in force," wrote the president of the Amana Church
Society in answer to a query put to him by mail.[36] "The business
affairs [are] being administered by a separate board of trustees
of the Amana Church Society." A specialty manufactured by
them and widely distributed are air conditioners and stoves.

One of the most intriguing women who was believed to
possess occult powers was Helena Petrovna Blavatsky (1831–
1891). While the sincerity of Ann Lee and Barbara Heinemann
could never have been impugned, the claims of the foreign-born
"seer" Madame Blavatsky have always been in doubt. Was she
an "initiate," who belonged to a totally different world, a world
of which ordinary mortals have no conception, as one disciple
claimed?[37] Was she an impostor and a fraud as some of her
servants asserted? Did her impulse in starting the Theosophical
Society have anything of the "religious" in it? She was an
atheist, but her statements had the fervor associated with religious conviction.

Madame Blavatsky was also directed to come to America,
not by heavenly voices as were the Shakers and the True
Inspirationists, but, as she tells us, by the command of a
"Master," or "Mahatma," who had been her mental guide and
mentor ever since she had met him "in the flesh" in London
on her twentieth birthday.

Hers was an aristocratic Russian family. When she was baptized, the priest's robe caught fire from a candle and he was

severely burned. It was interpreted as a bad omen, and a life of strife and trouble was predicted for her. Even as a child she was willful, daring, and unmanageable. A sleepwalker, she was subject to mysterious nervous diseases. She was supposed to have possessed psychic powers even in childhood. After the death of her mother she was brought up on the estate of her grandfather, who was a governor of a province on the Volga. He was unable to exert any control over her restless, nervous temperament.

As a result of a "joke," as she claimed, she became engaged to General Blavatsky, who was said to have been more than three times her age. She could not extricate herself from marrying him, but ran away from him in three months, and then embarked on an adventurous life that took her to Egypt, Eastern Europe, and London. There on her twentieth birthday she met "Master Morya," or "M," as he was called in the theosophical movement, a native of Tibet. He undertook to be her guide and mentor.

After a visit to the United States and two trips to India for a training period with her "Master," she was ordered by him to America. She was then forty-two and it was her second trip. The 1870s were a period of great interest in psychical phenomena in England as well as in America. In 1892 the English Society for Psychical Research had been formed, and in 1884 an American society of that name in Boston, in which William James took part. He was sufficiently attracted to psychical claims to investigate "ghosts, second sight, spiritualism and all sorts of hobgoblins."[38] It was Madame Blavatsky's privilege to bring to the world a new presentation of Theosophy. As she explains it, "Theosophy was 'Divine Wisdom'—the accumulated wisdom of the Ages, tested and verified by generations of Seers . . . that body of truth of which religions great and small, are but as branches of the parent tree."[39]

Starting out from Europe, she traveled in steerage. In America she lived in utmost poverty, trying to support herself through dressmaking and writing articles based on her experiences. According to one of her biographers, she had exchanged her first-class ticket to make it possible for a woman with a family who had been swindled out of her tickets to proceed to America where her husband awaited her.[40]

She was electrified when she read an article by Henry Steel Olcott, lawyer and spiritualist, who described some seances being conducted in Chittenden, Vermont. In haste she betook herself there, sought out Olcott, and convinced him of her powers. Olcott was sufficiently impressed to accompany her to New York, where they established themselves in a New York apartment. For him it represented a break with his family and his former life.

The Theosophical Society was founded in 1875 in New York by Olcott and Madame Blavatsky. The stated purpose was: "To promote the Universal Brotherhood of Humanity, to investigate the unexplained law of Nature and the psychical powers latent in man and to study comparative religion, philosophy and science." This was to be accomplished through contact with the Mahatmas (Masters) who would communicate from their Tibetan retreat with "True Believers" through Madame Blavatsky.

Henry Steel Olcott described their roles in the Theosophical Society in this manner:

She was the Teacher, I the pupil; she the misunderstood and insulted messenger of the Great Ones. I the practical brain to plan, the right hand to work out the practical details.[41]

Under the influence of the "Masters" she wrote in 1877 *Isis Unveiled: A Master Key to the Mysteries of the Ancient and Modern Science of Theology.* Her thesis was that all religions and cults are based on "Identical Cosmic myths and symbols."

The first edition of *Isis Unveiled* sold out within a few days.[42] But the Society failed to develop as the founders had hoped, and so she and Olcott decided to transfer it and themselves to India. She left the United States in 1878 and her connection with America came to an end.

In India she succeeded in attracting some English followers, but she antagonized the Indians by adopting Buddhism as the basic religion. She began to issue a magazine, *The Theosophist*, and to erect an international headquarters where she dispensed "psychic truths" and written communications from the "Mahat-mas," notably one Koot Hoomi.

In 1884 illness took her back to London and there the first outspoken attack on her was made. Two of her caretakers accused her of fakery and offered letters to prove it.

After that she would not return to India. She found new followers in the Countess Wachmeister of Sweden and in a wealthy Englishman who took her to his home in England. Another who opened her home to her was Annie Besant, Fabian socialist and reformer. There she completed in 1889 another book, *The Secret Doctrine*, which she called the "Synthesis of Science, Religion and Philosophy." Madame Blavatsky died in Annie Besant's home in 1891 of Bright's Disease.

After her death she was accused of fraud by one Vsevolod Solovyoff, who asserted he had obtained from her a decisive admission of "guilt."[43] But one of her biographers avers that she was "either incredibly wicked, or else was one of the most deeply wronged women known in history."[44]

She had sincerely devoted disciples as well. One was Alice Leighton Cleather, who lived in India and came to England in the late 1880s so that she could be instructed by Madame Blavatsky in the "truth and power of the soul." Mrs. Cleather said of her that she was a "lion-hearted woman" who "took one's breath away." She considered her "One of the true Saviors of the race; one of that 'deathless band of Great Ones' whose hands hold back the heavy Karma of the world—who remain unselfish to the endless end."[45] Apparently her name is still potent because today, more than eighty years after her death, an advertisement offers a book under the title *Dynamics of the Psychic World*, accompanied by her photograph.[46]

When she died in 1891, Mrs. Cleather's comment was: "She had been recalled because WE HAD ALL FAILED HER."

CHAPTER 5

In the Service of God and Man

To immigrants who were like "deaf-mutes"—because they could not understand what they heard and because of their inability to make themselves heard—their own clergy, who addressed them in words intelligible to them, provided the kind of support that steadied them throughout the crises of life. The help given to immigrants by their priests, ministers, nuns, and teachers of their own backgrounds raised many an individual from the depths of despair to the point of being able to carry on.

Ministers catered not only to members of their own ethnic groups, but during the early days of the Republic attempted to convert the Indians. The earliest attempt to reach the Indians was made by the Reverend John Eliot (1604–1690), pastor of Roxbury, who learned the Indian dialects, preached to them and turned some of them into Christians. But that did not prevent the periodic slaughter of the colonists.

Among the Catholic clergy, for instance, several Croatian priests, trained especially for missionary work in Austria, penetrated into the far West and the Northwest, where they opened missions for Indians in addition to ministering to their own people. An American Catholic Church existed since 1788, when the pope appointed the native American John Carroll the first Bishop of Maryland. One of the most serious complaints of newcomers was the lack of clergy of their own nationality. By the mid-nineteenth century Catholic leadership was firmly in the hands of the Irish, to the great unhappiness of Catholics from Germany, Poland, the Balkans, and Italy, who found it infinitely more comforting to deal with their own clergy.

Religiously inspired women did yeoman service in bringing

help to the poor, the sick and the discouraged. By organizing orphanages, schools, and hospitals they provided desperately needed social services.

The greatest of all Catholic benefactresses in America is probably Mother Francesca Cabrini (1850–1918), known as "Santina" to the Italians. This nun, of delicate appearance and frail health, possessed the kind of courage that caused her to attempt the seemingly impossible. More often than not she made it happen. In thirty years of unsparing labor she founded sixty-seven mission houses in North and South America and in Europe, and staffed them with more than one thousand sisters, who administered schools, orphanages, convents, and hospitals. It was an achievement of such magnitude that in 1938, nineteen years after her death, she was beatified and eight years thereafter raised to sainthood in the Catholic Church.

The youngest of thirteen children, nine of whom died young, she was born into the home of a farmer in Lombardy. The family was devout; an uncle who was a priest was treated with veneration. Her childhood and youth coincided with the "Risorgimento," which was an attempt to resurrect the time of Italy's greatest glory and to restore Italy to the position it had held during the period of its greatest power. Italy was then a divided country: the South under the rule of a Bourbon prince who was detested by the people; the North under the Hapsburgs who were resented no less than the French; and in the central portion ruled by the pope, who was opposed by all classes save the religious elements. It was a time when the Church had to tread softly.

By the time she was confirmed, she had promised herself to the Church, although she was told she was too delicate for the life of a nun. She began by earning a teacher's certificate at a school of the Sacred Heart in a neighboring town, then started teaching.

At thirty she founded a new order which grew so rapidly that she felt it ought to be represented in Rome. Although she was told a school for poor children was not needed, she was finally offered quarters in Rome in which to care for orphans and indigent children. But because she received no financial support, she and the other sisters were forced to go into the streets to beg for alms.[1]

The 1880s were the time of the great exodus from Italy to North and South America. It was then she received her first audience with the pope and was offered a mission in New York to assist in founding an orphanage for Italian children. The year was 1888; she was thirty-eight and only two years previously had been told she had only two years to live.

The immigration from Italy consisted overwhelmingly of the poorest elements in southern Italy, the "contadini," who had been agricultural workers and possessed no industrial skills. In America they would become laborers ("braccianti") and would encounter the most severe difficulties in the "little Italys" of congested urban centers. Tremendous prejudice existed against Italians, which would result in 1891 in the storming of a prison in New Orleans and the shooting and hanging of eleven Italians who had been suspected of murder but had been acquitted.[2] Italian immigrants found a poor welcome in the Catholic churches, which were staffed predominantly with Irish priests and nuns. The difficulties of adjustment to which Italians were prone were exacerbated by the lack of sympathetic Italian clergy.

After she was given a school to supervise, a stroke of unusual luck dropped a residence on Fifty-Ninth Street into her lap. It was given by Countess Palma di Cesnola, wife of the Civil War general, the holder of the Congressional Medal of Honor, and the first director of the Metropolitan Museum of Art, to use as an orphanage. Miles away from the Italian section, it was not the most suitable location for an Italian orphanage, but she accepted it and within several months had gathered together four hundred orphans.

Again the nuns had to go out to beg for food for the children. Their presence was resented so much that the archbishop suggested to Mother Cabrini that she discontinue her work and go back to Italy. But, finding her adamant, he did not insist.

After her first trip to Italy, where she returned regularly to recruit helpers, she purchased a large Jesuit estate, undaunted by the lack of cash and the absence of natural springs. The Lord would provide for His children, she said. Her prediction proved right, for a mountain spring appeared to her in a dream and when she investigated, it proved an adequate source of water.

Soon Mother Cabrini was presented with an unexpected opportunity to take over a small hospital. It had been started on East 109th Street by the Scalabrini Fathers, but was about to be given up because of lack of funds. She took over, moved ten patients into it and called it the Columbia Hospital after Christopher Columbus.[3] Doctors donated their services, and others contributed money and extended credit. Her nuns became nurses. When the Post Graduate Hospital became vacant, she took it over, turned it into a hundred-bed hospital, secured the approval of the State of New York, and built a training school for nurses.[4]

She also had the courage to start building a hospital in Chicago after $1,000 had been raised when over $100,000 was needed. A third hospital was started in Seattle. At the same time she kept adding orphanages and parochial schools in other cities of the United States—Newark, Denver, Seattle, Los Angeles, where she ministered to Mexicans as well as to Italians.[5]

She became an American citizen in Seattle in the early 1900s. After twenty-five years of residence in the United States her orphanages had taken care of 5,000 children and her hospitals had treated 100,000 patients,[6] some through epidemics of smallpox and yellow fever.

Her warmth, her joyous disposition, helped her in her work, but her most important personal endowments were fortitude and the capacity for incredibly hard work. She did not wait until she had the money with which to start new enterprises. While she trusted the Lord to provide, she expected that people would respond to real need. Her contributors, most of whom remained anonymous, were people of all faiths.[7]

When she died at sixty-eight in Chicago from a recurrence of malaria which she had contracted in the course of her work, she was buried on the grounds at West Park, New York, where she had started the orphanage on the Hudson. She had selected the spot where she wished to be buried. Several miracles directly attributed to her after her death brought her sainthood. But the greatest miracle lay in her accomplishments.

Other sisters of the Catholic Church—French, Irish, Polish, German—established schools, hospitals, orphanages, homes for the aged. One who preceded Mother Cabrini by almost three quarters of a century was a French nun, Rose Philippine Duchesne (1769–1852).[8] She founded the first American convent of the Sacred Heart which developed into an order known for its teaching institutions. Sister Anthony O'Connell (1814–1897),[9] served as a battlefield nurse during the Civil War. Josephine Dudzik,[10] a Polish immigrant in Chicago, after founding the Franciscan Sisters of Charity, established homes for the aged and schools for homeless orphans.

A laywoman who was a pioneer Catholic welfare worker was Adele Parmentier Bayer (1814–1893).[11] Her concern in seafaring men earned her the title "The Guardian Angel of the Sailors." Born in Belgium to a very devout Catholic family, she was brought to the United States in 1824, at the age of ten. Her family settled in Brooklyn, where her father was able to follow his bent as a horticulturist. It was a cultivated home which drew prominent Catholic visitors. The marriage of Adele Parmentier to the German-born Edward Bayer marked the celebration of the first nuptial mass in Brooklyn.

Mr. Bayer, a prominent merchant, who became a director of the Emigrant Industrial Savings Bank, encouraged his wife's philanthropic interests and shared in them. The first project, in which her parents participated, was to establish a Catholic colony, Vineland, in southeastern Tennessee. It attracted settlers from France, Germany, and Italy, but the Civil War arrested the project and it had to be dropped.

A childless woman, Mrs. Bayer sought activities that would satisfy her religious and humanitarian leanings. She started by concentrating on merchant seamen, many of whom were foreigners and Catholics. Soon her interest extended to all seafaring men, whose separation from home made them prone to loneliness and instability. She began to visit the Brooklyn Navy Yard regularly, offering the men her personal help. Encouraging them to save, she became their banker, kept accounts for them, made disbursements, and carried out their wishes in helping their families. In keeping each informed

about the state of his account, she maintained a large corre-
spondence with Catholics and non-Catholics alike. Her influence
is supposed to have been responsible for the regular celebration
of Sunday mass at the Brooklyn Navy Yard and for the appointment in 1883 of the first regular Catholic chaplain by the
United States Navy. When she died a requiem mass was offered
in the Brooklyn Navy Yard on board the ship Vermont. A
tablet in the Brooklyn Navy Yard perpetuates her memory as
the "Guardian Angel of the Sailors."

The dedication shown by religiously inspired women was not
limited to Catholics. At least two Protestant women of foreign
birth did their work, like the Catholic religious, "in the name
of our Lord and Savior." One, a Norwegian, Elisabeth Fedde
(1840–1921), was a deaconess—in the words of her biographer,
"a sort of Lutheran nun."[12] The other, an Englishwoman, was
Evangeline Booth (1865–1950), who had learned compassion
for the poor and the unfortunates from her parents, William
and Catherine Booth, the founders of the Salvation Army. A
vast difference in background and in what each was called
upon to do separates these two women. Miss Booth had been
introduced to the work of the Salvation Army in England,
where she became known as "The White Angel of the Slums."
Sister Elisabeth, a trained nurse, came to America in response
to an urgent appeal to work among Norwegian immigrants
who had reached the nadir of despair in the hovels of Brooklyn.
Elisabeth Fedde had lost her parents in her youth. While
working as a housemaid in a doctor's home in Stavanger, she
heard of the newly established Deaconess Institute in Kristiania
(later renamed Oslo), which was the first training school for
nurses in Norway. Nursing was then not regarded as a desirable
calling for young women. Girls from good homes were reluctant
to become nurses in public hospitals, because in addition to
attending patients, they were also expected to do menial work,
such as scrubbing floors.[13]
What undoubtedly influenced Miss Fedde in her decision
to dedicate herself to helping the sick was that she was a
Haugean Pietist.[14] The followers of Hans Nielsen Hauge, a lay
preacher who had served a year in prison for his defiance

of the prescribed dogmas of the Norwegian State Church, shared with their leader a devotion to the "living faith" rather than to the formalized doctrine preached by the regular clergy. The Haugeans did not propose an independent church, or separation from the established church.[15] Like the Quakers they were critical of high-church practices which smacked of aristocratic leanings. Hauge died in 1824, but the Haugean spirit was transferred by lay preachers to America, where it continued to have a deep influence on Norwegian immigrants.[16]

During her training period Elisabeth Fedde attended patients and was sent out on private cases as well, but at the same time she performed the humble work expected of her. Her next assignment took her to the State Hospital in Kristiania, where nurses were expected to serve an entire year without pay. They received board and room, but no allowance for their upkeep or other expenses.[17]

After completion of her course and a four-year stint in a hospital north of the Arctic Circle at Tromso, a brother-in-law in America suggested that she come to the United States to work among Norwegians in Brooklyn, many of whom were in such desperate straits that the Norwegian Seamen's Institute and the Norwegian Lutheran Church had become concerned. The idea of transferring her activities to the New World appealed to her, though the Deaconess Institute made it clear that she could not expect to receive any aid from them, because the request had not come to the institute, but directly to her.

Nevertheless she decided to undertake the mission and in 1883 started out alone for the United States. Upon her arrival in Brooklyn she found that no direct means for helping the indigent sick existed. But within days a Voluntary Relief Society for the Sick and Poor was formed and a little three-room headquarters provided for her, where she could offer homecare to the sick.

In the words of her biographer she was

. . . doctor, midwife, nurse, scrubwoman, evangelist and philanthropist who brought doctors for desperate cases, begged for food and clothing for needy families, worked late, often gave the last of her money away . . .[18]

She visited people in the most wetched hovels, where she emptied her pockets, frequently not even leaving herself money for carfare, and thus forced to walk home in the middle of the night. In her diary she wrote: "I gave to a poor widow with three children all I had—fifty cents."[19]

Also she went at least once a week to the immigrant hospital in Castle Garden and to the Ward Island Hospital to visit sick Norwegians. It made her resolve to work toward the establishment of a hospital where they would not feel that they were among strangers.

Two years after her arrival a house was rented in Brooklyn under the auspices of the Norwegian Relief Society; it contained nine hospital beds. It became the Deaconess Home and Hospital of Brooklyn. There anonymous donors left gifts of food, clothing, money, and equipment.

From there she made home calls, bringing help to the bedridden and performing such chores as cleaning, washing clothes, sending the children to school and making sure there was food. She tried to find jobs for unemployed men and homes for children. When there was no money to bury the dead, she went out and solicited alms.

Before a thirty-bed hospital could be erected in Brooklyn she and the members of the Board of Directors went out to solicit contributions. Among those who responded were Commodore Vanderbilt, John D. and William Rockefeller, and others.[20] In 1892 the hospital was renamed the Norwegian Lutheran Deaconesses' Home and Hospital and, eventually, the Lutheran Medical Center.

In 1888 she was prevailed upon to start another deaconess hospital in Minneapolis. However, after two years she returned to Brooklyn, where a most important task awaited her, that of persuading the legislature of the State of New York to grant state aid to the hospital. This modest woman, who must have been aware of her language insufficiency, went to Albany to plead for help on the basis that people of all faiths and creeds were given help at the hospital and that it ought therefore receive the same subsidy allotted to other hospitals. Her request was granted.

The difficulties with which she coped can be surmised from

an entry in her diary: "I'm almost distracted ... but your word, my God, will keep me alive. . . . How tired I was . . . God help me to carry my cross in patience."[21]

After undergoing serious surgery, she decided to return to Norway to marry a man who had waited for her for thirteen years. A highly respected individual, he had received recognition of his contribution as a citizen. By then the hospital in Brooklyn was treating two thousand patients annually, attended by twelve sisters.

When Miss Fedde resigned she had given twenty-seven years of service as a nurse. After her marriage she returned to America several times. In 1941, twenty years after her death, the pharmaceutical firm of Johnson & Johnson recognized her contribution as a nurse by including her picture with other outstanding nurses, among whom were Clara Barton, Florence D. Nightingale, and Lillian D. Wald.[22]

In 1904 Evangeline Booth arrived in New York to assume charge of the Salvation Army in America. Like the Salvation Army itself, she was thirty-nine years old, for it had come into existence on the day she was born, Christmas Day, 1865. It was then that William Booth, her father, left the Methodist ministry to establish the Christian Mission, which became the Salvation Army. At thirty-nine she had had extensive experience, not only in the slums of Whitechapel and Limehouse, but also as territorial commander of Canada. She was an outstanding administrator and such an efficient "troubleshooter" as to make her father feel that "to send Eva" was the best solution to any problem. She had also acquired the kind of inner strength that held its ground against insult, prejudice, and physical intimidation, as well as the sort of poise and charm that made her irresistible.

The story of Evangeline Booth in England and in America is tied to that of her parents, who created the Army, and to her family. The parents drew in the whole family as a unit. Of the eight Booth children—she was the seventh—all but one were active workers in the Army and all preached the gospel according to its precepts. One daughter was not considered strong enough for the strenuous work the Army required. Later four children would be lost through death and secession.

At the top of the pyramid which was the Army stood the two founders, William and Catherine Booth ("the mother of the Army"); below them were their children, including daughters-in-law and three sons-in-law who had accepted the name of "Booth" as part of their own names. Farther toward the base were the workers in the movement who sold the *War Cry*, a newssheet which referred to events in the newspapers and was sold on the streets, and those who sang, played various instruments, preached and prayed with the people. Evangeline's life and personality were formed by the upbringing she had received. Some of their convictions, such as the stand against liquor and gambling, she never modified.

The Salvation Army, which had spread throughout much of the world even during the lifetime of the founders, may be said to have grown from a tiny seed in the mind of a fourteen-year-old boy apprentice to a pawnbroker in London's East End. There he saw much misery. The boy had been raised in the Church of England, but may have been of Jewish ancestry as St. John Ervine suggests.[23]

William Booth's first pulpit was in the homes of his followers. Like other religious dissidents he began by gathering in cottages where those assembled sang hymns, prayed, read the Bible together, and listened to sermons. The next step in reaching out to people was through street-corner revivals. When a wealthy convert guaranteed him a pound a week for three months, he gave up his pawnbroker's job to devote himself fully to "God's work."

He was an extraordinary speaker who drew tremendous crowds. Mainly it was the compassion which his very being exuded that had a remarkable effect on his listeners. His message was an encouraging one: "Drunkards, utter heathens, if soundly converted, would win the world."[24] According to a present-day Salvationist who met him in person, he was the "embodiment of love for the poor" and the impression he created was that of a "father in God." The same individual declared Evangeline Booth to have been a "female reincarnation of him, a later generation embodying the same charismatic qualities."[25]

Mr. Booth met his wife among the Methodists, but she had Quaker antecedents. After hearing him preach, she married him despite her father's opposition. She designed the Army bonnet and was always considered co-founder of the Army. When she was, in the words of Salvationists, "promoted to glory," fifty thousand attended her funeral.

Up to 1865, the year of Evangeline's birth, William Booth called himself superintendent of the East London Revival Society. But his secretary fell into the habit of addressing him as "general." One day he wrote in a report: "We are a volunteer army," which Booth amended to "we are a Salvation Army."[26]

Although discipline in the Booth home was strict—dancing, smoking, drinking, playing cards, going to the theater were not permitted—in their daily relations with their children the parents were loving and understanding. Grace was said and everyone joined in the reading of the Bible. All the children sang and were taught various musical instruments, the piano, the violin, the concertina. Evangeline played the guitar and the harp and was the most talented musically.[27] The children were all privately educated; none was sent to college. Mother Booth, in particular, did not believe in higher education, because she felt it caused people to veer away from God.[28]

At fifteen Evangeline donned the Salvation Army uniform and was appointed sergeant. At seventeen she began to preach at meetings. A year later she was assigned to Marylebone in the slums. There she was frequently exposed to assault, because her preaching against liquor antagonized not only owners of saloons, but the poor themselves, to whom "the pint" was the only pleasure they knew. According to her biographer:

They snatched at the ribands of her uniform and on one occasion Evangeline Booth was struck by missiles and stunned. With blood flowing from her forehead, she was borne away for first aid. On other days she was seized by an angry constable who twisted her arms and dragged her roughly to the police court. They threw hot water from their windows, followed by curses and jests.[29]

Salvationists never retaliated with jeers or insults. Their answer was usually: "Glory be to God," or "God bless you. He can save you."

After her stint at Marylebone she was placed in charge of the International Training College at Clapton and became Field Commissioner of the region around London, where she had twenty-one thousand soldiers, six hundred officers, and three hundred cadets under her. She remained in this position for four years.[30]

Before she received her first foreign assignment in 1885 to Canada, she won an important victory for the Salvationists. As a result of her testimony before Parliament, a Public Health Act was repealed that prohibited Salvationists from holding processions accompanied by music and had led to many arrests. The turn of the century found the aging General Booth beset by many difficulties. His son, Ballington Booth, had been placed in charge of North America, but when reassigned elsewhere in 1896, he started with his wife a rival organization, "Volunteers of America." While Evangeline was building schools, hospitals, and immigrant aid stations in Newfoundland, her sister Emma Booth-Tucker and her husband were directing the Salvation Army in America. When she died in a train accident in Chicago, Evangeline was transferred from Canada to America to succeed her sister and brother-in-law. The Army then numbered 696 stations, which she was to build up into 16,000 within thirty years.[31]

Her American career presented several challenges. Financially, the Army was under severe limitations, the work being carried on in rented headquarters. She had other problems as well. Her brother, Bramwell Booth, had succeeded their father as chief of staff in London. Was the Army in America to remain international in character (under the direction of the Salvation Army in England as Bramwell Booth insisted), or would its development in America be fostered if it were allowed to become an American organization? The Volunteers of America, an evangelistic organization like the Salvationists, were establishing themselves as a strictly American organization, and were making steady progress. Ballington Booth was wooing the Salvationists to join his fellowship, and there was danger that the Army would fly apart.

Evangeline Booth managed not only to hold the Army together, but within thirty years built up its assets from $1½ million to $35 million and property valued at close to $50 million.[32] When she conducted her first national fund drive she was able to raise $16 million. Under her stewardship the Army headquarters on West 14th Street in New York City was begun and dedicated in 1930. She came to represent the Salvation Army to the whole world.

This she accomplished by winning and retaining the confidence of leaders in every walk of life—statesmen, lawyers, industrialists of all faiths, and others. She received contributions from such different philanthropists as John Wanamaker and Felix Warburg. Will Rogers gave the Army a cut from his radio receipts.[33] During World War I she sent a detachment of specially trained volunteers to France, where the soldiers were offered hospitality, restrooms, and hostels staffed by Salvation Army "lassies." In 1917 she went to visit the battle scene with the approval of the United States government. At the end of the war President Wilson awarded her the Distinguished Service Medal.

The Salvation Army's main contribution lies in its program for personal rehabilitation and its response to specific disaster situations. It was Evangeline Booth's decision to send help to the victims of the San Francisco quake and fire of 1906, and in 1923 to Japan in the wake of the disastrous earthquake. As a reaction to a more recent crisis the Army established and maintains the East Bronx chapel for drug addicts which is run by two Puerto Ricans who were themselves former addicts.[34]

A project in constant operation is the Family Service Department, which is a referral service. The Army maintains the William Booth Medical Center in Flushing; another project is a home for retired people. "Evangeline Homes" for young women, to be found throughout New York City, is an undertaking begun by Evangeline Booth herself.

She had the opportunity to prove that the future of the Salvation Army meant more to her than personal loyalty to her family when she gave her cooperation to those who felt that the reins held by her brother Bramwell over the whole structure of the Army should be loosened. When Bramwell Booth, whom his father had named his successor, became ill, the Army was governed by a regency which his wife controlled. Bramwell Booth's refusal to name a successor forced seven British commissioners in 1928 to invoke the arrangement by which a general could be removed from office. It was voted to depose him, and Evangeline concurred in the decision. But he would not relinquish his office and shocked Salvationists by submitting the case to the Royal Court in London. Edward Higgins, Bramwell's chief-of-staff, was the first head to be elected, but he found that by a codicil in the will of Bramwell, who died in 1929, he was eliminated as custodian of the property. A court fight ensued, which the Army won. But though Evangeline had not supported her brother, before his death she cabled her "undying love" to him.

In 1912 she obtained American citizenship and acquired a home in Hartsdale, New York. However, in 1934, when she became the fourth general of the Army and its second elected general, she had to return to London. When she departed for England, she vowed to return to the United States. This she did in 1939, when she retired at 74. She died in the United States in 1950.

CHAPTER 6

Immigrant Mothers and Wives

THUS FAR THE EMPHASIS HAS BEEN ON THOSE INDIVIDUALS AMONG foreign-born women who managed to raise themselves above the mass of immigrant women through ability, courage, initiative, and pertinacity. Undoubtedly these women possessed superior qualifications and fighting ability, or developed them unexpectedly as a consequence of their condition which called forth their strongest endeavors.

The special situation affecting foreigners, which required at the very least that they acclimate themselves to a new environment, a difficult enough task even when not complicated by poverty, held the most powerful of challenges. The spur to overcoming their handicaps was thus embedded in their special circumstances. Beset by the most trying difficulties, many succeeded not only in creating positions of respect for themselves, but in bringing large-scale benefits to others.

Admittedly those able to rise above the conditions by which they were surrounded were exceptional people. But what about those for whom it was a triumph just to survive the crises of each day? They were largely anonymous women—like the mother in Harry Roskolenko's story[1] who lost an arm trying to retrieve a block of ice which had fallen from an ice truck; or the mother of Edward Corsi,[2] who was unable to function in the American world and had to return to Italy leaving her sons in America; or the Slavic women whose existence was constantly threatened by mine accidents.

Though immigrant women may seem like peas in a pod, some striving, others passive, there were indubitably many distinct individuals among them whose "specialness" was submerged in a sea of unrelenting care and misery. It is these women with whom this chapter is concerned.

85

Clearly all immigrant wives and mothers may be considered a special group of women because of the incontrovertible fact that they were subject to a larger share of insecurity and anxiety than was the lot of other women. Economic crises were a part of their everyday lives. If they were agricultural settlers, they lived under conditions more primitive than they had known at home, miles away from where help could be summoned in time of sickness or accident. They worked unceasingly at hard physical labor, bore many children, and often lost a large number of them. But even in the cities where doctors were close, immigrants could not always afford to call them. They saw their children go off to work when they would have preferred that they continue in school, and accepted helplessly that children of school age must rush off to jobs before or after school to help eke out the family income. Even the wife of so steady and determined a worker as Samuel Gompers was periodically compelled, as he tells, to pawn everything of value save her gold wedding ring; was used to putting her children to bed hungry; frequently had to keep them from school because of lack of shoes, and could not have a doctor for a difficult confinement until her husband threatened one with murder if he did not attend his wife on the promise that he would be paid later.[3]

A touching story is told about this stalwart woman. During a strike a representative of the employers called on her and offered her thirty dollars a week if she would persuade her husband to drop the union. She showed him the door. When he returned she told him the story. "What did you do?" he asked her. Angered at his lack of confidence, she said: "What do you suppose I could do with one child sick and another coming? I took the money."

He was shocked. "My God!" she exclaimed. "How can you ask? Of course, I threw him out."[4]

Still, she was better off than many other women, because she was spared the worry that her husband, who was a cigar worker, might be brought home mangled or dead, a threat which hung over the heads of those whose husbands, and sons, too, worked in the mines, in the steel mills, or in packing plants, where an accident might put them in danger of life and limb.

The period when the industrial life of the nation was unfettered by regulation, and the open spaces beckoned to intrepid settlers who could visualize in the unbroken prairie princely kingdoms of 160 acres all one's own, was the time of the greatest trials for immigrant women in the cities and on the farms. It was during the decades between the end of the Civil War and the beginning of the twentieth century that the most severe depressions and labor upheavals took place. They affected urban workers as well as farmers. Though the earliest settlers undoubtedly endured deprivations that are beyond imagination, there was comfort in speaking the same tongue and in knowing that the dangers and want were shared by all. Social distinctions existed, and may or may not have been resented, but they were no more irksome than those they had known in England. And in a later period immigrant women could at least take comfort in the realization that husbands and children worked under regulated hours, under union wages, and under safeguards early workers would have considered utopian.

Admittedly the designation "immigrant wife and mother" suggests a perfect stereotype. In a world that seemed at best indifferent, if not hostile, even those women who may have been individualists to the core reacted in the same way. Prior expectations were pushed aside and the necessities of life became primary concerns. The most unworldly mother must have been aware that if her children could be kept at school, at least until they entered their teens, their chances for success would improve. It can be imagined how hard it was for a mother to wake a young boy at two in the morning, so that he could go out to sell the early newspaper edition to those returning from night shifts, as John Cournos[5] had to, or to send a boy to attend to his duties as lamplighter at four in the morning, which was Edward Corsi's job,[6] or to see a boy stumble out to deliver bread and rolls when it was still dark, which Leonard Covello[7] was compelled to do if he was to continue at school.

But there were families who lived under such despairing conditions that children were looked upon as a convenience to be used as necessity dictated. Everyone's work was needed just to keep alive. *McClure's*, a muckraking journal at the turn of the century (Samuel S. McClure, its founder and editor, was foreign-born himself and had spent a deprived childhood on a farm.), presented in 1910 a shocking picture of conditions among immigrant "home" workers living in New York City below 14th Street, an area which housed a thousand people to an acre.[8] Two to three rooms held families of seven to eight people and boarders besides, who were apt to add considerable strain and sometimes broke up marriages. In these homes "without windows even into an airshaft or into an adjoining room"[9] worked whole families from the youngest to the oldest, even when barely recovering from contagious diseases, at "finishing" men's and women's garments, at flower, feather and lace-making, the manufacturing of wigs and similarly malodorous work. The law prohibiting the work of children under fourteen did not apply to work at home. Children of preschool age as well as children of school age were kept home in order to aid in the family effort of earning a total of fifty to seventy cents a day, or about $4.50 a week.[10] Some of the wage rates were: fifty cents a gross for making silk pompoms; "finishing" trousers at seven cents a pair; "finishing" corset covers at thirty-six cents for six dozen; ten cents for rolling a thousand cigarettes in wrappers which were then passed off as "made in Turkey." Could any woman thus overwhelmed have thought of more than the day's food and the monthly rent?

Having large families might have comforted some parents into believing that they were assured of support in their old age, but could any mother fixing a lunch bucket for a young boy or boys departing with their father at daybreak for the mines feel an increased sense of security? No group of fathers could be less sure than miners of reaching a ripe old age and many of their women, despite their prodigious physical endurance, died at an early age from overwork and neglect. A recent study reveals that though there were minimum-age laws governing employment in the mines, they were violated by parents as well as employers, and that reformers were outraged because young children were working in the mines. It was not unusual for children of nine and ten to work a ten-hour day six days a week.[11] Did it bring less of a pang to see a young boy accompanying his father to a construction job, as Pietro di

Donato describes in *Christ in Concrete,* or boys and girls, too young to be employed, but nevertheless going off into the mills or other factory jobs, than the sight of children trudging off into the mines? When it was so difficult to provide the necessities with everyone in the family at work, it can be imagined with what apprehension one thought of strikes, layoffs, or unexpected illness.

Even life on the farm, where some kind of shelter could be taken for granted and food could be grown, was not free of anxiety. The fear of not being able to meet the payments on the mortgage was like living under the sword of Damocles. Whether or not drought, too much rain, or insects ruined the crops, or prices fell so low that crops were practically worthless, payment of the mortgage or other obligations had to be maintained. John Altgeld,[12] future governor of Illinois, for instance, while still in his teens was sent out to do a day's work for a neighbor, for money, of course, whenever his help could be dispensed with at home. His wages and every penny that could be spared went into the receptacle that held the "mortgage money."

It is a commonplace that all parents, except those too crushed by circumstances to nurture long-term expectations, shared the desire that their children at least would reap the "golden harvest" that was inherent in the American dream, whether it meant a mortgage-free farm, an honorable profession, or success in business. There must have been among immigrants many "mute, inglorious Miltons" who were forced to subjugate every personal interest to the hard reality of their lives. Behind the successful offspring of immigrants stood mothers who worried, counseled, upheld, scolded, and pushed. One such mother was Edward Bok's mother, whose advice he admits to having solicited and taken when he came to what was a crossroad in his life, the offer to become editor of *The Ladies' Home Journal.*[13] He was a very masculine type who worried about whether the job of editor of a magazine devoted exclusively to women's interests might not place him in a false light. She advised him to take the job. Another was the mother of Andrew Carnegie.[14] A determined, "managing" woman, her influence figured importantly in the way he shaped his life. Mothers made heroic efforts to keep their children on the right path, though they did not always succeed, as Morris Raphael Cohen admitted when he stated: "The same family produced saints and sinners, philosophers and gunmen."[15]

When it was not possible to help each child to take a giant step ahead, the effort would be concentrated on the males of the family, or at least on one of them, the brightest or the youngest, who might become the doctor, lawyer, or independent businessman whose glory would then reflect on all the members of the family.

When there was a choice between promoting the fortunes of a son or a daughter, it was most always the son, for whom all, including his sisters, were expected to step aside. We have Jerre Mangione's statement that among Italians of the immigrant generation "to give a daughter more education than required by law was an extravagant waste of time and money."[16] In his family, too, women worked as home finishers on men's clothing manufactured in the factories of Rochester, New York.

Immigrants harbored a preindustrial concept of the masculine-feminine role rather than an antifeminist one. As long as the world's important work rested on the shoulders of men, immigrant parents preferred to favor their sons over their daughters. Sometimes there was the fear that girls who became involved in outside affairs would not marry, as Rose Schneiderman's mother correctly foresaw. There was some justification in this, for among emancipated women (women labor leaders, women physicians), the number of spinsters was high. Daughters were expected to marry and thus to get a second chance to shine through the success of a husband, and still another, through their children.

What is more surprising than that immigrants led difficult lives, is that among the thirty-nine million foreign-born who entered the United States between 1776 and 1929, thousands upon thousands prospered beyond their wildest expectations. Many immigrant parents, even if good fortune eluded them, were richly rewarded in the satisfaction of seeing their children, or at least some of them, successful. Andrew Carnegie may have been one of the very few, if not the only one, to make a coach and driver available to his "lady" mother, but immigrants who provided their parents with automobiles and chauffeurs and settled them in mortgage-free homes, where the old days of toil were, like a bad dream, to be forgotten, were no rarity.

Many paid deference to their parents, particularly to their mothers, in fiction and in autobiography, where they present them in a variety of ways, either as wise and understanding, insistent and aggressive, weak and ineffectual, yet well-meaning. The writer Charles Angoff tells what thoughts ran through his mind while visiting his mother's grave: "Oh, that was one of the few things I was sure of in this world. Mother would be everlastingly with me, in me. . . ."

The remembrance that came to him was:

When I came home from school [Roxbury] chattering about all things that had happened . . . and Mother pushed one roll after another at me, some with poppy seeds, some with salt crystals, some plain . . . but I only nibbled at them . . . and she despaired of my health.[17]

Fathers may sometimes be disliked, even hated as in Jo Sinclair's *Wasteland*,[18] but not mothers. They were, as one of the early historians of immigration admitted, "the keystone of the home."[19] A son or daughter who had shared the hardships characteristic of immigrant life would not have said of their mothers: "What a radar on that woman! And this before radar. The energy on her."[20] Or to have declared snidely: "Properly practiced Jewish motherhood is an art, a complete network of subtly and highly sophisticated techniques."[21]

Women who lived in tenements of the large cities present a different profile from the wives of homesteaders struggling with the forces of nature, and from those whose lives were spent in mining towns against the backdrop of coal and sludge heaps and the redness of banked fires at night. Although those used to an agricultural existence undoubtedly found in the closeness to the earth and the care of barnyard animals a continuation of the old life, the primitive conditions and the change in scenery represented a sharp variation from the old environment. Norwegians, especially, were conscious of the difference between the breathtaking spectacle of mountains and sea to which they were accustomed and the flatness of the prairie states. "Oh, for a mountain with a view of forest and sea," one wrote in her diary.[22]

To Europeans coming from the smaller cities of the continent, where urbanization had either not yet begun, or was creeping forward at snail's pace, slum living was a shocking contrast to what they were accustomed. Those who came from the Balkans left one of the most picturesque regions of the world to come, frequently, to raw and ugly mining towns. Furthermore, for miners' wives there was the pall of fear of mine accidents that buried men alive or burned them as a result of explosions. The dread of working underground had communicated itself even to the people in little Balkan hamlets who knew of the mines in America only from hearsay. Louis Adamic tells that before his mother consented to let him depart for America, he had to promise her that he would never work underground.[23]

It is from the angle of the differences as well as the similarities in their American experiences that the lives of three groups of women, each functioning in a different environment, are herewith presented: the pioneer women who shared with their husbands the hardships of pioneer life, the Slavic women in the mining towns, and the Jewish women in the slums of the cities. Each group will be looked upon as representative of others who were subjected to similar experiences.

Among the foreign stocks who turned the Northwest into a fertile region, the Scandinavians predominated. Among them the Norwegians provided the largest percentage of agricultural settlers.

The mass of Norwegians had been agriculturists and fishermen at home, and the impetus to emigrate lay in the economic conditions in the homeland and in the lure of the Homestead Law, enacted in 1862, which granted 160 acres to everyone who pledged himself to become a citizen and to live on the land for five years. While some newcomers bought land from the railroads with money they had received by selling their ancestral farms, the bulk of Norwegian farmers, whose marginal farms had become too small through continuous subdivision, were attracted to "free land."

There had been a Swedish settlement in Delaware in colonial times, but after its absorption in New Netherland and the further takeover by the British colonies, the early Swedish pioneers lost their identification as Swedes. A new and steady influx during the midpoint of the nineteenth century contributed to the quick development of Minnesota and its admission into the Union in 1858.

As for the Norwegians, there were small settlements in New York State, in Illinois, and in Texas during the early part of the nineteenth century, but the bulk of Norwegians, as well as the Swedes and the Danes, who formed the smallest group of Scandinavian newcomers, began arriving after the conclusion of the Civil War. Like most other immigrants of all backgrounds, some Norwegians as well as Swedes settled in the cities where they worked as laborers, but the bulk proceeded to the Northwest, much of which was still in the territorial stage. Accompanied by their families, they were apt to settle on the frontier, if not in the heart of what was then still a wilderness. How intrepid were the wives of these settlers comes out clearly in letters and diaries written by some of the women themselves, in the fiction of the great epic writer, Ole Edvart Rolvaag, a Norwegian, and Vilhelm Moberg, a Swede, and from American descendants of settlers who heard about the pioneer generation from parents and grandparents.

These immigrants were rarely, if ever, able to move into waiting homes. Sometimes they moved in with another family, while the man worked as a hired hand until he had earned enough for the purchase of the most necessary supplies before making a land claim. Says Theodore Blegen, the authoritative historian and spokesman for the Norwegian people:

In the days of covered wagons weeks might pass with the family residing in the wagon boxes before cabins were made ready; sometimes tents were used. Sometimes it was a mere shed or perhaps an underground habitation with dirt walls on three sides. Ultimately a new and larger cabin was built and this, in turn, soon gave way to a frame house.[24]

Professor Blegen sums up the activities of pioneer women:

> The farmer worked hard, but his wife worked even harder. She did the housework, cared for the children, prepared the meals, helped to care for the cattle, pigs, sheep and chickens; milked the cows, churned the butter, did the canning in summer and fall, prepared cheese, carded and spun the wool [they brought their spinning wheels and looms—the author], wove cloth, dyed it with homemade dyes, knitted and sewed clothing, mended mittens and socks. On occasion she pitched in and helped to rake hay and bind the grain after it had been cut. . . . She bore children year after year; she cared for the sick when her home was struck by disease.[25]

Women also acted as midwives, as practical physicians, and as "helpers in emergencies." They sat up with sick neighbors, took care of the children of mothers who were incapacitated, and laid out the dead. In communities where schools were unavailable, the task of teaching the children to read and write also often fell on the women.

One of the deprivations which was deeply felt by Norwegian women was the absence of regular church services. Ministers dispatched from Norway traveled the circuit between settlements. The minister's visit was one of the highpoints in the frontier existence. It was then that marriages were performed and children baptized. Because of their dependence on the spiritual comfort derived from church attendance, the infrequency and irregularity of church services bore more heavily on women than on men.

Let us now examine the life of a pioneer woman who could with equal justification be considered a common as well as an uncommon type and who has recorded her experiences. She was Gro Svendsen (1841–1878),[26] who came with her husband in 1862 to a frontier settlement in Iowa. Her story emerges from the letters she wrote to her parents in Norway. She came from a superior home; her father was a teacher, and she had led a sheltered existence. Mrs. Svendsen was very fond of reading, but she could only indulge herself when she was in childbed. Once her eyes became "so sore" from continuous reading she had to stop. But since she had ten children in sixteen years, five of whom died, she was deprived of reading only between childbirths.

During the sixteen years of living in America she performed all the tasks of a frontier wife; she sheared the lambs for wool herself, carded it, made sugar from their own sugarcane, worried over the weather, the harvests, and the locusts, who "sometimes didn't even leave enough for seed," and over the illnesses of her children, half of whom succumbed to childhood diseases. She was so afraid of smallpox that she asked her father to send vaccine, which he did.

Her husband was called into military service, but was soon released because of the end of the Civil War.

As soon as her first child was ready for school, she began to attend English school herself, then taught three days a week in the various log cabins of the district. She had a sense of identification with America, because she sent all her children to English school and some to the Norwegian Sunday school. One of her sons was given an American name—"Steffen"—and she explained: "I thought I'd choose one that was a little more in conformity with American, so that he would not have to change it himself later in life if he should live to grow up." She also found time to be the "secretary of the community" by writing letters for them.

She died at thirty-seven after the birth of her tenth child. Her husband then sold his farm and moved to South Dakota, a state to which Norwegians were attracted. In his letter to her parents he enclosed the picture of their daughter's grave and promised that it would be well looked after.

Another woman whose information on the rigors of pioneer life is imparted through a diary was Else Elisabeth Koren (1832–1918).[27] She came to Iowa right after her marriage in the 1850s to a newly ordained minister who was to be the first resident Norwegian Lutheran minister west of the Mississippi. She, too, was the daughter of a cultured family. What emerges from her diary, which she kept for only two years, is a record of the way pioneers struggled with biting cold ("...so cold that the sheet had frozen and the pillow was covered with frost..."), wild snow and rainstorms ("I have never seen such rain nor have I ever heard such loud thunder..."), the prairie fires, the primitive accommodations. The reaction of the people at having a minister in their midst ("...there was such joy over the pastor's coming...") helped her to accept the hardships of isolation and primitive living conditions. Often she accompanied him in jolting, crude wagons. Even when the birth of her first child was imminent, she was still sharing a home with someone else. She was very brave and patient and eventually bore nine children. Like her husband she was highly respected by her neighbors. The Reverend Vilhelm Koren became one of the founders of Luther College in Decorah, Iowa.

Of all fictional presentations of Norwegian pioneer women the most striking is Rolvaag's creation of Beret in *Giants in the Earth*. She confirms Professor Blegen's admission that "insanity seems especially frequent among immigrant women, because they have less power of resistance,"[28] for she suffers a spell of mental aberration from which she recovers. One is reminded of the English pioneer women of whom Governor Winthrop spoke as "not keeping their wits," or "having grown turbulent with passion" without essaying a reason for this behavior. Rolvaag clearly implies that it was the change in the life of this simple woman that caused her to become temporarily deranged.

Two telling narratives of what was expected of wives of pioneers, one English, one Swiss, are presented by two different women. One story is told by the daughter of a Swiss settler, Jules Sandoz,[29] who built up the Nebraska Panhandle. The other is an autobiographical account by a Yorkshire woman, Rebecca Burlend,[30] about her experiences in Pike County, Illinois, in 1831.

Jules Sandoz was a year short of a medical degree at the University of Zurich when he came to America in 1879 after a violent quarrel with his father. A harsh, egocentric man, "Old Jules" drove his several wives and children almost to the breaking point. At the same time he acted as physician, delivering babies and tending the sick. In the following excerpt Mari

Sandoz, his daughter, presents the arrival of one of her father's unsuspecting brides in Nebraska:

> Train-weary, her body aching from the jolting lumber wagon, she crept into bed.
> Towards morning it began to rain. The roof leaked, a little at first, then more. Soon everywhere. Henriette sat on the wet straw tick all the next day with a purple umbrella over her head, crying noiselessly while Jules raged that there was no fuel. Plainly the white hands of his wife would be incapable of wielding a successful axe against the toughness of wet wood.... At last he got the fire going and while one stoveful burned, he dried another in the rusty oven, his socks steaming behind the stove. He made half a gallon of coffee and dug out the remainder of the crackers and cheese. As he pushed the cup towards Henriette, he warned her he was not the man to wait on a woman....[31]

It was a situation she had to accept. Also her educated husband was not above striking her when she annoyed him with ill-chosen remarks.

A Yorkshire woman, Rebecca Burlend, told the story of an incident in her life in America which had occurred fifteen years before to her son while on a visit to England. The son wrote it up and had it published in England under the title "A True Picture of Emigration." Later it was republished in Chicago.[32]

She and her husband came to Pike County, Illinois, with five of their seven children, ranging in age from infancy to nine years. They took over a site from another man and, after paying him for the house and the improvements he had made on the property, they had hardly enough money left with which to purchase tools and supplies. Then just when the wheat was ready for reaping her husband suffered a severe knee injury. The man got rapidly worse. What was she to do? This is Mrs. Burlend's description of her predicament:

> My situation required no comment: I could not but perceive that I was likely to lose my dearest earthly friend, and with him all visible means of supporting myself, or maintaining my family. I was almost driven to frenzy.... My eldest child alone manifested

any signs of sympathy; the poor boy went up to his father's bed and with affectionate and child-like simplicity said, "don't die, father, don't die . . ."

But her husband improved and she goes on:

On perceiving this, I felt myself the happiest woman on earth, although my situation was still embarrassing. Our wheat was quite ripe, indeed almost ready to shake, and if not cut soon, would be lost. We had no means of hiring reapers, and my husband could not stir out. I was therefore obliged to begin myself; I took my eldest child into the field to assist me, and left the next in age to attend to their father and take care of the youngest, which was still unweaned. I worked as hard as my strength would allow; the weather was intolerably hot, so that I was almost melted. In a little more than a week, however, we had it all cut down.[33]

No group of foreign-born women was subjected to a more painful adjustment than European women who had converted to Mormonism and were shipped into the Salt Lake Basin to become members of the Church of the Latter-Day Saints, or as the "Gentiles" called them, "The Latter-Day Fools." It was Mormon policy to send missionaries overseas for the purpose of making converts. Thousands among the English, Irish, Scotch, Scandinavians, Germans, French, and Swiss, many single women among them, embraced the new religion. Maureen Whipple, one of the Mormon chroniclers, confirms that a mixture of dialects and brogues could be heard in the camps. They, she reports, were "chattering in Swedish, Welsh or German."[34]

It was in the 1840s, during the Nauvoo period, that Joseph Smith announced it was "the will of Heaven that a man have more than one wife." It became the underlying principle of "celestial marriage." But it was bruited about that polygamy was practiced by Mormon Elders long before Joseph Smith had made it official, and it was one of the reasons for the violent persecutions to which the Mormons were subjected and which compelled them to abandon the prosperous community of Nauvoo for the wilderness of the Salt Lake region.

In the "States," as the Mormons referred to the Eastern part of the United States, many of the amenities of life were freely available, but Mormon women were expected to submit cheerfully to the deprivations characteristic of pioneering. They were exhorted to prepare themselves to fulfill the following expectations:

Mothers in Israel . . . Teach your daughters to sew, spin and weave; to cultivate vegetables as well as flowers; to make soap as well as preserves; to spin, color and weave and knit, as well as embroidery; to milk, make butter and cheese, and work in the kitchen as well as in the parlor. Thus will you and your daughters show yourselves approved and prove helpmeets in every deed, not only in the domestic relations, but in building up the Kingdom also.[35]

For European women conversion to Mormonism represented not only a break with the old associations—family and church— but also the adoption of "celestial marriage" which must have been startling, if not abhorrent, to most. The acceptance of the Mormon way of life has been called "a compound fracture."[36]

There are fictional accounts of Mormon life in plenty, many of them highly sensational. Some were written by women whose hurt and embarrassment are not glossed over. The following words spoken by a second wife to the first wife, a Swiss girl who is deeply hurt over the appearance of a second wife, suggests how plural wives may have felt:

We must be friends, because we shall both be utterly wretched if we quarrel. I know you do not want me here and I would much prefer a husband who belonged wholly to myself. But what can we do? The men rule—they decide our lives. We have no other home; we are bound to do as those who rule us say . . .[37]

Before Utah was admitted to the Union, it was required that plural wives and children of such unions be repudiated. Many men, aware of their responsibilities to women who had trusted them, were loath to comply. But they were compelled to do so. Though there were many protest meetings, polygamy was declared illegal in 1890. Hard as it may have been to cast off wives who had been assured that their marriages were for "eternity," the Mormons, including Brigham Young, the putative husband of nineteen to twenty-seven wives, submitted. In 1896, when compliance was assured, Utah was accepted as the forty-fifth state in the Union.

The Slavic group included the various nationality groups which ringed the Austro-Hungarian Empire in the Balkans, the Czechs and the Slovaks in the North, the Ruthenians on the eastern flank of the Dual Monarchy, the Poles, whose ancient kingdom had been partitioned among the Austrians, Germans, and Russians.

The appearance in America of the Yugoslavs (South Slavs), who form the second largest group of Slavs residing in the Western Hemisphere (the Poles are the largest), coincides with the rise of heavy industry, such as the manufacture of steel, and coal mining, meat packing, and so on. They did not begin to arrive in large numbers until the last decades of the nineteenth century. Many were illiterate, but they possessed what Louis Adamic, a native of the region known since 1918 as Yugoslavia, calls "heartculture"—kindness, a sense of fairness, and a strong attachment to their traditions. These people, who were predominantly farmers and shepherds and were accustomed to an outdoor existence, turned out to be prodigiously hard workers. In the anthracite areas their coming drove out many of the old English, Welsh, and Irish elements. Whereas in 1880 the English speaking groups of foreign-born made up 94 percent of the total in the hard coal regions, twenty years later the figure had dwindled to less than 52 percent.[38]

In this influx males predominated. Many of them were single men or men who had left their wives behind. That was because of the hope of returning to their homelands after accumulating savings with which to enlarge their farmholdings, their homes, or both. Other single men wanted to survey the situation in America before breaking the ties to their natal places permanently. Then if they decided to remain and had saved the money for the "Schiffskarte" for wives and children, they sent for them. Emily Greene Balch, that stout friend of the Slavs, states that the ratio of women to men was one woman to twenty-five men.[39]

In the mining towns a woman had a high economic value. She was expected not only to make a home for husband and children, but also for other unattached males, which brought additional income into the family till. Single men were apt to await the arrival of the wife of one of the married ones among them with almost as much eagerness as that of the husband, for then they could become boarders of the family. A man with a wife who kept boarders was much better off than any single man, for in addition to his pay he collected board from the men, pocketing the money, while his wife took care of the domestic needs of as many as six to twelve boarders.

Of course, not all Slavs worked in the mines. Those who did not lived on the outskirts of industrial centers in the same sort of squalor which characterized the mining towns—outhouses, open sewers, unpaved streets. In industrial cities like Pittsburgh, at the turn of the century, twenty-two thousand women, including a large number of Slavs, were employed at jobs that were considered inferior and unpleasant, such as tobacco stripping in stogy factories, work in laundries, in canneries and in metal trades.[40] This work force consisted of single and married women. They worked a ten-hour day, at an average wage of between one dollar and one dollar forty cents a day, depending upon the unpleasantness of the work. The Slavic women were docile workers. In describing Polish women in grimy factories a foreman is quoted as saying: "We never have any trouble with them; we can't give them enough work to do."[41] The explanation provided is this: "They are there too much on sufferance for grievances to be worth their while."[42]

Among married women, miners' wives bore the heaviest burdens, because in addition to normal concerns affecting working people—strikes, layoffs, wage cuts—there was also the dread of mine accidents. Both men and women were fatalistic. Their feeling was, as the author of a novel about the lives of miners in Pennsylvania puts it: "When the time comes to go, you go. It's up to God."[43]

A young college graduate came to a mining town during the depression of the 1930s to observe the effect of a strike on the miners and their families. Inquiring about causes of fatal mine accidents, she received this answer:

. . . Choke dust gets in with the air when you're firing a shot, and there's a mine explosion. The roof can cave in. You can get electrocuted. May be there's a premature shot. When there's a big fall, the air'll go up the entry sixty miles an hour, knocking down everything. Maybe you're walking up the main entry, and you get knocked down by a motor and killed.[44]

Slavic girls were primarily "peasant girls."[45] Poverty and meanness were their portion in America. "Work gives them no time to live," remarks Thomas Bell. Their homes were unpainted, ugly shanties made of scrap materials, and they considered themselves lucky to have a patch of ground on which to grow vegetables and to be able to keep a cow, a goat, and some chickens. Every room but the family room and kitchen was rented out to four or five bachelors who paid two to four dollars a month per room. This excluded the purchase of food, but included the cooking of it.[46] Water had to be carried from a common fountain, and bread was baked at a communal bake oven.

Women served the males under their roofs like slaves. It was not unusual for husbands to beat their wives. On Saturday nights when men went to the tavern, "women waited in the passageways, shawled, quiet, patient, to take their husbands home."[47]

Such was the even tenor of their days. When accidents came, it was with terrific suddenness. A siren or a bell announced an accident which brought all the women running. Thomas Bell tells of the death of a young miner, whose wife, the mother of several young children, received compensation of $1,370, which was considered a large sum.[48] In addition she was tubercular. Her duties bore down on her so heavily that in spite of the shock of her bereavement, the day after the funeral she had to do a large wash because it could not wait.

An even greater tragedy than the loss of a husband was the loss of a husband and son or sons in the same accident. One Croatian woman was said to have lost three or four sons in the same mine disaster.[49] The Croatian artist, Maxo Vanka, who had been professor of painting at the Zagreb Academy of Art and a pupil of Ivan Mestrovic, was so affected by the misfortunes of Croatian mothers in America that he devoted one of his murals on the walls of the Saint Nicholas Croatian Church at Millvale, Pennsylvania, to the picture of a mother weeping over the body of a son killed in a mine accident.[50]

No discussion about Slavic wives and mothers can ignore their behavior during the fierce strikes of the late nineteenth and early twentieth centuries. Contrary to allegations that the Slavs did not support their strikes, recent historiography maintains that rather than being strikebreakers, they made heroic sacrifices in support of their unions.[51]

Women played an extraordinary role in the "Long Strike" of 1875 and the "Latimer Massacre" of 1897, when strikers were fired upon and brutally manhandled. To ascertain whether their husbands and sons were among the dead or the injured

Frantic, kerchiefed women, trailing bewildered children behind, searched among the blood-spattered beds for their husbands and sons. When they found the ones they sought a pitiable wailing arose.[52]

A woman of heroic stature was "Big Mary" Septek. Employing the tactics of Mother Jones, who was a well known strike leader among miners, "Big Mary" placed herself at the head of a caravan of women supplied with rolling pins and pokers, some carrying their infants, and prevented strikebreakers from entering the mines. According to Professor Greene:

At five separate points . . . a score of women armed with clubs, rolling pins and pokers led over a hundred men and boys in chasing immigrant workers on the South Side.[53]

Louis Adamic tells a more optimistic story about a Croatian woman whom he calls Manda Evanich.[54] Manda worked just as hard as any woman among the Slavs, but she succeeded in bringing her husband and sons to a peak of responsibility and affluence.

Manda was, like so many of her countrywomen, unusually strong; she could haul, lug and lift as well as any man. She could also read and write, which many Slavs, men and women, could not, and she was adept at healing, at setting bones and taking care of injuries. This was greatly valued in any immigrant colony.

Her marriage to Mike Evans at nineteen was her second marriage, and she had a child from a previous marriage. Mike Evans preceded her to Michigan by two years. The first Croatian in Michigan, he worked in the copper mines. His intention was to return to his homeland. But when he contracted an eye disease no doctor seemed able to diagnose, he wrote to his wife to come posthaste with her herbs so that he might be cured.

Upon her arrival she found an abandoned log cabin waiting, which her husband and a dozen prospective boarders had made ready for her. In two weeks her husband's eye infection was cured.

His daily wage was a dollar and twenty-five cents, but with the income from the boarders they were able to save six hundred dollars. For three dollars a month she cooked, baked, cleaned, washed and ironed for them, working sixteen to eighteen hours a day. In addition she nursed their colds, stomachaches and injuries such as broken arms and open wounds. She offered an additional service to her boarders, washing their feet once a week.

She was alert to every opportunity to improve their situation. When she heard that other mines paid better, she prevailed upon her husband to change his place of work. Then she found another home, her boarders faithfully following her. Later she bought a large house in Calumet. By then she had saved twenty-five hundred dollars, with which they decided to open a saloon, a business much favored by Slavs. She was then in her early thirties and had spent eight years in America.

In the meantime several American-born children—all sons— had made their appearance. Twelve of them grew to manhood. When the last, a pair of twins, were born, President Theodore Roosevelt wrote her a letter of congratulations.

A saloon keeper was expected to act as an intermediary for his countrymen. He sold not only beer and wine, but provided a social center where meetings and weddings took place. The saloon keeper cashed paychecks, often collected union dues, sold steamship tickets and money orders, wrote letters, acted as banker, prepared people for naturalization, and accompanied would-be citizens to the place of examination. Gambling was not allowed at the Evans saloon, and Mrs. Evans herself was capable of disposing of drunks.

As the saloon became a thriving establishment, Manda was busier than ever, attending to a variety of duties with the help of girls she kept bringing over from Croatia. They stayed with her until they were married. She promoted the building of a Roman Catholic Croatian church, organized a Croatian Women's Club, and at the same time kept an eye on her twelve sons.

One of her jobs was to go to Chicago twice a year to purchase at wholesale the wearing apparel twelve growing sons required. Guided by her good sense she cautiously bought copper stocks which eventually added considerably to the family wealth.

After twenty years she began to think of giving up the saloon and returning to farming. The Canadian government was offering one hundred and sixty acres in Saskatchewan to every adult male who would settle on the land and improve it. With twelve sons she visualized a princely estate of several thousand acres. Her husband and several sons had already begun the building of a home when Mike took ill and died. The undertaking was dropped. It was the only plan she had ever abandoned.

Mrs. Evans's greatest achievement was that all her sons became successful and respected men. Several were sent to college and law school. Three became lawyers, one ending up as a well-thought-of member of the Chicago Bar. One served in the legislature of Wisconsin, another in the state government of Michigan. However, none became a priest, though three were sent to the seminary. One struck oil in Texas.[55] At eighty-one Mrs. Evans was still alive, a financially independent woman who was still practicing her healing art.

Though the Jewish mother has some close competitors for the designation of the most self-sacrificing mother and wife among all foreign-born women, she would surely be entitled to front rank, particularly when shawled and bewigged women were not an unusual sight in the ghettos of our cities. Hapgood Hutchins,[56] a journalist who was, like Lincoln Steffens, fascinated with the Jews of the East Side, describes the Jewish woman as "drab and plain in appearance with a thick waist, a wig and as far as possible for a woman, a contempt for ornament." But he also realized that "they are predominantly serious in nature and, if they lack alertness to the social nuance, have yet a compelling appeal which consists in headlong devotion to duty, a principle or a person."[57] This was his estimate of the Jewish immigrant mother of the turn of the century, but if he were living today he would not find it applicable to Jewish women of American birth. The Jewish immigrant mother, then, made up for aesthetic deficiencies in intensity of purpose and in fanatic devotion to her family.

During those decades when the flow of immigrants kept rising, filling the cities to the bursting point, the hardships were very real. The greatest number of Jewish newcomers huddled mostly in the large cities, particularly in New York, because of the greater availability of work, closeness to others of their own kind, and the ease in maintaining religious observance.

Anti-Jewish prejudice was comparatively light until the 1880s, when Jews and other undesirable Europeans began to pour into the United States. But it was not entirely absent. When the first group of Sephardic Jews from Brazil arrived in New York harbor during the days when Peter Stuyvesant ruled "Nieuw Amsterdam," he would not admit them until specifically told to do so by the Dutch West India Company. But prejudice remained. In Maryland, for instance, there was a restriction against Jews in public office until the "Jewbill" of 1826 removed that disqualification. Social prejudice was even more firmly entrenched, as the banker Joseph Seligman found out. President Grant, who was accused of being an anti-Semite because of his order in 1862 expelling Jews from the Department of the Tennessee,[58] offered the office of Secretary of the Treasury to him; but in 1877 the Grand Union Hotel in Saratoga Springs refused him admission.

The Jewish population remained small until 1880. By 1820 America was home to 4,000 Jews[59] who were living in New York, Philadelphia, Portsmouth, Charleston, and in some of the lesser towns. The influx of German Jews—Forty-eighters who hoped to find America hospitable to their idealism, and those who sought an expanded outlet for their entrepreneurial skills—raised the number to 150,000 in 1860.[60] During the next twenty years, which formed the prologue to the drama of hundreds of thousands fleeing from persecution and hunger, the number rose to 280,000.[61]

The reason for the avalanche that began in the 1880s was two-fold. The Jewish population in Europe had kept pace with the general increase of population throughout Europe and had grown by more than five million. This exacerbated the Jewish economic situation. The second and more directly frightening occurrence was a series of terrible persecutions in Russia and in Poland, called "pogroms," between 1881–1883 and again between 1900–1907. While the Jews of Austria did not experience the awful government-inspired terror suffered by the Jews of Russia and Poland, their economic situation was precarious. Another center of merciless persecution was Rumania.

In 1900 the Jewish population in America stood at one million, and during the peak years between 1904–1907 a new wave of "pogroms" added 642,000.[62] In 1925 the number had grown to four and a half million.[63] By 1915 the East Side of New York alone had acquired 300,000 Jews who had compressed themselves into an area of two square miles.[64]

The German Jews, many of whom had by then wrested for themselves respect, influence, and wealth, were dismayed by the extent of this inundation, by the outlandish appearance of these entrants, and by their desperate poverty. Aware of their moral obligation to help them, an obligation to which Jews rarely failed to respond, the American Jews made noteworthy efforts to facilitate the settlement of the newcomers, some of which were not always appreciated.

An attempt was made to disperse these new arrivals and to turn some of them into cultivators of the earth through the National Farm School and the Jewish Agricultural Society. But farming and industry had not been a Jewish way of life for centuries, for they had been barred from owning land. However, some of the new immigrants became passionately attached to the "Green World," as Maurice Hindus called it, and made significant contributions to agricultural progress. Hindus, of Russian birth, happily forsook ghetto life to become

a "hired hand" on a farm.[65] Another, also of Russian birth, was
Dr. Joseph G. Lipman, plant geneticist and head of the Department of Bacteriology at Rutgers State University.

Though by 1870 Jews were to be found in every state of
the Union,[66] they preferred urban life, notably New York City,
which toward the end of the century was becoming the hub
for the manufacture of women's wear, and Chicago, the center
of the men's wear industry. Most of them made a living by
working in sweatshops or through petty trade. It was this
dense concentration of people competing for jobs and scarce
housing that was in large part responsible for their hardships.
The ready-to-wear industry was a seasonal one and the availability of more workers than jobs kept wages abysmally low.
Not until their unions gained in strength did their situation
improve. Their places of work were unsanitary and dangerous,
and sweatshop owners, grubbing away at saving pennies per
garment so that they might be in a better competitive position,
spared neither themselves nor their workers. They were usually
immigrants themselves, and sometimes not more than "one
ship ahead" of their workers.

The intolerable conditions inhering in the immigrant situation
may have been partly responsible for rousing those Jewish
mothers, in whom adversity had not killed every spark of
ambition, to their greatest exertions. The dirt and squalor of
their living quarters were awful, and often the earnings of
a whole family were insufficient for their needs. These immigrant mothers kept before the family the goal of constantly
bettering themselves. Though some died struggling, many lived
to see a tremendous improvement in their situation. Rose
Schneiderman's statement of her mother's role in the family
is not unusual. In describing the family's progress to a steam-
heated apartment on Second Avenue, she states: "How did
we get such luxury? Again it was Mother's doing. Throughout
the years she struggled to pull us up one rung of the ladder,
even if it meant we were forever moving."[67]

It was generally the mother who saved pennies to make
music lessons possible for one child or another, who purchased
an instrument on credit and somehow managed to get it paid
for, who fiercely pushed as many of her children as she could

through high school, some through college, even through professional schools, exhorting the rest to work and sacrifice without
stint, so at least one of the family could forge ahead of the
rest. The genteel, golden or white-haired Christian mother who
draws all to her by gentle persuasion and a soothing tone of
voice was rarely to be encountered in immigrant life. Sometimes
Momma is presented as gentle, occupied with cooking and
baking the traditional Jewish dishes; sometimes as a raging
virago; but most always she appears as counselor, consoler,
arbitrator and the tie by which the family was kept together.
Occasionally we hear of fathers being feared or even hated,
but rarely were children disloyal to their mothers. The following
statement appears in a novel by a first generation American
woman:

> The old man was no tie. He was a hate. He was a hate all tied
> up with shame, but he couldn't tie Jake to the house. . . . It was Ma
> who was the tie. . . .[68]

Jewish authors lead in the number of fictional accounts of
the immigrant experience. The reason may lie in the severity
of the "psychic wound" from which immigrants were apt to
suffer, and to which the Jews seem to have been more sensitive.

One Jewish author was Michael Gold, in reality Irving
Granich, who became editor of the *Masses*. In his autobiographical novel, *Jews Without Money*, he presents a Jewish
immigrant family on the lower East Side during the early
decades of the twentieth century and creates an indelible
picture of a woman continually struggling with misfortune.
She is naive, direct, without guile—a woman who exemplifies
Thoreau's apothegm, "The heart is forever inexperienced." The
realization is inescapable that what the author experienced in
his youth propelled him into the Marxist camp and drove
him to write about it.

His father was a house painter, a romantic who enthralled
his two children with stories of his old life in Rumania, whose
hopes were as volatile as helium but who couldn't earn enough
to pay the rent half the time, a man who attracted misfortune.
One time he was taken sick with lead poisoning; another time

he fell off a scaffold. Instead of working himself up, he worked himself down, ending by peddling bananas, but as everyone could have guessed, including himself, he could not make a living at it. Like so many immigrant parents he wanted his son to become a doctor (always a doctor, because doctors were looked up to and it was a profitable skill anywhere). But the boy had learned to be a realist; he knew it was an idle dream.

His mother, he states, had "a wonderful heart . . . she could be sorry even for a landlord." But,

> She was a buttinsky. She tried to "reform" everybody and fought people because they were "bad." She spoke her mind freely and told everyone exactly where the path of duty lay.

When someone was evicted she wrapped herself in her shawl and went begging for pennies. Her son was aware:

> She would have stolen or killed for us. She would have let a railroad train run over her body if it could have helped us. She loved us with the fierce painful love of a mother wolf and scolded us continually like a magpie.[69]

A writer who ascribes to his mother the financial success of some of her sons is Harry Roskolenko. When he returns to his home in New York after years as a sailor he finds "my two older brothers had bought a luncheonette from a Greek on New Street—my mother had urged, coaxed and finally forced them into the venture. . . . In a few years they owned a chain of restaurants from Manhattan to Brooklyn. . . ."[70] This particular mother had lost an arm after crawling underneath a wagon for a piece of ice.

Alfred Kazin, writer and literary critic, presents his mother in two different autobiographical works. His mother, a dress-maker in the Williamsburg section of Brooklyn, seemed to have a built-in energizer within her that drove her to ceaseless activity. Brooklyn, the first stop in the peregrination of Jews toward respectability, represented a slight step ahead of the slums of the Lower East Side, which were more congested than

the slums of Brooklyn and housed a more heterogenous assort-
ment of immigrants. She had worked in the Triangle Shirtwaist
factory and bore the stigmata of her work in a hand that had
been injured and remained maimed. Both descriptions show
her in the kitchen at her sewing machine, working as if she
were being pursued, not only by Time's Winged Chariot, but
by an unrelenting demon.

The kitchen gave a special character to our lives: my mother's
character. All my memories of that kitchen were dominated by the
nearness of my mother sitting all day long at her sewing machine. . . .
Year after year as I began to take in her fantastic capacity for
labor and her anxious zeal, I realized it was ourselves she kept
stitched together. I can never remember a time when she was not
working. She worked because the law of her life was work, work
and anxiety. She worked because she would have found life meaningless without work.[71]

In another book:

In my mother's world . . . no one was ever bored or lazy; no one
was ever cynical; no one ever laughed. She was an indentured servant
of the emotions, and always a slave to other people. . . . My mother
was bent, arthritic, and always walked as if she were controlling
pain. . . . Her whole being expressed so momentously her awareness
of the grimness of life.[72]

A different mother-son relationship existed between Louis
Dembitz Brandeis, Justice of the Supreme Court, and his
mother. His parents were both born in Prague, Bohemia. They
became engaged in Europe, but were not married until they
arrived in the United States.

His parents were educated people. Neither they nor their
children suffered privation. Within a short time the family
was prosperous and, though they underwent financial reverses
during the depression of 1873, they overcame them.

On his mother's birthday in 1888 when he was thirty-two,
Louis Brandeis wrote to his mother as follows:

I must send you another birthday greeting and tell you how much
I love you; that with each day I learn to extol your love and your

worth more—and that when I look back over my life, I can find nothing in your treatment of me that I would alter. . . . I believe, most beloved mother, that the improvement of the world, reform, can only arise when mothers like you are increased thousands of times and have more children.[73]

For over forty years until his death at eighty-five, the Justice is supposed to have kept on the walls of his study in Chatham, Massachusetts, a picture of his mother with some small children, including himself, which his mother had given him before her death.[74]

It was not only for their children that Jewish women made heroic sacrifices. Sometimes it was for their husbands. In immigrant annals there are many instances of young women working on sewing machines for years to enable their husbands or husbands-to-be to become members of the "safe professions"— doctors, dentists, pharmacists, teachers, or members of the federal, state or city bureaucracy. Or was it for the purpose of insuring a better future for the children they would have? Sometimes these intended husbands decamped after reaching their goals, leaving these poor women devastated.

There's a story about a midwife from Russia who came to America with a husband and child in the 1880s. In Russia her husband had been a locomotive engineer. Quickly perceiving the educational opportunities that were open to strivers, she urged her husband to try to become a physician. While working during the day, he went to college at night, and then to Jefferson Medical College in Philadelphia. She continued to work as a midwife.

Her work was extremely demanding. Frequently awakened during the night, she trudged through dark streets, up flights of stairs, or into basements, to find women in the kind of poverty Jacob A. Riis described in *How the Other Half Lives* and *The Battle With the Slums*. After delivering a baby she often had to go out and buy a bottle of milk at her own expense so that the woman would have some food. It was an uphill fight for her and her husband all the way.

On the day on which her husband received his medical

diploma, this valiant woman died. Her husband practiced medicine in Philadelphia until his death at sixty-nine.[75]

The end of the nineteenth century was a period of mounting immigration. Immigrant labor provided the muscle for the industrial expansion which characterized the period. When immigrant women found that industrial work was open to them as well as to men, they looked upon it as one of America's special blessings. They were willing to work at anything, particularly those who were young and without responsibility to young children. The relative, friend or neighbor who could help find work for a recent newcomer was a new immigrant's greatest benefactor.

The rewards even for onerous work were great. But a letdown was inevitable when workers realized that they were being unmercifully exploited, and that no matter how diligently one worked, the wages were insufficient to cover the most essential needs. The remedy was obvious: increased wages. But this was not to be achieved on request.

Consequently, the period at the turn of the century constituted a time of gigantic labor struggles which were instigated by leaders who came from immigrant workers themselves. Though young and inexperienced they possessed the courage that won for them and their fellow workers better wages, improved working conditions, shorter hours, and job security.

Thus a group of new heroines was created.

CHAPTER 7

Strength in Union

THE ATTEMPT AMONG WORKERS TO BAND TOGETHER AS A COUNTER-weight to exploitation is as old as the Republic, but even limited success in establishing a firm national labor movement eluded workers until after the end of the Civil War. The early labor leaders were mostly natives. Among the best-known before the emergence of the American Federation of Labor in 1886 were Uriah Stephens, founder of the Knights of Labor in 1869, and Terence V. Powderly, who succeeded him. Although during the first half of the nineteenth century several English, Irish and Welsh labor leaders met with some success, the first foreign-born individual to capture first place in the labor movement was Samuel Gompers, a native of Great Britain. Not until the second decade of the twentieth century did the colossi Sidney Hillman and David Dubinsky, Eastern Europeans both, come upon the scene. A third foreign-born man who began as a union leader, then turned to politics, is Alex Rose, another native of England. However, John Mitchell, Eugene V. Debs, "Big Bill" Haywood, William Green, Philip Murray, John L. Lewis, Walter Reuther, George Meany, among others, were (and are) all native Americans of the first generation.

Among early leaders of working women, we find mention of Lavinia Waight and Louise Mitchell, both New England work-ing girls who attempted as early as 1825 to form an association of "tailoresses." Another, Sarah G. Bagley,[1] born in New Hamp-shire, was a factory girl in a cotton mill in Lowell, Massachusetts. She began to attract attention by contributing to the *Lowell Offering*, which consisted of the writings of mill girls. Later she broke away to start her own publication. Was the *Lowell Offering* intended to bolster their yeoman pride or to disarm them? It did not silence Miss Bagley. A natural-born protester,

114

who was sympathetic to Fourier's communitarian ideas, she became the president and founder in 1845 of the "Lowell Female Labor Reform Association," which managed to draw under its wing several hundred members in branches in Massachusetts and New Hampshire.

Though American women factory workers did not make their appearance in considerable numbers until the 1820s, when the introduction of machinery made large-scale production of textiles possible, at no time did women function exclusively as housewives. There had always been midwives who were accustomed to hurrying day or night, on snowshoes if need be, to their tasks. Their tombstones contain the information that some of them brought a thousand, two thousand, even three thousand babies into the world. They looked upon their work as their contribution to the growth of their New England communities.

Even during the colonial period there were "tailoresses" who filled such essential needs as sewing shrouds and might have been as skillful at fine sewing and embroidery as Hawthorne's Hester Prynne who compensated for the disgrace of having to display the letter "A" (adulteress) on her bosom by turning her symbol of identification into a work of art. "Dame schools," where young children received their earliest instruction, provided an outlet, if scant remuneration, for the more genteel of their sex. In addition to working as shopkeepers, as compositors in print shops, some were apothecaries. One eighteenth-century widow, Martha Smith of Long Island,[2] continued her husband's business in whale fishing.

A form of mass employment existed before the end of the eighteenth century. As early as 1764 a Philadelphia establishment is said to have employed more than one hundred spinners,[3] producing yarn, not cloth. It was the "factory system" at the start of the nineteenth century with the introduction of the power loom that brought the women out of their homes in large numbers and marked the beginning of textile manufacturing. The city of Lowell subsequently became known as "The City of Spindles." The Boston Manufacturing Company, started in 1813 by Francis Cabot Lowell, actually solicited young women to leave the farms and come to work in the factories. A very appealing argument was judged to be one that suggested their accumulated earnings would improve their chances for marrying and furnishing homes. But, instead, some of these women put the money they earned to use in helping to educate their brothers—so that they could become ministers, town officials, and clerks—or in augmenting their own education. In order to keep the virtue of these working girls unimpaired, companies provided boardinghouses which made church attendance mandatory. The Merrimack Company, for instance, owned thirty-five such residences for their workers.[4] The mother of Lucy Larcom,[5] a mill girl, was a supervisor of a dormitory. Lucy worked in the mills for ten years, then went to college, and afterward taught and wrote verse, as well as a critical work on poetry, *Landscape in American Poetry*. She gained considerable reputation as the author of two autobiographical volumes: *Among Lowell Millgirls* and *A New England Girlhood*.

There were also factories in Paterson, New Jersey, and in New Hampshire. The wages girl workers received were around two dollars a week and no more than four.[6] The first strike occurred when three to four hundred girls in Dover left their jobs. They were not union members. Girls also struck when their board was raised, which reduced their net earnings. They also attempted to secure a ten-hour workday (instead of 13½) and better wages, but were unsuccessful.

By the 1840s, with the influx of Irish into Massachusetts, there was a considerable number of Irish immigrant girls working in the mills, and as the century progressed, the work force became representative of the newcomers who had settled in Massachusetts. Irish, Canadian, and Portuguese women worked side by side. By 1850 the first complete industrial census indicated that over 250,000 women were employed in industry as against 750,000 men.[7] By 1912 the mixture in the New England textile mills was English, Irish, French-Canadian, Portuguese, Polish, Lithuanian, Syrian, Armenian, Belgian, Greek, Turk, and Italian.

The two oldest organizations to which women were admitted were The International Typographers Union, formed in 1868,[8] and The Cigarmakers International Union in 1867.[9] Both consisted of skilled workers. Whereas the Typographical Union was composed largely of English-speaking women, the Cigarmakers

Union included Bohemian and German women who were cigar-makers in their homelands. In 1866 the Collar Laundry Workers of Troy also succeeded in establishing a union, but three years later they lost a strike which the union could not survive.[10]

In 1869 the Knights of Labor came into existence with high hopes of finally establishing a viable labor organization. It was to be an industrial, not a craft union, which was open to all workers, regardless of race, color, or sex. Excluded were only liquor dealers, lawyers, bankers, and stockbrokers. Started by Uriah Stephens as a secret order (so workers could not be identified and/or blacklisted) secrecy was abolished when "Grand Master Workman" Terence Powderly was elected in 1878 after having served as mayor of Scranton, Pennsylvania. To signalize that the attitude to women workers was to be one of perfect equality with men—"equal pay for equal work"—the wife of Terence Powderly was the first one to join.[11] In 1886 when the A.F. of L. was already a serious threat to the Knights of Labor, eight to nine percent of the total membership were women. At the highest point of membership they numbered about 50,000.[12]

The Knights of Labor organization was seriously injured during the Haymarket incident of 1886, when a membership card was found on the person of one who was arrested and suspected of being an anarchist. The appearance in 1881 of the "Federation of Organized Trades and Labor Unions of the United States and Canada," which in 1886 became the "American Federation of Labor," helped to undermine the Knights. It was led by Samuel Gompers and Adolph Strasser, both cigarmakers. Though the A.F. of L. declared in favor of the principle of "equal pay for equal work" for women, it was considered "complacent" about admitting women.[13]

In 1870 a foreign-born woman already in early middle age appeared on the labor scene. She was Mary Jones (1830–1930), and was soon called "Mother Jones." She was destined to become a legendary figure. No one believed more fervently in the power of labor unions to make workers strong, or worked harder at the task of organizing them to be able to withstand the pressures of the coal and mining interests.

A friend and partisan of miners and a determined foe of child labor, she was to be found in the midst of the fiercest labor battles of the nineteenth century. She did not come into the labor movement until she had lost her husband and four children. When she went to observe the conditions under which children of tender age worked in the cotton mills of the South, she witnessed such wretchedness and exploitation that she wrote: "My ears wearied with the stories of brutality and suffering; my eyes ached with the misery I witnessed; my brain sickened with the knowledge of man's inhumanity to man."[14] An intrepid fighter who feared neither guns nor the police, she chose to exert herself in behalf of the most exploited workers—the anthracite coal miners—despite imprisonment and threats to her life.

Born in County Cork, Ireland, Mary Jones was brought to America at the age of ten. By then her father had become naturalized, and although he was working as a railroad laborer in Toronto, he retained his American citizenship. She went to school in Toronto, including Normal School, in order to be able to teach. At the same time she learned dressmaking and became expert at it. Except for two stints of teaching in Canada and in Memphis, she stuck to dressmaking until she became a union organizer.

In 1861 she married a native of Tennessee, an iron molder and a member of the Iron Moulders' Union, who soon became an official of the union. Bob Jones was an idealist and a devoted trade unionist who converted his wife to the belief that trade unionism was the cure-all for the evils of industrialism.

In 1867 an outbreak of yellow fever robbed her of her husband and their four children. Because of her apparent immunity, she stayed on in Memphis to nurse the sick. When the epidemic was under control, she went to Chicago and set up a dressmaking emporium. She was struck by the misery of Chicago's poor. This is what she observed as she stitched away:

. . . I would look out of the plate glass windows and see the poor, shivering wretches, jobless and hungry, walking along the frozen lakefront. The contrast of their condition with that of the tropical comfort of the people for whom I sewed was sinful to me. My employers seemed neither to notice or to care.[15]

In 1871 the disastrous Chicago Fire occurred, which made 70,000 people homeless. She was one of those who lost everything—home and business. Within two years a new catastrophe struck—the financial crash which caused "The Panic of 1873." The legacy was a recession which lasted six years, created four million jobless, and ushered in wave after wave of the fiercest strikes that kept erupting throughout the rest of the century like delayed-action fuses. Having kept up her affiliation with the Knights after the death of her husband, she became a K. of L. organizer.

The first theater of operation was the strike on the Baltimore and Ohio Railroad in 1877. It provoked the violence of a tornado as it spread from Martinsburg, West Virginia, to other rail centers. In Pittsburgh such havoc was caused by rioters and looters, who burned railroad stock and buildings, that the militia was called out and, finally, federal troops. The presence of "federals" was a virtual guarantee that any strike would be lost.

Immensely sympathetic to striking workers and their families, she condemned rioting because she knew that the strikers would be blamed for excesses committed by strikebreakers and hoodlums for whom a strike was an excuse to go on a rampage. Though Mother Jones was a militant, she insisted the law be observed. She wanted strikers to win by strictly legal means. She was also fiercely patriotic. Washington was to her the "immortal Washington," as was Lincoln, and "Uncle Sam" was her very own uncle. America was our "great and enlightened country." It was on judges, bosses, governors that she was apt to heap the greatest scorn. Bosses were "steel Gods," or "the grand dukes of the region," any judge who supported the companies was a "scab," the governor of Colorado was "the obedient boy of the coal companies," and "God Almighty" her personal friend, whom she would inform about the state of affairs when she arrived on "the other side."[16] Her judgment of John D. Rockefeller, Jr., was that he was "a nice young man who reads the Bible."[17]

While she may have been sympathetic to anarchists as people

who were "poverty stricken, in rags and tatters and wretched shoes," she had no use for anarchism as a means of improving the social order. After watching a parade of anarchists she observed:

I thought the parade an insane move on the part of the anarchists as it only served to make the feelings more bitter. . . . It had no educative value whatever and only served to increase the employers' fear, to make the police more savage and the public less sympathetic to the real distress of the workers.[18]

She was conservative in regard to the status of women. "A great responsibility," she asserted, "rests upon women—the training of children. This is her most beautiful task. If men earned money enough, it would not be necessary for women to neglect their homes and their little ones to add to the family income."[19] But she also preached: "No matter what your fight / Don't be ladylike."[20]

She became so well-known and respected that trainmen, newspaper men, even soldiers, warned her of danger and tried to help her as she traveled from one strike headquarters to the next. Generally she was called in when a strike had begun in order to help in lifting the morale of the strikers and their families. Her method was to move in with a striker's family, to share what they had, to help in taking care of the sick and the injured, in laying out the dead, in keeping men away from the saloons, and in sundry other tasks. She would organize processions of strikers' wives, their babes in their arms, one holding aloft the American flag, the rest carrying brooms and mops with which to belabor strikebreakers and chase them off their jobs. When she succeeded in organizing a union and there was no money to pay for the charter, she would pay for it herself.

Her speeches were always peppery and daring. The appellation "ladies" did not appeal to her. "God Almighty made a woman," she would say, "and the Rockefeller gang of thieves made the ladies."[21] Once when she gave an incendiary speech in a church and was upbraided for it, she replied, "Oh, that wasn't God's house. That is the coal company's house. Don't you know God Almighty never comes around to a place like this?"[22] She refused to call a judge "Your Honor," until she was convinced that he was honorable.

From 1900 on she immersed herself in one coal strike after another. The coal strike of 1902 was one of the most vicious, and the first strike in United States history in which a President of the United States decided to act as mediator. According to the employers, President Theodore Roosevelt was on the side of the workers. When after five months of bitter struggle neither side showed any signs of softening and coal supplies were getting dangerously low, the President forced the employers to accept arbitration by threatening to send a general to run the mines. John Mitchell, the strike leader, was in favor of arbitration, but Mother Jones was not, because she suspected rightly that only complete victory would force the companies to grant union recognition. Though the miners gained a 10 percent increase in wages, the employers refused to recognize the union. She criticized Mitchell severely as being unworthy to lead the miners.[23] In this she may have been unfair because other equally determined unionists considered Mitchell "the great idol of the labor movement" and admitted their "high esteem for him."[24] Mitchell became so incensed at Mother Jones that the next time she criticized him he fired her.

This happened during the uprising of the miners in 1903 against the Colorado Fuel and Iron Company, owned by the Rockefeller interests. Two groups of miners were involved, those of northern Colorado, who were mostly English-speaking, and those of southern Colorado, who were mostly foreigners (Mexicans, Poles, Hungarians, and others). Although the leaders had pledged not to accept separate settlements, this is just what Mitchell did, abandoning the southern contingent to certain defeat. She made a fiery stand against Mitchell, accusing him of betrayal, and Mitchell dismissed her as an organizer of the United Mine Workers. But she joined the Western Federation of Miners, representing the miners of southern Colorado, upholding their cause until they were forced to give up. When John Mitchell's term as president expired in 1908, she returned to the United Mine Workers.

Child workers aroused her deepest compassion and her most

perfervid condemnation. She observed them in the cotton mills of Alabama and in 1903 she helped in a textile strike in Pennsylvania, where a large number of children were employed. At a demonstration she assembled the children and holding up their crushed hands with missing fingers, she stormed at the crowd. "Philadelphia mansions were built on the broken bones, the quivering hearts and drooping heads of these children. . . ." Then she thought up the idea of taking them within sight of President Roosevelt. She took them on a tour for a week, marching with them to the tune of a child's drum and fife. On the campus of Princeton she made a speech on "Higher Education" and pointing to a child, said: "There's a textbook on economics." She brought the children eventually within sight of President Roosevelt's home in Oyster Bay, explaining: "We want President Roosevelt to hear the wail of children who never had a chance to go to school, but work eleven and twelve hours a day in the textile mills of Pennsylvania." Though the textile workers lost their strike, she had her reward not long afterward when the Pennsylvania legislature passed a child labor law banning children from work until they were fourteen.

When she returned to the Colorado coal mines in 1911 she found herself sentenced to prison. Her descriptions of prison conditions outraged the imagination. But it did not succeed in breaking her dedication to the miners and other exploited workers in the American industrial world.

In 1913 occurred the Ludlow massacre, when the Colorado National Guard set fire to a tent colony occupied by evicted strikers. Sixty-five[25] people were killed, forty-three of whom were women and children. This outraged her so that she decided to go to Washington to tell the story to the House Mining Committee. The ensuing publicity caused President Wilson to dispatch federal troops to replace the state militia.

Even when she was past eighty-five she continued to be active in strikes in New York. But she recognized in the last years of her life that the number of severe strikes had dwindled. Her comment was that "both employers and employees had become wise."

At ninety-three she addressed the convention of the Farmer

Labor Party and told them "the militant, not the meek, shall inherit the earth."

When she died in 1930 she was one hundred years and seven months old. She died in the home of a worker where a miner's wife took care of her. It was in the tradition of the labor movement for comrades to open their homes, however crowded, to one another. She was buried in the cemetery of the United Mine Workers at Mount Olive, Illinois.[26]

During the forty years between the appearance in 1860 in America of Darwin's *The Origin of Species* and the beginning of the twentieth century, the United States became a Darwinian paradise. Between 1890 and 1914 a total of fifteen million immigrants arrived who became grist for the mills of our expanding industrialism. They came largely from Russia, Austria-Hungary, Italy and the Balkans.[27] In 1907 alone, 1,285,000[28] streamed in eager to secure for themselves some of the wealth they had heard about. These hordes of ragged, mostly unskilled people had to find any kind of work or starve, and often when they worked to the limit of their endurance, their wages were insufficient to purchase the necessities of life. The realization that while the individual worker was helpless, thousands united in their purpose were not, was not long in impressing itself on the consciousness of workers. Consequently the early twentieth century brought not only increased industrialization that made possible (for many) the "Two-Chickens-in-Every-Pot" prosperity promised by the backers of McKinley, but also increased pressures for better wages and greater security for all workers. It was from among this group of new immigrants that a number of militant leaders arose who became fighters for union recognition and the benefits that result from collective action. These militants consisted of men and women, but the emphasis in these pages is limited to women of foreign birth.

The initial result of the huge influx of Eastern Jews to the United States between 1882 and 1914 was a phenomenal acceleration in the growth of the garment industry. Among these newcomers tens of thousands were young girls, some of whom came alone in the vanguard of brothers, sisters and parents.

Most of the adults had received scant or no schooling in Europe and many of those who were brought by their parents as children attended the American public schools only until they were thirteen. In the factories they began to realize that their only hope lay in acting together for the good of all. This involved taking part in strikes and picketing, and submitting to arrest and police brutality, without which union recognition was rarely achieved. At the turn of the century they demanded bread, not roses. But in 1912, during the textile strike at Lawrence, Massachusetts, the girls would carry the slogan: "We Want Bread, and Roses Too." The rallying cry for early garment workers was the "Solidarity Song," set to the "Battle Hymn of the Republic." "What force on earth is weaker than the feeble strength of one, / But the Union makes us strong."

Between 1900 and 1915 occurred a series of severe strikes in the needle trades, which brought significant victories to the strikers and strengthened their unions so that they could bring more advantages to their members. The success of the strikers was due not only to the courage of the members and their seemingly inexhaustible amount of stamina and determination, but also to the help given them by a group of women who were not themselves of the working class, but whose sympathies were stirred by the struggle of those who had to work in order to survive. That group of women were the members of the Women's Trade Union League (WTUL), a volunteer organization whose generosity matched their understanding of the workers' problems. Without their help, progress would have been slower and more dehumanizing in the process.

The Jews from Eastern Europe were only part of the stream that converged on the United States at the turn of the century. Italians and Slavs from the Balkans and Poland contributed to the avalanche of peoples who came in search of economic betterment. Though many Slavic women—Polish, Bohemian—did enter factories, their numbers were not nearly as large as those of the Jewish women. Nor were they as audacious. Italian women were also numerically less impressive as well as more retiring, because the familial pattern among Italians favored keeping young women chained to "homework" as far as it was possible. By 1902 immigrants had helped to swell the ranks of unionized women workers to over 15,000 as against slightly over 313,000 men, and in 1913 the number had risen to 78,522 women to almost six million men.[29] In 1920 the International Ladies Garment Workers Union (ILGWU) alone had a membership of 105,300.[30] Also, by 1900, more than five million women were employed in 296 occupations out of 303 listed.[31] Of the women employed in the needle trades the Australian-born Alice Henry, an official of the League, declared:

. . . as far as women are concerned, it is to this group of aliens in particular that is due the recent tremendous impulse towards organization among the most poorly paid women. In the sewing trades and in some other trades, such as candymaking, it is the American girls who have accepted conditions and allowed matters to drift from bad to worse. It is the foreign girl and especially the Slavic Jewess who has been making the fight for higher wages, shorter hours, better shop management, and, above all, for the right to organize.[32]

When the National Women's Trade Union League was established in 1903, to be followed a year later by a New York branch, it was an event of incalculable importance to working women. It proved no less a spur to the women's movement than to the labor movement. If one remembers that the first decade of the twentieth century was dominated by the "muckrakers" who called attention not only to political corruption, but to social and economic inequalities as well, the work of the League may be viewed as in the tradition of a reform movement of a distinctly concrete nature. The League pledged itself to upgrade the economic status of women through union organization and to bring other benefits to working women as well. In this endeavor it succeeded so well that in a relatively short period it was conceded "the League should be credited as the strongest single influence in the marked growth of trade unionism among women, especially since 1911."[33]

A precursor of the Women's Trade Union League was the "Working Women's Society" begun in 1886 by the native Leonora O'Reilly, who was a garment worker and became an organizer for the American Federation of Labor and a dedicated member of the League. In 1904 the sum of $289 represented the average annual earnings of women.[34] Though the A.F. of L. was officially on record as favoring the entrance of women into male-dominated unions, it was lukewarm about prevailing upon existing unions to accept women. Women workers were competitors. The growing army of women rivals obviously needed allies and they found them in the League.

Patterned on the model of the British Women's Trade Union League, its American counterpart was open to union members as well as to men and women who had no connection with the trade union movement, save that they were sympathetic to workers. As Mrs. Raymond Robins, the moving spirit behind the League, declared, "the entire trade union movement is a great democratic training school open to all." Jane Addams had been the first president of the League; she was followed by Mary McDowell, who was president until 1907, when she gladly relinquished her job to Mrs. Robins. By 1904 there were local branches of the League in New York, Chicago, Boston, and Philadelphia; later one was formed in St. Louis.

Margaret Dreier Robins, a Brooklyn woman, who was the daughter of German liberals, was the League's outstanding personality for fifteen years. Mary Anderson, one of Mrs. Robins's protégées, says of her: "There was one friend who stood out above all—Mrs. Raymond Robins. From the first time I knew her until the day of her death in 1945, she was our inspiration and support."[35] Alice Henry, whom Mrs. Robins took on as editor of *Life and Labor*, the League monthly magazine, and later placed in the League's educational department, comments on the role of Mrs. Robins as national president of the Women's Trade Union League as follows:

> Mrs. Robins familiarized the women of privilege with the difficulties and the needs of their working sisters and educated the General Federation of Women's Clubs of the United States to an understanding of the problems. But she also realized that to be a success as an essential part of the labor movement more and more women would have to be drawn into trade unions.[36]

Margaret Dreier Robins was a brainy, resolute woman executive of a forceful personality, an impressive but likable manner, who was able to influence wealthy women to contribute money. There seems to have been an unspoken commitment among the leaders of the League to extend social acceptance to working girls whose lack of social sophistication could not have escaped them. Before Mrs. Robins became a member of the League she had done serious volunteer work in a Brooklyn hospital among immigrants. Rose Schneiderman, about whom more will be said later, discloses how Miss Dreier, unmarried in 1905 and president of the New York League, sought her out in the midst of a strike by the United Cloth and Cap Makers Union and offered the union favorable publicity. It was accepted, and at the end of the strike, Rose Schneiderman joined the League by paying the special union membership of one dollar. In the spring she was surprised to receive an invitation to the wedding of Miss Dreier to Raymond Robins. It was Rose's first party "in a house where everything was beautiful." She admitted frankly: "I had never known such places existed."

Raymond Robins was also social-minded. He had amassed a modest fortune during the Klondike Gold Rush, and when he returned, it was with the intention of using it for worthwhile purposes. After their marriage he brought his wife to the "Bloody Seventeenth Ward" of Chicago, where he did his political and social work.[37] At the end of World War I he was appointed by President Wilson to the Red Cross Mission in Russia, later becoming chief of the mission. When he returned he made an effort to persuade President Wilson to recognize Russia, but the President refused to see him.[38] During the Republican Twenties he became an adviser to President Coolidge.[39]

As a woman of means, Mrs. Raymond Robins, as she was generally called, had entree into social circles where she could play an active role in proselytizing the causes she espoused. Money enabled her to take trips at her own expense and to underwrite some of the League's special projects. In Chicago, as a newly married woman, she worked at Hull House at first, and met many of the socially active women of her time, among them Julia C. Lathrop, who became the first head of the Children's Bureau, and Grace Abbott, who succeeded Miss Lathrop. Others were Florence Kelley, whom Governor Altgeld had appointed chief factory inspector for the state of Illinois,

Dr. Alice Hamilton, who was an expert on industrial diseases, and Mary McDowell, social worker, who was known as "The Angel of the Stockyards."

When Mrs. Robins assumed the presidency of the National Women's Trade Union League in 1907, it was with the endorsement of the A.F. of L., but the WTUL could never depend on the A.F. of L.'s financial backing. What financial help they received from the unions was always exiguous. According to Rose Schneiderman, "It wasn't given graciously."

For instance, in 1912 the A.F. of L. granted the Women's Trade Union League $150 a month for a year; the United Mine Workers, the United Brotherhood of Carpenters, the International Boot and Shoe Workers promised $50 a month for a year, and smaller sums were pledged by other internationals.[40] It was a time when all unions were willing to accept the League's help in organizing workers (but brooked no interference in their affairs). Regular payments from the A.F. of L. stopped in 1915, though they undertook to pay for a woman organizer who would be selected jointly by Samuel Gompers and Mrs. Robins.[41] During the 1930s all League branches suffered acutely from a "starvation diet." By then, Mrs. Robins, who had been an excellent fund raiser (as was her sister Mary Dreier), had retired from active participation in League affairs.

It was Mrs. Robins who set the pace during her term of office for all other officers of the various regional offices to follow. She gave all her energies to the job, which required that she speak on labor issues, march in parades, attend labor conventions, and travel to raise money. She also supported women's suffrage, as did all the leaders of the League. Mrs. Robins remained at the helm until she retired in 1922 to live in Brooksville, Florida. When she died in 1945, the League was still alive, but steadily losing ground.

The League's accomplishments went beyond the stated purposes, "to organize women locally into trade unions and to assist already organized workers to secure better conditions." Far from being an impersonal organization, it became the staunchest ally working women ever had. With the help of women from some of the most prestigious families, among whom were Anne Morgan, sister of the financier and daughter of the man who had founded the banking house which became J. P. Morgan & Company in 1895, Mrs. Thomas Lamont, Mrs. Gifford Pinchot, Mrs. Willard Straight, Miss Irene Lewisohn, Mrs. Franklin D. Roosevelt, and many others, the League was able not only to carry out its stated program, but to enlarge on it. During the decade of 1910–1920 requests were constantly received to start new unions and to guide already existing ones.[42] During strikes they furnished speakers, arranged for favorable publicity and for picket lines, helped to provision strikers' families, arranged for bail for strikers who were put under arrest and for legal help to represent them, dumfounding the police, the judges, and employers by showing partisanship to people who were obviously not of their class.

In spite of Mrs. Robins's identification with working people, she was not even faintly radical. She was, however, a genuine progressive. Mr. Robins was Republican by inclination and during the twenties he was a trusted adviser of several of the decade's Republican Presidents. To a question by a friend whether she and Mr. Robins were Socialists, Mrs. Robins replied:

You think Raymond and I must be Socialists. But we are not, and for this reason. Economic socialism appeals neither to our minds nor to our sense of integrity. . . . We believe that there are two kinds of wealth. One kind is individual, produced by human brain and hand under the domination of a human will, and that wealth belongs to him who will produce it. The other kind is produced by the community and is social or common, as distinguished from individual wealth. This latter belongs to the people in a common heritage regardless of individual merit and should be taken for the whole people in the form of taxes and used for their benefit in the state and national undertakings for the common good. We believe that private industry should be carried on by private individuals, firms or corporations, under free competition for private profit.[43]

After 1909, when the Supreme Court upheld an Oregon law limiting maximum working hours of women in *Muller vs. Oregon,* the League embarked upon a program of legislative action to meliorate working conditions for women. Today women reject special consideration, but seventy years ago attempts to provide rest rooms, to limit working hours of women, and to establish minimum wages for women when a wage differential between men and women doing the same work was taken for granted, were objectives worthy of any reform program.

Some of the local Leagues provided special instruction, such as English classes for women at a time when such programs were not available. In 1911 Mrs. Robins personally undertook to find backing for a monthly magazine which was to be called *Life and Labor*. It replaced the Women's Department which the League had conducted in the *Union Labor Advocate* of Chicago.[44] Though Mrs. Robins had pledged to maintain the monthly *Life and Labor* for five years, it continued, under different editors until suspended in 1921.[45]

The League also undertook to conduct its own investigations. For instance, in 1913 when the Calumet Copper Mines in Michigan were on strike, and horrendous tales of brutality were being circulated, the League dispatched the very competent Mary Anderson, accompanied by an attorney and a representative of the Consumers' League of Illinois to investigate the situation.

A very significant project was also started in 1913—that of providing training courses to organizers at Northwestern University and the University of Chicago. There working women were taught economics and trade union affairs, the League supplying the scholarships.[46] The League also secured scholarships for individuals. Irene Lewisohn provided one for Rose Schneiderman through an arrangement with the League, which enabled her to give up her job as a sewer of linings in caps and concentrate on getting an education.[47]

From 1918 on, a legislative office was maintained in Washington headed by Miss Ethel Smith, a woman experienced in the federal civil service. It functioned until 1926 when it was given up for lack of funds. When it was decided that a Women's Bureau in the New York State Department of Labor would be of direct benefit to working women, money was raised to pay the salary of a director for a year. By then the need for such a service had so thoroughly proved itself that the Commissioner included her salary in his budget.[48] Also it was evident that the interest of women claimants for workmen's compensation were being neglected, and money was raised to pay the salary of a compensation adviser. She was Mrs. Maud Swartz, and during her tenure she handled close to 4,000 cases.[49] Later Mrs. Swartz was appointed Secretary of Labor of the State of New York, a job which after her death was offered to Rose Schneiderman.

The League's influence extended to the federal level as well. The agitation for a women's division in the Department of Labor in Washington began in 1916. In 1918, when war work inflated the ranks of women workers, the "Woman in Industry" service, later called the "Women's Bureau," was established and placed under Mary van Kleeck who came from the Department of Industrial Studies of the Russell Sage Foundation and was a League member. Mary Anderson, who had been a shoe worker and was then an organizer for the League, was made assistant director and within a year she became head of the Bureau. Many other League members were called into national service. The 1919 convention of the League reported thirty-eight appointments.[50]

League officials did nothing in half measures. The leaders of the WTUL not only trained promising young women, but they also befriended them, possibly because they were aware that the confidence of socially inexperienced people was bound to be augmented through contact with people of social experience and sophistication. This was true of the friendships extended to individual girls by Mrs. Robins, Mary Dreier and Eleanor Roosevelt (a League member after 1921), and by other women as well. Clearly they realized that democracy without social democracy is no democracy, because social barriers were dropped and invitations to various social functions were constantly extended. Rose Schneiderman, Maud Swartz and other League members found a welcome at Hyde Park while Franklin D. Roosevelt was Governor of New York and at the White House when he became President. For instance, in 1936, when the convention of the Women's Trade Union League was held in Washington, members were invited to be guests at the White House, where they had breakfast with Mrs. Roosevelt every morning. The President frequently talked to some of these women about pending legislation and similar matters.[51] How broadening such contacts were to people of limited formal education may be inferred from a remark made by Rose Schneiderman that she loved listening to Mrs. Roosevelt reading aloud during visits to her home. This is how Rose became acquainted with *The Education of Henry Adams.* It provoked the comment that "it should be required reading in our high schools."[52] Mrs. Roosevelt was "Dearest Eleanor" to her, as many letters testify.[53]

The League's important contribution to the strengthening of the labor movement was that it acted as an adjunct to the trade unions and that it furthered the careers of many individuals, so that in many cases the success of certain women may be said to be attributable to the opportunities the League opened to them. On the other hand, other women owed their rise to executive positions in the labor movement primarily to the unions in which they were active. The next two chapters will deal with the careers of specific workers who were responsible for significant changes in the lives of working people.

The attainments of two women exemplify the advancement the League made possible for some of its members. They are Rose Schneiderman and Mary Anderson. As for Rose Schneiderman, her spectacular rise makes clear that without the dynamic influence of the League, the trade union movement and her own role in it would have been an inching forward rather than the series of leaps it was. She admits that her own story and that of the New York Women's Trade Union League cannot be separated.[54] Mary Anderson is no less emphatic that she owed her spectacular career to Mrs. Raymond Robins, the dynamic president of the League and the opportunities provided by that unique organization.

CHAPTER 8

Graduates of the Women's Trade Union League

WHETHER OR NOT ROSE SCHNEIDERMAN (1884–1972) IS NOW to be regarded as a forerunner in the movement for women's liberation, as a New York *Times* editorial marking her death suggested, she was undoubtedly one of the outstanding foreign-born women of the early twentieth century. The editorial in the *Times* reads in part as follows:

A tiny red-haired bundle of social dynamite, Rose Schneiderman did more to upgrade the dignity and living standards of working women than any other American. . . . She pioneered in the mission of emancipation that reached flower two decades later in the campaign for women's suffrage and the current movement for women's liberation. . . . The upward march that Rose Schneiderman did so much to start had now progressed to a point where women felt able to stand on their feet, with walls of protection as unwelcome as walls of prejudice. That progress is her monument.[1]

Though only four and a half feet tall, she was attractive, high-spirited, and determined. She enjoyed dancing and fun. When Governor and Mrs. Franklin D. Roosevelt became her friends, she would arrange parlor theatricals in which she would underscore their foibles. Apparently they liked it, for she commented: ". . . they enjoyed our performance very much, almost as much as we did ourselves."

She did not begin as a worker in a factory. In 1890, at the age of six, she arrived with her family from Poland. Unfortunately, her father, a tailor, died shortly thereafter and all the children had to be sent to an orphanage. She remained there a year; her brothers longer.

133

At the age of thirteen, after staying out of school for long periods, but nevertheless completing nine grades in four years, she was ready to be sent to work. The United Hebrew Charities helped her to find a job as errand girl in Hearn's department store. Her wage was $2.16 a week for a sixty-four hour week. Within a short time she lost her job, because she brought the wrong change to a customer.

At her new job in another store she received $2.75 a week. During those years she educated herself by reading the Jewish newspaper and also English novels in ten-cent paperback editions, for which she saved pennies from her lunch money. By going to lectures and listening intently, she "learned to speak English properly."

What made her turn to factory work was the desire to earn more money, though workers at sewing machines had to buy their own machines and their own thread. Someone taught her how to make linings for men's caps and in a short period she was able to earn $5.00 a week. But her mother was unhappy because she considered it more genteel to be a clerk than a factory worker.

While stitching away she quickly picked up the rudiments of trade unionism. The men workers belonged to the United Cloth Hat and Cap Makers Union, and, she was told, if the lining makers, all women, could join the union, they would be vastly better off. It seemed simple to her—why not request to be taken into the union? She led a committee of four, herself included, to union headquarters and asked to be organized. When a young man "all smiles" told the girls they would need at least twenty-five women from a number of factories in order to acquire a charter, it did not strike her as a hard requirement to fulfill. She and her coworkers stationed themselves at the doors of various factories employing lining makers and solicited the girls to join the union. Within days they had the necessary number of applications, received a charter, and she found herself elected secretary of her local. Even when the local eventually acquired two hundred women members, it was still considered a very small group.

The United Cloth Hat and Cap Makers Union became a very idealistic union, in which women were elected to important posts. Rose Schneiderman became their first woman vice-president. The union was very lucky in having several able men at the helm, one of whom was Max Zaretsky, and another, Alex Rose. In 1936 Alex Rose founded the American Labor Party with David Dubinsky and Sidney Hillman. When it was infiltrated by Communists, Alex Rose, David Dubinsky, George L. Childs, Adolph Berle, and others established the Liberal Party in 1944.

Rose found it was "exciting" to be a union member. To quote her:

A new life opened up for me. All of a sudden I was not lonely any more. I had shop and executive board-meetings to attend as well as the meetings of our unit. I was also a delegate to the Central Labor Union of New York, which was a remarkable experience for me...[2]

It was not long before other of her abilities were discovered. After having made her first speech, she was asked to address meetings, and to act as her union's delegate to annual conventions. At twenty-two she was elected a member of the general executive board, which was akin to vice-presidential office.

She did not have to wait long before she could participate in an important strike that would prove her mettle and demonstrate that she was "a bombshell of a speaker." In 1905 the employers decided to follow the stand taken by President Theodore Roosevelt, who had declared the government printing office an "American shop," neither union nor nonunion, where employees could either accept or reject union membership. The Cloth Hat and Cap Makers Union called a strike, which lasted thirteen weeks during the coldest months of the year. Rose not only picketed and made speeches, but was sent to other unions to solicit their financial support. She was thrilled to receive a donation of $1,000 from the Hatters' Union.[3] It enabled the union to subsidize the married men among the strikers at the rate of $6.00 a week.

Though the strikers made some gains as a result of the strike, it did not represent a clear-cut victory, because the strikers did not gain the union shop. This boon, which was one of the most important objectives of the early labor movement, was not attained until the enactment of the N.R.A. under the Roosevelt administration.

When Rose Schneiderman joined the Women's Trade Union League, Mary E. Dreier, sister of Mrs. Robins, was very active in the New York branch. As Mary Dreier and Rose Schneiderman began to realize that they could depend on one another, their friendship grew. Rose was thrilled when she was invited to take the first vacation of her life in the Dreier farmhouse at Stonington, Connecticut. Though Rose became increasingly drawn to the League, she remained at the same time a devoted member of her own union. In 1908 the League secured for her a scholarship from Irene Lewisohn that sent her back to school to secure an education. What time she had left she spent as organizer for the League. Her stipend was $41.00 a month, which was what she earned when she worked full-time.

In between organizing white goods workers and dressmakers she dreamed of going to college and becoming a schoolteacher, but an entirely different kind of future awaited her. The event that determined a lifelong career with the Women's Trade Union League was the epoch-marking strike of shirtwaist makers in 1909. The favorable outcome of this strike had immense consequences in opening up unexpected positions of leadership for those who had participated in bringing this strike to a successful conclusion, as well as for many other young women. More of them later.

The significance of the Women's Trade Union League itself to the growing labor movement was demonstrated by the League's participation in three great strikes in the garment industry at the end of the first decade of the twentieth century: the "Uprising of the Twenty Thousand" in 1909, which affected primarily young shirtwaist makers; "The Great Revolt" of 1910, in which sixty thousand cloakmakers participated; and the strike in the men's clothing industry triggered in the Hart, Schaffner & Marx factories in Chicago in 1910.

The strike of the shirtwaist makers broke out in November of 1909 and lasted until February 1910. The League arranged for a picket line of seventy-five women—"The Mink Brigade"—

which included J. P. Morgan's sister and Mary Dreier, and it gathered a volunteer legal staff of prominent attorneys and a publicity committee of young Vassar women. Rose Schneiderman received the assignment to raise money in Massachusetts for the strikers and proved very successful. Addressing students at Radcliffe, Wellesley, and Mount Holyoke colleges, she brought $10,000 into the strike fund. The New York *American* donated one of its editions to the cause, which the strikers sold on street corners, bringing $5,000 to the union coffers. Of the $100,000 the strike is supposed to have cost, the League raised almost $20,000.[4]

The brutality that was loosed on the striking girls shocked the public. They were clubbed, manhandled, and hundreds were arrested daily. What the strikers won after ten weeks of heroic suffering was a fifty-two hour week, an increase in wages, and the agreement that all strikers would be taken back. It was admitted that the victory resulted from the "significant alliance between socially minded women of the middle and upper classes and the American working women; in fact between the liberal community as a whole and organized labor."[5]

It was in this strike that a wealthy young woman, Carola Emma Woerishoffer, played an important part by providing bail for arrested strikers. Another who furnished bail was Mrs. Henry Morgenthau, Senior. But the greatest surprise was provided by Carola Woerishoffer. Hers is such an unusual story and so tragic in its outcome that it deserves telling. She was a Bryn Mawr graduate, whose mother had fostered advanced ideas in her daughter. Her father was the millionaire railroad builder and banker, Charles Woerishoffer, who died when she was eight months old, leaving her a million dollars. Her grandmother was Anna Ottendorfer, whose first husband, Hermann Uhl, had founded the *Staatszeitung* and who was greatly respected for her philanthropies.

Carola was so deeply interested in the lives of working women that she had worked in a New York laundry for four months during the heat of the summer when temperatures were close to 100, and also as a domestic in a summer boardinghouse in order to acquire information at first hand about laundresses, waitresses, and domestics. She became a member of the League by walking into the New York office one day, depositing her membership fee of one dollar and leaving a $500 check without comment.

When the strike broke out, she put up a house worth $75,000 given to her by her mother as bail for arrested strikers, then spent her days in Jefferson Market Court acting as bondsman. After the end of the shirtwaist strike, she gave the secretary of the New York League a check for $10,000 with which to establish a permanent strike fund.

The job to which she settled down was that of special investigator under the auspices of the Labor Department of the State of New York. When she was returning from Albany on a wet day, her car skidded and went over an embankment. She died the next day at the age of twenty-six. In her will she left $750,000 to Bryn Mawr.[6]

Though the League played a lesser role in the cloak makers' strike of 1910 than in the shirtwaist strike which had preceded it, the distribution of over 200,000 quarts of milk was the League's contribution. The strike lasted from July 7 to September 2 and was settled when Louis Marshall, a well-known lawyer, and Louis D. Brandeis, the future Justice of the Supreme Court, browbeat the manu.acturers into accepting "The Protocal of Peace," which provided for recognition of the union and arbitration of grievances.

The League played a most significant part in the Chicago strike of the United Garment Workers which began in the Hart, Schaffner & Marx factories. It was triggered by a wage cut of one fourth of a cent and was started by girl workers, of whom the future Mrs. Sidney Hillman was the leader. Eventually it affected 40,000 workers, one quarter of whom were women.[7] The League was called in to help and again responded by launching a publicity campaign, by furnishing the services of the very able Mary Anderson, and by raising funds. Mrs. Robins became chairman of the strike committee. Of the total strike fund of $100,000 more than $70,000 was collected by the Women's Trade Union League.[8]

The strike was called off when Hart, Schaffner & Marx agreed to an arbitration committee, of whom Clarence Darrow, the famous labor lawyer, was a member, but this was not accepted by all the employers who were being struck. A belated result of the strike was that in 1914 a group seceded from the United Garment Workers, the parent union, to form the Amalgamated Clothing Workers Union. Since 1910 some members of the United Garment Workers had nursed the feeling that the union had betrayed their cause. It caused some ill feeling between the League and the officials of the United Garment Workers because the latter felt the League had differed with them over strike policies.

On March 25, 1911, a tragic event took place that highlighted the conditions to which workers in the sweatshops were subjected. It involved the Triangle Waist Company owned by Harris & Blanck on Greene Street. This firm was one of thirteen which had held out against the strike settlement of February, 1910, although three hundred fifty manufacturers had agreed to the strikers' terms. It was there that 146 young girls, mostly Jewish and Italian, died as they jumped from the tenth story to escape from a devastating fire. There was no sprinkling system; the doors were kept locked (to keep organizers out and to prevent girls from escaping with a spool of thread or a bit of lace). One narrow doorway was left open and there was only one fire escape. It is estimated that it would have taken three hours to evacuate the floor using these two exits. The Triangle Waist Company was a burning hell within twenty minutes and girls started to jump out of the windows.

In the aftermath of this dreadful occurrence which sent a shudder through the nation, the League and Rose Schneiderman played conspicuous roles. Local 25 of the ILGWU and the League jointly received permission to hold a mass funeral for those who could not be identified. More than 120,000 people marched on a cold, wet April day in a funeral procession that lasted six hours. The League also cooperated with the Red Cross in establishing a relief committee to deal with the families of the dead girls. What added to the horror was that early in March the Joint Board of Sanitary Control of the ILGWU, which had been set up as part of the Protocol of Peace won by the cloak makers at the end of their strike, had sent a complaint to the Mayor of New York City regarding the dangers in the factories.[9] The fire broke out the same month.

During a mass meeting at the Metropolitan Opera House sponsored by Miss Morgan, Rose Schneiderman delivered a speech which held the vast audience spellbound and turned her into a celebrity in labor circles.

. . . I would be a traitor to these poor, burned bodies, if I came here to talk good fellowship. We have tried you good people of the public and we have found you wanting. . . . This is not the first time girls have been burned alive in the city. . . . The life of men and women is so cheap and property is so sacred. There are so many of us for one job it matters little if one hundred forty three[10] [sic] of us have been burned to death.

We have tried you, citizens; we are trying you now, and you have a couple of dollars for the sorrowing mothers and daughters and sisters by way of a charity gift. But every time the workers come out in the only way they know how to protest against conditions which are unbearable, the strong hand of the law is allowed to press down heavily upon us . . .[11]

In a letter to Rose, dated June 14, 1938, Mrs. Robins reminded her of what a policeman had said about her when asked if he knew her. "Oh yes," he said, "one of them furriners, but she herself can make you weep. She is the finest speaker I ever heard."[12]

The disastrous Triangle fire had important consequences. The Governor of the State of New York, John A. Dix, appointed a Factory Investigating Commission to which Mary Dreier was the only woman appointed among several prominent men, among whom were Samuel Gompers, Alfred Emmanuel Smith, Robert F. Wagner, and Dr. George Price. The League organized a legislative campaign which produced a significant victory. Frances Perkins, one of the investigators, piloted a bill through the legislature which recommended a new Industrial Code. It became the code for the lives, health, and welfare of millions of workers in New York State and a model for other states to follow. Frances Perkins so impressed Governor Franklin D. Roosevelt that when he was elected to the Presidency she was appointed Secretary of Labor and the first woman cabinet member in the history of the American nation.

Though Rose Schneiderman accepted other temporary assignments on and off, she always returned to the League when she was finished. In 1912 she took time out to help promote woman suffrage. She also undertook a stint as organizer of the ILGWU, because it would take her out of town and she wanted to see a little of the country. She admits she also wanted "a little freedom from my family." In 1917 she returned again to the Woman's Suffrage Party as chairman of the industrial section.

In 1917 the greatest honors were still ahead of her. Her election as president of the New York League during that year gave her the opportunity to meet Eleanor and Franklin D. Roosevelt, to become a friend of the family, and eventually to be appointed by him to the Labor Advisory Board when he became the President of the United States. She was one of the delegates representing trade union women at the Peace Conference, which gave her the opportunity to travel in Europe. In 1921 the long-hoped-for plan for the Bryn Mawr Summer School for Working Women materialized. Also in 1920 she found herself nominated as a candidate for the U.S. Senate under the banner of the New York Labor Party.

The plan to enlist the help of the colleges in training women workers during the summer months had been put forward in 1913 as the result of a resolution during a convention of the Womens' Trade Union League in St. Louis. Mrs. Robins wrote to all the colleges, but didn't receive a single answer. In 1920, however, the project came to life. Miss Schneiderman received an invitation from Miss M. Carey Thomas, president of Bryn Mawr College, to discuss plans for a summer school for working women. The final plan admitted one hundred students, all of whom were to receive scholarships for which Miss Thomas undertook to raise funds. All were to be industrial workers, twenty to thirty-five years of age, with a minimum of a sixth grade education, and were to receive instruction in economics, labor problems, history, literature, and elementary science.

The summer school, which represented a most unusual opportunity for working women, remained in operation until Miss

Thomas's retirement in 1939. It was then that Hilda Smith, Dean of Bryn Mawr, and her sister offered their country home in West Park, New York, for the continuation of the program. Christened the Hudson Shore Labor School, men were admitted for the first time. The arrangement continued until 1952 when Rutgers University took over the program as part of its course on Labor Management.[13]

The other event of 1920 that contributed to a rise in self-confidence was that Rose found herself chosen by the Labor Party of New York as a candidate for the United States Senate with Dudley Field Malone being asked to run for Governor of New York. Though she knew her defeat was certain, she suspected that campaigning might be "a lot of fun." She was not disappointed and she received an unexpectedly large vote—between fifty and seventy-five thousand.[14]

In 1921 working women wishing to extend their education had a choice of attending three schools—the National School at the University of Chicago, sponsored by the League, the summer school at Bryn Mawr, and Brookwood College, the only one of the three that did not owe its existence to the League. Brookwood College was such an interesting experiment in educating people for the labor movement that it deserves further discussion.

William Finck, who had been pastor of the Second Avenue Labor Temple of the Presbyterian Church in New York, his wife, Helen Finck, and Toscan Bennett established Brookwood College on Finck's property at Katonah in Westchester County. A two-year college course for men and women offered instruction in economics, history, public speaking, trade union administration, labor legislation, dramatics, and other subjects. The teaching staff included several respected liberals, men as well as women. Sinclair Lewis was on the lecture staff for one year.[15] The school was endorsed by Rexford Tugwell, Harry Elmer Barnes, Donald Richberg, John R. Commons, and Mary Mc-Dowell, among others.

Within five years they had eighty graduates, all members of unions, and in 1932 the list of students and graduates included about two hundred fifty people. The support came from the

unions, who paid $450 annually for maintenance and tuition
for every member they sent. Workers who did not have the
financial backing of unions paid at least $250 yearly. Rose
Schneiderman was an executive member of the board, but
resigned in 1929 giving as the reason the pressure of her responsibilities to the League. She mentions that in "the thirties
Brookwood was another victim of Communist infiltration," but
communism seems to have come to the surface earlier.[16] In
1928 the school was attacked by the A.F. of L. for teaching
theories to which the A.F. of L. objected.

Rose Schneiderman, who was politically conservative, probably
also disapproved. She admits she had believed in the principles
of socialism when she was young, but when she became politically
mature she prided herself on her loyalty to Democratic candidates, or those of the Liberal party. The leadership of the
A.F. of L. was so aroused over what they termed communist
influence at Brookwood that unions were advised to "disassociate"
themselves from it, and in 1929 a member of the Carpenters'
Union was expelled[17] because he would not sever his connection
with the school.

Many graduates of Brookwood became prominent in labor
and other fields. One of whom Rose Schneiderman speaks glow-
ingly was Clint Golden, who was appointed by President Truman
to help administer the Marshall Plan in Greece and, says Rose,
"was looked to for help by captains of industry and labor alike
when they were in trouble."[18]

Rose had assumed the presidency of the New York Women's
Trade Union League in 1917 and she proved to be a dedicated
and inventive president and an excellent fund raiser. She asserts
that she would not ask for anything for herself, but she had
no hesitancy in appealing for financial help for the League.
Her first effort as president was a luncheon at Delmonico's,
at which Mrs. George D. Pratt was chairman and Ethel Barry-
more chief speaker. It brought $7,000 into the League coffers.
It was only one of many benefits to which a variety of prominent
women gave their support.

In 1921 she decided that the League, which had been occupying cramped quarters at the Rand School, should have a club-

house of its own. Though this struck the board as a bold undertaking, Mrs. Willard Straight, chairman, and Mrs. Thomas Lamont, secretary, undertook to raise funds. Thomas Lamont seems to have approved of his wife's activities on behalf of the League, for in a letter to Miss Schneiderman he was most cordial.[19]

It was at a tea given by Mrs. Straight that Rose met Eleanor Roosevelt for the first time and received Mrs. Roosevelt's promise that she would help. The next time she saw Mrs. Roosevelt again was when she was invited to one of her famous scrambled-egg suppers. From then dates the extraordinary friendship between them. After Maud Swartz succeeded Mrs. Robins as president of the National Women's Trade Union League, she also found herself invited with Rose to Hyde Park and once to Campobello. Rose explains the cordial acceptance by the Roosevelt family very simply: "It was to bring new and stimulating ideas after his [FDR's] illness," but Frances Perkins provides a much more detailed explanation:

... He was soon learning from these girls a great deal about the trade union movement...

Through the eyes of these girls he saw the exploitation of the sweatshop and how the tuberculosis rate had shot up in the printing industry before the union stepped in with regulations of hours and wages.... He heard how the trade unions had been the first to demand that little children under ten should not be employed.

He learned why labor leaders are sometimes rough—often quite rough. He learned that in the days of organizing against severe opposition the police and hired thugs were often set upon trade union organizers. It took a "roughneck" to stand up to that kind of thing...[20]

Within a short time the committee to provide the League with its own home had raised, to Rose's amazement, $20,000 and arranged for a mortgage of $35,000 on a five-story brownstone at 247 Lexington Avenue. The house was large enough to make possible a cafeteria in the basement and to rent out a floor and a half. The parlor floor was being used for evening classes and meetings as well as parties, and the second floor for clubrooms. The education program was enlarged. Girls flocked to the League building.

Social events, dances, and gatherings took place in the club-rooms. There, once a week, Eleanor Roosevelt could be found reading aloud to the girls and afterward offering them cocoa and cookies she had brought from her own home. It was a custom she kept up until Franklin D. Roosevelt was elected Governor. In 1925 she gave a Christmas party at League head-quarters for poor children at which the youngest Roosevelt children, Franklin and John, were hosts. Franklin D. Roosevelt was present at the first party and read Dickens's *A Christmas Carol* to the children. Ice cream and cake were served and each child went home with a present and a cornucopia filled with candy. The Christmas celebration became an annual event which was kept up throughout the Depression years until the beginning of World War II.[21]

In 1929, the twenty-fifth anniversary of the League's founding, the Roosevelt family was responsible for a memorable climax in the life of Rose Schneiderman. Mrs. James Roosevelt, of whom she remarks, "I am sure that she did not really approve of FDR's friends, but she always made the best of it and always entered into the gaiety,"[22] invited the whole membership to a celebration at Hyde Park. Two hundred people came. FDR made a speech, and Mrs. Lamont and Eleanor Roosevelt presented the League with a check of $35,000 to pay off the mortgage on the League building. On the eve of the Great Depression the building was cleared of debt.

Soon League members would be in desperate need of financial help. When the Depression hit, single girls were in the worst situation, for relief plans were aimed principally at helping families. The League responded to this emergency by providing one hot meal in the middle of the day with the help of some of the unions. After President Roosevelt's election, organizations supplying meals received surplus food which was allotted to the unemployed. But much more than that was needed.

Again Mrs. Lamont and Mrs. Roosevelt came to the rescue. Mrs. Lamont gave $3,000 to set up a loan fund and Mrs. Roosevelt donated her fees from a series of radio broadcasts, giving the League $300 for each of twelve weeks and the rest of her fees to needy individuals.

The new President remembered his mentor in trade union

affairs, and Rose Schneiderman was the only woman appointed to serve on the Labor Advisory Board, composed of the most prominent figures in the world of labor. As she had done on previous occasions, she took a leave of absence from the League, Mary Dreier taking on her responsibilities at the League, and moved to Washington. In 1934 she was asked by General Hugh Johnson to go to Puerto Rico for the Labor Advisory Board to look into the situation of women employed in the needle trades. It was a disheartening experience, not only because of a contract system under which women and young girls received abysmally low wages, but because she realized that the contract system could not be dislodged. Eventual progress was achieved by Puerto Rican needle workers through their membership in the ILGWU.

The invalidation of the NRA sent her back to the League to fight her last big battles in organizing the laundry and hotel workers, both of whom had been terribly exploited. She succeeded in consolidating all laundry workers under the aegis of the Amalgamated Clothing Workers, who had been representing a small section of laundry workers and would be able to bring many benefits to the whole group. The hotel workers gained immensely when the League helped in organizing the Hotel Trades Council, which secured an excellent welfare program and other advantages for the workers.

In 1923 Rose Schneiderman had been instrumental in having Maud Swartz appointed to help women secure compensation from the State of New York. Mrs. Swartz continued with that work until she became Secretary of the State Department of Labor. When she died in 1937, her job was offered to Rose Schneiderman. In taking it, Rose remained a volunteer president of the New York League without salary, but continued to exert herself to raise money with which to meet the League budget. In 1943 she resigned voluntarily when Thomas E. Dewey became Governor.

She returned to the League in time to aid in its dissolution. The national office of the Women's Trade Union League, which had moved to Washington in 1930, was on a "starvation diet," and in 1947, twenty-five years after Mrs. Robins had resigned and two years after her death, it was decided to give up. The unions were doing so well they no longer required help in increasing their membership.

Though the New York branch of the League went on until November 1955, the last of the local leagues to close its doors, it became increasingly harder to raise the needed money for its continuation. As Rose explains, donors were apt to ask: "What are the unions doing for the League? They have millions of dollars now." But organized labor's help was grudging and insufficient. Also, some of the services supplied by the League, such as instruction in various subjects, had become superfluous when adult education classes were available all over the city.

In 1947 Rose Schneiderman decided to retire. From the most prominent individuals of the nation came messages of appreciation and praise for the role she had played. At a farewell luncheon at Sherry's she received a check for $8,500 which, she was told, came from her co-workers in the labor movement as well as from people who had no affiliation with labor.

Rose Schneiderman spent the last five years of her life at the Jewish Home and Hospital for the Aged in New York. She died there on August 11, 1972, at the age of ninety. In June, 1972, the author visited her in the presence of a social worker who had warned that she was not always lucid. In a wheelchair sat a small white-haired woman looking at television. It was clear that she must have been pretty. The only thing she said with some spirit was: "I wrote a book too, you know." After that she could not be roused. Nothing seemed to matter to her. It was hard to imagine that this inert little figure had been able to accomplish so much. In her mirror was the picture of the beautiful, young Mary Dreier with her aristocratic chiseled face and on the windowsill reposed a small bust of Franklin D. Roosevelt, his face thin and careworn, and another of an exuberant President Kennedy. It was obvious the fire had gone out completely from the small huddled figure. Within two months she was dead.

A spectacularly successful trade union woman who was steered by Mrs. Robins and the League into a job with the federal government was Mary Anderson (1873–1964). She had been a member of the International Boot and Shoe Workers Union for fifteen years, when Mrs. Robins, as president of the National Women's Trade Union League, tapped her at the conclusion of the Hart, Schaffner & Marx strike in 1910 to be the League's representative in implementing the terms of agreement between the United Garment Workers Union and the employers. In accepting the post Miss Anderson quit factory work and never went back to it. In 1917, when women were urged to come into the defense industries, Mrs. Robins pushed her almost against her own inclinations to act in an advisory capacity to Samuel Gompers in matters affecting women's interests. In Miss Anderson's own words: "Here again it was Mrs. Robins and the League that were the deciding factors in starting me in a new line of work."[23] Thus, while her union membership was the initial entrance ticket into the WTUL, the League rather than her union was responsible for her phenomenal accomplishments in the world of labor.

Her transformation from a domestic into a stitcher on shoes, and on to the directorship of the Woman's Bureau in Washington, makes her a Cinderella among working women. Her outstanding traits were uncommon good sense, practicality, and patience. In her dealings with people—workers, union and government officials—she was a John Dewey kind of pragmatist. Her motto, "If it works it's good; if not, do the best you can," sounds as if it might have been said by the great pragmatist himself. In her own words:

I always did whatever job I had to do as well as I could under the circumstances and I never found that it was any help to anyone to get upset if things did not come off exactly as I wanted them to. I think my work in trade union organization taught me not to expect too much and be satisfied with part of a cake when I could not get a whole one.[24]

With her abundance of "good sense" she could even educate a professor. This particular professor was one Hart, Schaffner & Marx had brought in to be their labor representative. An impatient man, he antagonized the workers until Miss Anderson got him "educated" to realize that

. . . to deal with labor you have to be patient while everyone learns to work together. I think patience is one of the greatest disciplines in working with human beings.[25]

She was born on a farm in Sweden and received a meager education in a Lutheran parsonage. When her parents lost their farm, she and a younger sister decided to follow the example of an older sister, who had been the first to emigrate to America. The year was 1889, the heyday of Swedish immigration, and she was sixteen. She had hoped to find something other than housework, which she disliked. But when she realized that no other work was available to inexperienced girls, she became a domestic like her sisters.

After several years and several moves she landed in Chicago, and there found work as a stitcher in a shoe factory. She liked factory work immediately, because she could make "contacts" with other people. After meeting Jane Addams, then president of the League, and coming away with the feeling that any organization in which Miss Addams was active would be of great help to working women, she became a member of the League. Also she joined the International Boot & Shoe Workers' Union, became a shop collector, and in a year was elected president of her local, a job she retained until she retired from factory work. She was also the elected delegate to the joint council of the union which determined all important decisions, and a delegate to the Chicago Federation of Labor. Her trade union activities were her only source of education because, as she explains, and many others have similarly claimed, union meetings at night left no time for going to school.

The 1910 strike of men's clothing workers in Chicago spread so rapidly and involved so many workers (more than 40,000) that the Chicago WTUL and the Chicago Federation of Labor were asked to help. By her response in gathering funds, supplying commissary relief, and furnishing organizers, Mrs. Robins so impressed Hart, Schaffner & Marx that when they finally decided to grant union recognition to the strikers, Mrs. Robins and John Fitzgerald of the Chicago Federation of Labor were asked to be cosigners of the agreement, so that they might continue to exert a good influence on the workers. Miss Anderson, who had worked very hard during the strike, was asked to act as the League representative. In this demanding job she had the help of Bessie Abramowitz, later Mrs. Sidney Hillman of the United Garment Workers.

These two women were no prima donnas, a species for whom Miss Anderson has scathing words. It was important for the agreement to succeed because it was binding for only two years, and the fear was that if the employees proved too fractious, it would not be renewed. But a new agreement was signed in 1913 and between 1913–1917 Miss Anderson acted as general organizer for the League. Her duty was to conduct strikes, to help in investigating working conditions, as she did during several miners' strikes in Michigan, to arrange for bail, and to help strikers in every way possible. Like the "Mink Brigade" in New York, Chicago had its own nucleus of prominent women to call upon when help was needed. Among them was Mrs. Mary Wilmarth, the mother of the first Mrs. Ickes, as well as Mrs. Ickes herself, Mrs. Frank Lillie, wife of a professor at Chicago University, and others. Miss Anderson herself was arrested together with Ellen Starr Gates, one of the founders of Hull House, and it was Harold Ickes who sent Donald Richberg to defend Miss Anderson in court. During those years she organized garment workers, girls in a broom factory, waitresses in a chain of restaurants, and employees in a state institution for the insane.

This period was a preparation for the big opportunity looming on the horizon. She was engaged in helping with a strike involving 1,000 women workers on small machine parts when Mrs. Robins called her hurriedly and told her to take a train for Washington. She protested; how could she leave the striking girls at this point? But Mrs. Robins was adamant and volunteered to take her place until she returned.

Thus began her "trail to Washington," where she was to spend the next twenty-five years, serving five Presidents, three Republicans and two Democrats. During the meeting of the Gompers committee she became acquainted with Mary van Kleeck from the Russell Sage Foundation, who was studying the feasibility of employing women in ordnance storage plants. She struck Mary Anderson as a "very crisp, intelligent-looking person." Soon Miss van Kleeck had organized a woman's division in the Ordnance Department and became its head. Realizing she ought to have a "labor woman" in this new women's division, she asked Mary Anderson to join her. Thus in January, 1918, began a new phase of her career.

What was to be the function of the new bureau? Certain standards for the employment of women had been formulated and accepted by the chief of ordnance. It was the responsibility of the women's division to see that these standards were put into effect, to inspect conditions in ordnance plants, and to adjust problems arising from improper working conditions.

It was not long before Miss Anderson sensed that many of the men "who were running the show" resented them as women and were distrustful of them. She was ready to go back to Chicago when she received a luncheon invitation to the bachelor apartment of Felix Frankfurter. He was then working with the Secretary of Labor in creating new divisions in the Department of Labor that were being recommended by the Committee on National Defense. She knew a "Woman in Industry" division was about to be set up as soon as Congress appropriated the funds, and she surmised he wanted to look her over for this new job. She must have passed muster for she was soon notified that she and Mary van Kleeck were to settle it among themselves who was to be the director and who the assistant. She chose to become the assistant.

The job was a demanding one that called for a full working day inspecting factories, and spending nights in Pullman berths. She attended meetings of the War Labor Policies Board whenever Miss van Kleeck was absent. Her experiences confirmed what she had always known: "If the jobs were desirable there was usually a good deal of opposition to women's employment ... but if the jobs were low grade and no one else wanted them, there was much enthusiasm about women taking them over."[26]

One very important contribution that proved to be a permanent one, made by the "Woman in Industry Service," was the setting up of standards for the employment of women. It remained in force over the subsequent decades, except that working hours were shortened, and stipulated the eight-hour day, equal pay for men and women, a minimum wage rate, and other specifications. Though the code was accepted in December of 1918, the equal pay provision continued to be evaded. As she says, "The men always felt they were inferior if they did not get higher wages than women. . . ." Even when she tried to bring pressure on Felix Frankfurter, he told her that if men and women were paid the same "there would be a revolution."[27]

When Mary van Kleeck resigned in 1919, Miss Anderson became the new director of the Woman in Industry Service at a salary of $5,000 a year. In 1920 it was renamed the Women's Bureau.

Not until the National Recovery Administration (NRA) was launched in June, 1933, could the battle for equal pay for women be launched in earnest. But the "best" she could get with "persistent nagging" was to reduce the differential between men's and women's wages, to obtain the same minimum in about seventy-five percent of the codes, and to get the differential decreased in the rest.[28] It was again a matter of accepting a part of a cake when she could not get a whole one.

The lack of equal pay was not the only instance of discrimination against women workers. Though she succeeded in eliminating the exclusion of women from sixty percent of the Civil Service examinations, there was still another hurdle—the power of the appointing officer to decide whether a man or a woman should be chosen. Another was that veterans were given preference even when their ratings were lower. Other discriminatory practices included prejudice against married women, especially during the Depression when Congress legislated that two persons in one family could not be employed in government service. In order for both to be able to retain their jobs, many families chose to break up, if only temporarily.

She was reappointed by President Harding and remained in her job under President Coolidge. Under President Hoover, whom she knew personally, and with whose wife she was friendly, she submitted her resignation, but she was asked to remain.

Like so many of the women active in the League, Miss

Anderson had an affectionate relationship with Mrs. Roosevelt, who called her "Mary." She often stood at Mrs. Roosevelt's side at receptions for women in government, and she represented the Department of Labor when Miss Perkins was unavailable. She was sometimes asked to address women reporters at Mrs. Roosevelt's press conferences. The "most interesting party" to which she was invited at the White House was when the King and Queen of England were guests of the President and Mrs. Roosevelt. When introduced to both of them, she says, she shook hands in "American fashion" and was glad she didn't have to curtsy. Then, when the Queen was alone, Mrs. Roosevelt beckoned her to talk to the visitor and Miss Anderson described her work and thought the Queen seemed interested, which suggested to her that she would be "a staunch friend of women."

In 1941 she received the honorary degree of Doctor of Law from Smith College. Mrs. Dwight Morrow, a trustee, presented her for the degree.

In 1944 she retired and was succeeded by Frieda Miller, Labor Commissioner for New York State and a friend of Frances Perkins. She also received a scroll of honor from the General Federation of Women's Clubs at the golden jubilee. On her ninetieth birthday Labor Secretary Arthur J. Goldberg presented her with the Department's Award of Merit.[29] It would be hard to disclaim the statement that among foreign-born working women she came closest to the top.

While most of the women in the trade union movement were driven to battle by the desperate need to improve their economic situation, there were those who were drawn to the labor field by dormant feelings of kinship with workers. One of those who was brought to the cause of aiding women workers by the direct influence of the WTUL was Maud O'Farrell Swartz (1879–1937).[30]

She was of Irish birth, came of a good family, was well-educated, though her father, dogged by ill fortune, found it hard to support fourteen children. William R. Grace of New York, founder of the Grace Steamship Company and later mayor of New York, was her mother's brother, and he provided regular assistance.

Maud O'Farrell was educated in convents in Germany and in Paris with the goal of becoming a governess. When she accepted her first post in Italy, she acquired still another language. In the work she eventually adopted, knowledge of foreign languages proved very useful.

The job of governess did not appeal to her and she decided to try her luck in America. In 1901 she was a young girl of twenty-one when she again took a post as governess, but she liked it no better than in Europe. According to Rose Schneiderman she was very attractive, which made some of her employers too attentive. After an interval she found employment as a proofreader in a foreign language printing firm. There she met Lee Swartz, a printer, and married him, but the marriage didn't work out well and she left him.

In 1912 she was introducing the idea of woman suffrage to Italian women when she met Rose Schneiderman, who was then also doing her stint for suffrage. Mrs. Swartz joined the WTUL and a close friendship developed between the two women. She became full-time secretary of the New York League, a job she held until 1921. It was there Eleanor Roosevelt discovered her and she and Rose became frequent guests at the Roosevelt home in Hyde Park. It was there that they tutored Franklin D. Roosevelt in trade union affairs. Miss Perkins asserts that "while well disposed ... he never understood with real detail the purpose of this movement."[31]

It was in the job as "compensation adviser," which was created for her by the League to help women seeking compensation from the State of New York for industrial accidents, that she found her calling. Rose Schneiderman asserts that she did "superbly" in this job, handling thousands of compensation cases annually. For instance, upon investigating the death of a man who had apparently died from tuberculosis, which was not considered an industrial disease subject to compensation, she found that the cause of death was lead poisoning. She won the case and gained compensation for a woman who could not speak a word of English and had several small children to support.

In 1922 she succeeded Mrs. Robins as president of the National Women's Trade Union League, but retained her job

Phillis Wheatley
(1753-1784)

Mother Jones
(1830-1930)

Needle Trades Workers' Demonstration

General Evangeline Booth
(1865-1950)

Eleanor Roosevelt and Rose Schneiderman (1884-1972)

Bessie Abramowitz Hillman (1889-1970)
and Sidney Hillman

Drs. Gerty Teresa Cori (1896-1957)
and Carl Cori

Dr. Elizabeth Blackwell
(1821-1910)

Rose Pastor Stokes
(1889-1933)

Mary Anderson
(1872-1964)

Anzia Yezierska
(1885-1973)

Dr. Valentina Suntzeff
(1891-   )

Clara Mannes (1869-1948)
and David Mannes

Suzanne Bloch
(1907-   )

Nadia Reisenberg
(1904-   )

Rosina Lhevinne
(1880-   )

Jennie Grossinger
(1892-1972)

Pauline Trigère

as compensation adviser. Her main value to the League was in appearing at Congressional hearings and at legislative conferences.

While acting as secretary of the New York State Department of Labor she died of coronary thrombosis in 1937. Her job was then offered to and accepted by Rose Schneiderman.

CHAPTER 9

From the Ranks of the Union

WHILE THE PROMINENCE OF SOME WOMEN IN LABOR CIRCLES MAY be attributed to the training and encouragement they received from the various branches of the Women's Trade Union League, other competent women found the opportunities for their development under the aegis of their own unions. It is not surprising that the International Ladies Garment Workers Union (ILGWU), with its large membership of women workers on all manner of women's and children's wear and accessories, should have been the training ground for innumerable women organizers and administrators.

A woman who qualifies for the seat of honor among women of foreign birth is Pauline Newman. Though she served the Women's Trade Union League as organizer, vice-president, and member of the National League's Executive Board, she is primarily a trade unionist whose first loyalty has always been to her own union, the ILGWU. Her connection with the ILGWU gave her the training for the job she has occupied for fifty years, that of Educational Director of the Union Health Center. A crisp, no-nonsense woman, she is a rarity among working women—an intellectual by inclination who has educated herself through self-study and an unabated interest in reading. She summed up her educational background in *Life and Labor* (the magazine published by the League), to which she was a regular contributor: "College at the Triangle Waist Company at thirteen; M.A. from the ILGWU; graduate work at the university of a cotton mill in Connecticut [on the suggestion of the Bridgeport *Herald* that she investigate working conditions at the plant of Atwood Brothers]; the Ph.D. from the Women's Trade Union League in New York."[1]

156

Even as a totally inexperienced immigrant she was able to present her impressions of the East Side of New York so vividly that the Jewish *Forward* published them. Later she became a succinct writer who contributed informative articles chiefly on labor to many magazines, most of them no longer extant—*The American Hebrew, Labor Age, The Progressive Woman, Life and Labor,* and others. In *Justice,* the official organ of the ILGWU, she filled a column which she devoted to health education.

She qualifies for a seat in the pantheon of outstanding foreign-born women on the basis of two achievements—as a trade union organizer and as Educational Director of the ILGWU Health Center. Starting as a trade unionist she was responsible for organizing a large number of new unions, ranging between workers at sewing machines to women machinists who worked on ball-bearing tools. In 1913 she was one of the founders of the Health Center and in 1924 she went to work on it full time and helped to develop it into the huge institution it has become, where union members are given complete diagnostic care and treatment without cost. The center has long been considered a "living monument" to Pauline Newman and to Dr. George M. Price, its first director.[2]

Her birthplace was Lithuania and she arrived with her mother and two older sisters in 1901 when she was in her very early teens. It was her father who had taught her to read and write. From then on she was on her own, always reading, first the Russian classics, and in America, poetry, the English classics, biographies, and whatever she could lay her hands on. She also attended classes under the auspices of the Socialist Literary Society, which helped to strengthen dormant inclinations toward socialist principles.

She had to get a job immediately. Even when she worked for the Triangle Waist Company, which was her second job, she was too young to qualify for working papers. Her job was to trim threads from finished blouses, which was tedious rather than strenuous work. For this she received a wage of $1.50 a week. She never worked at a machine.[3] To avoid being fined for employing girls under age, the employers would hide their young workers in large wooden hampers where unfinished work was piled up as soon as an inspector was known to have entered a building.

In the summer of 1907 she had a chance to prove her mettle. When the rent in the tenement building in which she lived was raised without giving tenants corresponding benefits, she organized a rent strike. The excitement created by the teen-aged girl came to the attention of the *Evening Journal* and to her surprise she was shown an article about herself which had appeared without her knowledge. The strike was won when the landlord dropped the attempt to extort additional rent from tenants occupying several buildings in the block.[4]

During the "Uprising of the Twenty Thousand" in November, 1909, she went out on strike with the rest of the workers, but her main assignment during the strike was to solicit funds in upstate New York among unions, women's clubs, and other sympathizers. She had had some experience as a soapbox speaker in front of factories. Though it was scant preparation for wringing hearts and opening pocketbooks, she did very well.

After the strike was settled, she was appointed by the ILGWU to be their first organizer, and she never returned to a factory job. Instead she was sent off to preach the gospel of unionism to unorganized workers in Philadelphia, to help striking cloak-workers in Cleveland, to promote a strike by corset workers in Kalamazoo, and to fill other assignments.

Unlike baseball players she was never sold, but her services were frequently loaned by the ILGWU to organizations to which she and her union were sympathetic. As an organizer for the Philadelphia Women's Trade Union League she brought candy makers, textile workers and women working on small tools into the protection of their unions. For the Socialist party she did a stint of proselytizing among the miners of Philadelphia, and for the Federation of Jewish Philanthropies she conducted a money-raising campaign among the unions.[5]

Interludes of "fun and games" were not lacking in her life. When nominated in 1918 (the year before passage of the Nineteenth Amendment) for the Office of Secretary of State by the Socialist party, and later for Congress, an article in the *Evening Sun* written in a very condescending tone provided amusement for her, as it was undoubtedly intended to do. The

quaint headline, "A Skirted Secretary of State," can make her
laugh even today. The *Evening Sun* suggested:

Why not place one or two women in office and observe the results?
Then if things become too efficient, or too moral, or too headstrong,
or too capricious those who want to oppose equal suffrage will know
on what ground they are standing.

By losing the elections to various offices, Miss Newman
was saved for the Health Center, to which she returned full
time in 1924 after a year's trip to Europe, where she represented
the National Women's Trade Union League before the International Women's Congress in Vienna.

The Health Center established in 1914 was an outgrowth of
the Joint Board of Sanitary Control charged with investigating
conditions in the factories. Miss Newman was one of the
inspectors and Dr. George M. Price, a pioneer in industrial
medicine, was a member of the board. He had presided over
the Factory Investigating Commission following the Triangle
Fire. He was aware through treating cloak makers that they
were prone to some form of pulmonary tuberculosis. In 1913
the United States Public Health Service in conjunction with
the Health Center conducted a series of free examinations
which disclosed a tuberculosis rate of two percent[6] and thus
underlined the need for regular medical care that would provide
diagnosis and treatment.

In 1920 the need for expanded health services led four of
the larger locals of the ILGWU to purchase a four-story building
on East Seventeenth Street in New York City, which received
a charter from the State Board of Social Welfare. It was expected that the facilities would be sufficient for future needs.

The demand for services soon exceeded the budget and
the job of keeping the Health Center in financial health was
entrusted to Miss Newman. Hers was the additional task of
maintaining the educational campaign for health improvement
and the prevention of disease.

The worst period was between 1928 and 1933 when the
country began to move toward and then to settle into depression.

It was then, she says, she practically lived in the halls of union offices begging for help from the giant unions with large reserves—the Typographers', the Pressmen's and Electrical Workers' unions. In order to survive, the House of Health extended its facilities to members of other unions, who, in paying for services to their members, kept the center alive.[7]

With the decision of the ILGWU in 1934 to assume full responsibility for the complete financing of all health facilities, the Health Center found itself in calm seas. In 1935 it moved to larger quarters in the garment district. In 1945 the ILGWU bought an entire seventeen-story building, two and a half floors of which (23,000 square feet) were given over to the care and treatment of patients. More than 50,000 people are taken care of annually; x-ray examinations, electrocardiograms and other diagnostic tests are given; physical therapy is administered; all prescriptions are filled at no cost to patients. The Center is equipped to take care of all illnesses, except those requiring hospital, surgical, or institutional care. The budget is met through a payroll tax paid by the employers, which also includes paid vacations and severance pay.[8]

Even during the years when Miss Newman was the moving spirit behind the functioning of the Health Center she accepted other assignments, with the approval of the ILGWU. In the 1930s, for instance, she was appointed by Mayor La Guardia to study the taxicab industry.[9] She served on the New York State Minimum Wage Law Commission which set minimum wages for different industries—laundries, cleaning and dyeing establishments, hotels, restaurants, department stores, and other businesses.

At an age when all her former friends are either dead or have retired from active work, Miss Newman still may be found at work every day. Her job now is mainly to emphasize the prevention of disease through lectures and written presentations. Now that the center requires less of her attention, she is thinking of completing the story of her life which she began but did not finish. It is intended to recreate the turbulent years of the early twentieth century, when people were forced to work seventy to eighty hours a week, including Sundays, and lived and worked under conditions of indescribable squalor.

Her intention is to appear as a witness, to testify to what it was like to be a struggling worker in the days when employers could exploit workers at will.

Two young women found in the more masculine precincts of the United Garment Workers, later the Amalgamated Clothing Workers, the opportunity to develop leadership qualities that would turn them into two of the most respected labor personalities of their time. They were Bessie Abramowitz Hillman and Dorothy Jacobs Bellanca.

Bessie Abramowitz (1889–1970) was of Russian birth. In 1905 when she was sixteen and Russia was seething with pogroms and revolutionary unrest that drove hundreds of thousands to flight, she decided to accompany a friend to America. For a young and inexperienced girl this was an act of great courage. Her destination was Chicago, where a relative kept a boardinghouse. She found employment in a clothing factory where she sewed buttons at the rate of two and a half cents per garment. Sixty hours of work was required to earn a weekly wage of $3.00. When she formed a committee to protest these wages she was fired. In addition she found herself blacklisted as well. To get another job in the clothing trade she would have to take an assumed name. Her next place of employment was in the factories of Hart, Schaffner & Marx. Despite Mr. Schaffner's reputation of being a fair-minded employer, the system in the workshops as enforced by shop foremen was as rigorous as anywhere else. Miss Abramowitz thought that perhaps Mr. Schaffner was unaware of how the workers were treated by their immediate supervisors and volunteered to inform him, but was dissuaded.

When the rate of four cents per garment was cut a quarter of a cent in September of 1910, she again reached a degree of anger that was a prelude to strike action. This was standard management procedure when workers attained efficiency and speed with the resultant increase in earnings. She decided to walk off her job and sixteen girls joined her. Soon most of the 8,000 employees of Hart, Schaffner & Marx were idle.[10] More and more workers from other factories followed suit and within a week close to 40,000 were on strike.[11]

The clothing workers were then affiliated with the United Garment Workers Union, whose president was Tom Rickert, an old-fashioned type of unionist who believed in the superiority of craft unions and distinguished between workers on the basis of the work they performed. He had little respect for the newly arrived immigrants whom he suspected of being socialists, and was known to favor the earlier workers (Germans, Bohemians, and others), who made up the membership during its halcyon days. He was high-handed, autocratic, and contemptuous and the newer elements were dissatisfied with his leadership. Almost as soon as he was made aware that he had a strike on his hands that he had not authorized, he was ready to accept the first offer made by management. The workers rejected the first as well as the second settlement he recommended, neither of which granted union recognition which the workers considered the sine qua non of their demands.

After more than four months of bitter controversy and much suffering on the part of the strikers, Hart, Schaffner & Marx offered to recognize the union, to set up a board to deal with grievances, and to reinstate all strikers. However, not all manufacturers were equally reasonable. While negotiations were still in progress with the other employers, officials of the United Garment Workers called the strike off suddenly, forcing the rest of the workers to accept a "hunger bargain" (one into which they were forced by the threat of hunger). Having lost the strike, the workers seethed with resentment. In 1914 this faction was to break away and to form a new union, The Amalgamated Clothing Workers Union with Sidney Hillman as president. He had been a cutter in the factories of Hart, Schaffner & Marx.

Several events of importance to Bessie Abramowitz happened during this strike; she met Sidney Hillman, whom she married six years later, and she established herself as a labor leader, organizer and conciliator whose good sense became invaluable. At the conclusion of the strike, she and Mary Anderson were given the responsibility to see that the workers adhered to the agreement. They were often balky and unreasonable and it was the task of the two organizers to listen to grievances and to pacify grumblers. At the same time she was acting as business agent for the vestmakers' local 152 of Chicago. In 1913 she became a naturalized citizen.

In 1914 a crisis erupted which was of personal significance in the life of the young union leader. At the 1914 convention of the United Garment Workers at Nashville, a faction of dissatisfied union members was excluded. Miss Abramowitz, who had been seated, was sympathetic to those who had been locked out. Sidney Hillman was not present, because he was then in the employ of the ILGWU as chief clerk of the cloak makers' Joint Board, which was part of the grievance machinery under the Protocol of Peace gained for the workers by Louis Marshall and Louis D. Brandeis after the cloak makers' strike of 1910.

The insurgent faction sent for Hillman and asked him to take over the leadership of the breakaways. Hillman hesitated, but when Bessie Abramowitz wired him to accept,[12] he followed her counsel. The new organization became the Amalgamated Clothing Workers Union with headquarters in New York, Hillman its president, and she a member of its General Executive Board.

After her marriage Mrs. Hillman became a volunteer worker who attended meetings, made speeches, picketed, and helped in various organization drives. Between 1932–1937 she helped to organize shirt workers in Connecticut, Pennsylvania, and upstate New York. Between 1937–1942 she acted as the educational director of the Laundry Workers Joint Board, who had become affiliated with the Amalgamated.

During the war years she presided over the War Activities Department of the Amalgamated which promoted blood donations and conducted various bond drives. She was also a member of the Defense Advisory Committee on Women in the Services of the United States Department of Defense, a member of the advisory board in New York for the Office of Price Administration, by appointment of Governor Lehman, and a member of the wartime Child Welfare Committee of New York which provided child-care centers for the children of workers in war plants. She was also associated with the women's division of Russian War Relief.[13]

When Sidney Hillman died in 1946, she was elected vice-president of the Amalgamated. She was then in her fifties and her intense vitality, warmth, progressivism, and interest in people that had made her an outstanding labor leader, were at their peak. As vice-president she continued with the same work she had done as a volunteer, only more of it. The education of trade union members became her most important concern, especially the broad program of labor education carried on by the union since its founding. She was traditionally the chairman of the education committee at conventions and was a regular speaker at seminars and conferences, not only on labor matters, but also on politics, child welfare, world peace, duties of citizenship, women in society and how to become effective citizens. She was particularly successful in her relations with minorities who sensed her warmth and sincerity.[14]

In 1962 she was asked to sum up her views in a chapter for a book which consisted of articles on "Gifted Women" in a variety of professions. Mrs. Hillman's chapter is called "The Gifted Woman in the Trade Unions," where she urged women to assume top labor leadership posts.

Mrs. Hillman worked until she was stricken. After a lifetime of dedication to the goals to which she had committed herself in her youth, she died in December of 1970 at the age of eighty-one.

Dorothy Jacobs Bellanca (1894–1946),[15] the daughter of an immigrant tailor, consolidated her career in the labor movement by marrying a worker-organizer of Sicilian background, who gave her all the help and encouragement he could. As Dorothy Bellanca she became known as an outstanding woman in labor, reform, and political circles.

Born in Latvia, she was brought to Baltimore when she was six. She attended the public school until she was thirteen, then began to work as a buttonhole sewer on men's overcoats. After working as a "learner" without pay for four weeks, she received a wage of $3.00 a week.

Her quiet, gentle manner and an attractive appearance accompanied an uncommonly forceful personality which was honed by the struggle she observed all around her. Her father and the people in whose midst she earned her pittance were all caught in the vise of exploitation. In spite of her youth, and though sixty-five percent of the people with whom she worked were men, she organized Local 170 under the United Garment Workers and became its head. When the Amalgamated Clothing Workers Union was formed by the breakaway faction from the dissatisfied United Garment Workers, she led Local 170 into the newly established Amalgamated.

There she made rapid progress. A year later she had gained sufficient respect to be chosen secretary of the Amalgamated Joint Board and within another year she was placed on the General Executive Board. As an organizer she proved so compelling an advocate of trade unionism that she brought under the jurisdiction of the Amalgamated many of the "runaway shops," which employers had deliberately removed to non-union states in order to be able to lower costs. She was an equally effective agitator within the union, for when she saw the need for innovations she did not rest until she succeeded in implanting her point of view on the administration.

Upon her marriage in 1918 she resigned, but it was to be only a temporary withdrawal. She returned to bring almost 30,000 shirt workers in New York, New Jersey, Connecticut, and Pennsylvania into the union. In 1934 she was appointed the union's only woman vice-president. At the same time she maintained her membership in the Consumers' League and the Women's Trade Union League.

She entered the labor reform movement during the Depression decade. Mayor Fiorello La Guardia appointed her to a commission on unemployment and also to his committee on ethnic problems. Governors Lehman and Dewey consulted her on discrimination in employment. She also served under Frances Perkins on the advisory committee on maternal and child welfare, on several industrial committees to set minimum wages and also on the Women's Policy Committee of the War Manpower Commission.

In the mid-thirties she was drawn into reform politics, first by supporting the fusion movement; later she was among those who founded the American Labor Party in 1936. Two years later she was placed on the American Labor party and Republican party tickets as a congressional candidate.

Hers was not a long life. A year after being cited by the

New York Women's City Club for unusual service, she died at the age of fifty-two. To honor her memory and to keep it alive the Amalgamated made a contribution to Memorial Hospital by endowing two beds in the children's ward in her name. The contribution of union members went to pay for an auditorium in an institution for homeless boys in Rome, Italy.[16]

Obviously among hundreds of thousands of women workers it is not possible to include all who stood out from the mass in one way or another. Many more deserve to be pointed to as outstanding, but because their experiences and stories were similar to those described herein and because even unusual tales, if repeated, become commonplace, a halt seemed advisable. The women cited in these pages deserve to be considered standard bearers, but at the same time they must be looked upon as representative of others like them—young, untried, eager to make their mark in the group of which they were a part, most often meagerly educated, if not entirely untutored. In their struggle to overcome their handicaps they elevated themselves and their fellow workers.

Let it be remembered that building strong labor organizations called not only for principal players, but for a large supporting cast.

CHAPTER 10

Two Women Who "Wouldn't": Emma Goldman and Rose Pastor Stokes

IN 1916 THERE APPEARED A PROLETARIAN DRAMA "THE WOMAN Who Wouldn't" by Rose Pastor Stokes, a woman born in Russia whose marriage in 1905 to the millionaire James Graham Phelps Stokes was an event to which immigrants alluded with reverent wonder. The theme was supposed to have been influenced by Emma Goldman's critical work, *The Social Significance of the Modern Drama.* The play was produced by the Washington Square Players. What the heroine, a mill girl, would not do, was to tell the man to whom she was engaged (but who seemed to be in love with another girl) that she was pregnant, nor would she marry him eight years later when she returned with his child to her childhood home. Both Mrs. Stokes and Emma Goldman could be called women "who wouldn't." Of the two, Emma Goldman, the notorious anarchist, had a more unusual mind and was a far more incisive thinker than Rose Pastor Stokes.

Both women were ideologists dedicated to hastening the millennium through the implementation of their respective ideas. While Miss Goldman had the immovable convictions of the true zealot, Mrs. Stokes was a shopper among ideas. But both were sincerely involved in the class struggle. They knew each other, and during Emma Goldman's campaign in favor of family limitation, Mrs. Stokes, then still in the socialist camp, distributed birth control pamphlets at some of Miss Goldman's meetings. She also protested Miss Goldman's frequent arrests, which everyone knew were intended to harass her. Yet Miss Goldman gives Mrs. Stokes only one mention in her long autobiography. Both women had adoring friends who idolized them;

167

Miss Goldman especially received material help as well as adulation from people who were not anarchists like her, but were impressed by her idealism and fighting spirit. As Emma Goldman asserts, she was "a multimillionaire in friends," which is reminiscent of the sweatshop poet Morris Rosenfeld's "a millionaire of tears am I."

Both had been manual workers—Rose Pastor since the age of four, and Emma since thirteen. Both ceased being workers— Emma Goldman when she was past her teens, and Rose Pastor after her marriage to the converted socialist Graham Stokes. It was then Mrs. Stokes turned political by pinning her hopes first on Socialism and after 1919 on Communism. Emma Goldman embraced the anarchist faith at the age of seventeen after the execution of the Haymarket victims in 1887 and never deviated from her views.

Rose Pastor, however, twisted and turned from one set of ideas to another and from one ambition to the next until too ill to care. She was a flame, like Edna St. Vincent Millay's candle that burned at both ends. At her death she left an unfinished autobiography entitled "I Belong to the Working Class," on which she had worked for ten years. It was her last act of defiant assertion. Emma Goldman survived the publication of her memoirs for nine years.[1] The stories of these two women which follow are taken from their respective memoirs.

While Miss Goldman has had many biographers, nothing has been written about Rose Pastor Stokes. Emma Goldman (1869– 1940) was born in Latvia, but was brought up in Königsberg, Germany, where, for a short time, she attended a secondary school. But it was soon necessary to join her father in St. Petersburg and go to work. While still in Russia she read the radical Russian writers Tchernyshevski, Goncharow, and Turgenev. She continued to educate herself by reading and studying in a serious way; even in her later years she never neglected a chance to add to her library or to exploit any opportunity to learn.

She had had what she called a "ghastly childhood," a harsh violent father, and a mother who, though more restrained, showed little understanding of her children. When she lived in Königsberg with a grandmother and an uncle, he, too, treated the young girl with unbelievable callousness. It is possible that the violence she had encountered was to blame for her uncontrolled outbursts, such as leaping at a woman's throat when the latter made a callous remark about the Haymarket victims and, even after being restrained, throwing a pitcher of water into her face "with all my force." She publicly horse-whipped Johann Most, the "pope of American anarchism," when he refused to retract criticism of Alexander Berkman for his attempt to assassinate Henry Clay Frick. Another of her lovers had a chair thrown at him which barely missed. At the same time she was meltingly attached to those she cared about, and tenderly sympathetic to all who appeared to be "victims of the social order."

After threatening to jump into the Neva if not permitted to accompany an older sister to America, where still another sister was living in Rochester, she left Russia in 1885. In Rochester she found a job sewing buttons on men's coats at $2.50 a week and within a short time married a Russian who had become naturalized. The marriage turned out badly, and she left him. But it brought her a valuable advantage, American citizenship, through her husband. Not until after 1924 was the law granting citizenship through marriage rescinded.

She was twenty when she arrived in New York, which was to become her "beloved city." She had five dollars and the address of Johann Most's anarchist paper, *Freiheit*, which she had begun to read in Rochester. The execution of the Haymarket victims in 1887, which she considered "judicial murder," so outraged her that henceforth she committed herself irrevocably to anarchism. She was unalterably convinced that the present social system needed to be replaced, that the "state was the worst enemy, a machine that crushes," while anarchism was "a beautiful ideal ... which stood for release and freedom from conventions and prejudice ... the right to self-expression."[2] In her later years she stated that she considered herself "an American in the truest sense, spiritually rather than by the grace of a mere scrap of paper ... who had lived, dreamed, and worked for that America."[3]

She had two instructors in anarchist theory—Johann Most

and Alexander Berkman. Berkman was by far the more intellectual. The wild, frustrated, undisciplined Most knew immediately that Emma would make an effective speaker, and he began grooming her and almost immediately to send her out on speaking tours. But their friendship was not to last because Emma fell in love with Alexander Berkman.

Her idyllic existence with the intellectual Berkman was broken in 1892 when Berkman attempted to assassinate Henry Clay Frick with a homemade bomb made according to the recipe Most published in *Freiheit* and failed. To her it was a heroic act, even though Most and other anarchists disavowed it as a useless act. As a young woman Emma advocated the use of the bomb as when she suggested to Berkman: "Don't you think one of the rotten newspaper offices should be blown up—editors, reporters and all? That would teach the press a lesson."[4] But he pointed out to her that they must "strike at the root" and not at "hirelings of capitalism" such as the press.

While Emma had watched Berkman fashion the bomb in their home, she was aware of the danger to the tenants in the house, but decided that the end ("the sacred cause of the oppressed and exploited people") justified the means ("what if a few have to perish—the many would be made free and could live in beauty and comfort"). If they had had enough money for two fares to Pittsburgh, she would have accompanied Berkman, then twenty-one years of age, and shared his fate. Frick was only wounded and Berkman, who seemed to have been destined for the role of *l'homme malheureux*, was sentenced to twenty-two years.

Emma was overwhelmed by guilt feelings that her beloved and noble "Sascha" had to bear all the punishment and she none. At first she wept, stormed, conducted mass meetings, publicly horsewhipped Most, lashed friends and foes with speeches on Berkman's ability, but eventually settled down to practical ways of trying to help him, including to escape, but it was foiled.

Never had a man had a more consistently devoted friend. After his release she opened her home to him, as well as her magazine *Mother Earth* (she had begun to publish it while he was in prison), though his love for her had died during his prison years. She let him manage and edit *Mother Earth* while she was away on "lecture trips" gathering money for its upkeep, and let him mismanage finances, for which he seemed to have had a conspicuous talent. For instance, after their deportation to Russia his clothes were stolen while he slept, and their entire fortune of $1,600 which he was supposed to guard was lost, rendering them helpless until faithful relatives and friends sent more. Later his trunk containing everything they owned, for which he was also responsible, was also stolen. But if she felt any anger at what must have been a serious setback for them, the tone of her writing does not reveal it.

She raised the money with which to publish his book, *Prison Memoirs of an Anarchist*, traveled with him as a stateless person from one European country to another, sharing everything with him, nursing him in illness, and upholding him with her devotion and unwavering admiration. When he committed suicide in Nice in 1936, justifying it by "right of revolutionary ethics," it was a bitter blow.

Her existence in America was one of continuous strife. There were times when no one would rent a room to her (once she could find no place to live save in a brothel) and she found herself barred from lecture halls across the country. She was arrested so many times she said she never knew whether she would sleep in her own home and for that reason always carried a book with her to read if she should find herself detained by being arrested. However, she served only three prison sentences.

The first time it was in 1893 as a result of declaring at a mass meeting that "if they do not give you work, demand bread. If they deny you both, take bread. It is your sacred right."[5] Sentenced to one year at Blackwell's Island on the charge of inciting a riot, the state inadvertently provided her with an honorable profession. When sent to the prison hospital, the physician in charge discovered how intelligent she was and decided to train her to become the prison's hospital nurse. After her release she went to Vienna to study midwifery and nursing at Das Allgemeine Krankenhaus and became very adept at it. In her professional capacity she carried out all tasks expected of her even when they violated her precepts as an anarchist.

After President McKinley's assassination, for instance, she let it be known to the sardonic amusement of reporters that she would have been willing to nurse McKinley "because he is merely a human being to me now."[6]

Like many anarchists she looked upon the courts as pillars of the capitalist society who could be expected to be hostile to nonconformists. She would not sue, appeal for redress, ask for leniency, and, when on trial, preferred to conduct her own defense which she did very ably. This was her attitude to court proceedings:

We did not believe in the law and its machinery, and we knew that we could expect no justice. We would therefore completely ignore what was to us a mere farce; we would refuse to participate in the court proceedings. Should this method prove impractical, we would plead our own case, not in order to defend ourselves, but to give public utterance to our ideas.[7]

To anarchists it was the system that was at fault and not those charged with carrying it out. For instance, during the period when President McKinley hovered between life and death, she was again arrested in Chicago and while being transferred to Cook County jail was assaulted by an enraged guard who knocked out a tooth. She refused to identify the man.

By the time she was arrested the second time in 1915 her citizenship had been revoked by the expedient of denaturalizing her dead husband. The reason for her arrest was her noisy advocacy of birth control, in which she was supported by Rose Pastor Stokes. She received fifteen days in the workhouse, during which she prepared material for six lectures on American literature.

The third and last time she was arrested was in 1917 before the draft bill became law. She and Berkman had formed the No-Conscription League to protest conscription, but she insisted she had never urged individuals not to register.

Another gesture that infuriated the authorities was that the June issue of *Mother Earth* appeared draped in black, its cover bearing a tomb with the inscription: *IN MEMORIAM— AMERICAN DEMOCRACY*. Both she and Berkman were arrested. Their sentences were two years in prison and a fine of $10,000 each, with the recommendation that they be deported at the expiration of their prison terms. She was sent to the state prison in Jefferson City, Missouri; he to the federal penitentiary in Atlanta, Georgia.

After serving their sentence they were ordered expelled from the United States. With 247 radicals they were placed on the S. S. *Buford*, which had been a troopship during the Spanish-American War and was thoroughly dilapidated. They left on December 21 and on the twenty-eighth day were dumped in Finland, where they crossed into Russia.

In Russia they found, instead of a glorious new world order, people starving, the jails filled, the Cheka in control. At night they heard the sound of guns, suggesting that mass executions were taking place. When they inquired, they were offered such spurious explanations that they began to suspect "the shiny Soviet medal" had an "obverse side" which was ugly. When they were finally received by Lenin, she was taken aback by his manner—his "amazing glee" in putting them into a position of disadvantage. He "shook with loud laughter" so as to "compel one to laugh with him," and told them they should have remained in the United States. It was clear he had no use for them, though he professed to be delighted to have their services. A recent commentator states that Lenin wanted to bring Baruch to Russia to develop industry and natural resources.[8]

There followed a period of desperate maneuverings to be permitted to go anywhere where they would remain unmolested. They were forced to wander all over Western Europe on temporary visas. During this period she managed to write her impressions of Russia, which she called *My Disillusionment in Russia*. Published in America, it was republished in a Swedish and in a British edition, the latter with a preface by Rebecca West. In 1925 on English soil she married a Welsh miner, the anarchist James Colton, who was an old friend, clearly in order to be able to claim an English passport.

She finally settled in a little cottage in St. Tropez which friends had bought and presented to her. There she wrote her autobiography. But before she started her memoirs, she visited Canada for fifteen months. In 1940 she was in Canada again to raise money for the Spanish Loyalists when she suffered a stroke and died.

In death she returned to America, being buried at the Waldheim Cemetery, the resting place of the Haymarket victims. The sculptor, Jo Davidson, who was her friend, designed a plaque for the headstone of her grave. According to one of her biographers, she never overcame her longing for America.[9]

Rose Wieslander (1879–1933),[10] who took her stepfather's name—Pastor—may be said to provide the proof for all time that the most fanciful possibilities could indeed happen in America. That a poor immigrant could become a millionaire in his own lifetime was fantastic enough, but not as incredible as that an immigrant girl without background or formal education, accustomed to hunger and deprivation, should marry a young millionaire, the son of a family of old lineage, who had been given all the advantages of wealth and background and was a physician to boot. Equally incredible was that such an unbelievably lucky girl could throw it all away, then succumb to an incurable disease and become so poor again as to have to depend on the help of friends, none of them rich, for minimum comfort during her terminal illness. Rose Pastor Stokes's story has some of the elements of the classical concept of tragedy— the fall from the highest to the lowest and the evocation of sympathy and/or pity, if not fear.

She was born in Russia, but at the age of three was taken to London by her mother, who seems to have been a rebel. She had divorced Rose's father whom she had been forced to marry against her will. In London her mother proved again how spunky she was by leading a victorious strike, setting her young child an example she would not forget. She worked at making satin bows for satin slippers and Rose began to help her when she was four. Like so many of Whitechapel's poor children whom she heard begging for "bread with treacle," she knew real hunger, which she explains as "a gnawing that would make me restless when I tried to play." She speaks of an orange as a real luxury. She attended a free school for poor children where Israel Zangwill had been a pupil and later a teacher. Even as a child she revealed unusual determination. When a teacher struck her for laughing and injured her hand, she would not go back to school, preferring to become a truant until she could go to another school. As a young child she was taken on at the Princess Theatre to play in a child's pageant. She owned one book, Lamb's *Tales From Shakespeare,* which she says she read and reread for years. Her life in London must have been extremely barren, for she says:

> During my eight years in London I did not remember seeing a tree or a blade of grass near my home, save in a graveyard. . . . Those eight years there was never enough to eat.[11]

Upon arriving in America and docking at Castle Garden, she asked: "How and why is this a garden?" In Cleveland, where they settled, she was immediately taken by a neighbor to work in a cigar factory to be taught stogey-rolling. When a factory inspector was due she was told to stay home.

In her environment she learned quickly that employers were "bosses" for whom one could only have contempt. This is what she observed around her:

> There was much talk, and my child's horizon began to widen through the equal sorrows and bitter economic struggles of the little proletarian world about me. . . . There was always someone losing a job, or hopelessly in search of one. Or the schoolchildren were without shoes or decent clothing. Or there was nothing to pay the grocer who refused further credit. Or someone came to borrow an egg for a sick child. Or the eternal Installment Plan Agent had been and threatened to take away everything unless something were paid on account and with more than half already paid out! . . . Or there was nothing toward the rent, most of the next month gone and the landlord knocking daily at the door. Or there was an eviction threatened, and not a dollar to move with . . .[12]

At first she earned one or two dollars a week, later nearly four dollars, but had to work ten or eleven hours daily and got "hunger and cold for my portion." She went to work for a "buckeye," a cigar factory in the owner's home, because it was near where she lived and she could thus save time and earn a dollar more a week. But she found that by working fast, she "sped up" the others. As soon as their output increased, their piece wages were cut.

The agonies of the depression of 1893 hit them particularly hard because her mother's husband, a man for whom Rose felt immense sympathy, began to drink and to leave home at intervals. At first when he returned, he would be abject and conscience-stricken, until one day he disappeared for good. The burden of keeping up a home fell entirely on Rose. That these experiences burned themselves into her very being can be gleaned from these words:

How we went through that winter of crisis and tragedy—on what we subsisted; of the days of stark hunger; of the endless trudgings from one closed factory to another; of our struggle with my poor stepfather giving himself more to drink, the more his hope of livelihood vanished; of the nights without sleep because of hunger and despair; the days in a frozen flat; of the children who cried for bread in the cold . . . I cannot tell of them now.[13]

She tried work in a shirtwaist factory, but could not stand the noise of the electric sewing machine. "Stogey-rolling" was quiet work that was apt to induce what Samuel Gompers, himself a cigar worker, called "mind-peace." One could mull over problems; one could also sing if one felt like it. She had tried selling millinery in a department store, but after ten months went back to the cigar factory.

In the shop she was introduced to socialism. A copy of Edwin Markham's "The Man with a Hoe" fell into her hands. She also came upon the poems of Morris Rosenfeld, an immigrant poet who wrote of the woes of immigrant sweatshop workers in Yiddish. In 1914, she and a collaborator published an English version which they had translated into English.[14] She pounced on every bit of reading matter that came into her hands. When she began reading about the struggle between capital and labor, she discovered she was a "Socialist by instinct." She had no social outlets, except for a club for working girls, called "The Friendly Club." She and other stogey workers in several factories applied for membership in the Cigar Workers' Union, but they were rejected as "unskilled workers."

What she wanted, she asserts, was a "decent world to live in, not a fine house."

One day in 1901 a copy of a Jewish newspaper, the *Jewish Daily News*, fell into her hands, in which the editor of the English page urged his readers to "write a letter." Rose did, received $2.00 and continued sending letters for a year and a half under the pen name, "Zelda." Her letters became so popular that when she stopped, readers swamped the paper with inquiries as to what had happened to "Zelda." The editor offered her $15 a week to come to New York and work full-time on the English page. In 1903 the family left Cleveland and moved to the Bronx. Rose became a newspaper writer.

That Rose Pastor really cared for the poor and the hopeless, her "class," as she frequently reiterates, emerges from a story told by a young woman physician, Emily Dunning Barringer, who was the first woman intern to serve on an ambulance. One day Dr. Dunning was summoned to appear in the office of Police Inspector Max F. Schmittberger to disprove or confirm an allegation made by Rose Pastor in her newspaper that the police had been dilatory about getting an old derelict into a hospital.

Inspector Schmittberger,[15] proud of the efficiency of his department, had been stung by Rose's sizzling story. Dr. Dunning, who had been on the ambulance when the old man was picked up, watched the confrontation between a young woman with an English accent, surely more effective than the usual East Side intonation, whose sense of social justice had been outraged, and the inspector who took Rose's allegations as an attack upon himself. Though Dr. Dunning exonerated the police, she was impressed with the "striking and convincing little figure," whom she describes as "not beautiful, but definitely attractive." She noted: "Her great physical charm was her superb, copper-tinted hair."[16]

One day Rose received an assignment to interview a Mr. J. G. Phelps Stokes, who was much in the news. A turn-of-the-century rebel, he was the scion of an aristocratic family of Puritan background, who had studied medicine at Columbia's College of Physicians and Surgeons, but was not practicing. He had left his father's mansion at 225 Madison Avenue, renouncing luxury to live at the University Settlement and devote himself to the underprivileged. She objected to her assignment, but was told that unless she did she need not come in on Monday.

As she tells the story, on the way to the settlement she met Edward King, the East Side's popular Scotsman-lecturer and hero figure, and he allowed himself to be persuaded to accompany her. He drew Stokes out while she listened, "enchanted," as she says, "by the very tall, slender young man, who both in his features and in general appearance was so like the young Lincoln, full of sympathy for the poor."

James Graham Phelps Stokes had been brought up on abolitionist sentiment and his family had always aided social betterment. Booker T. Washington had been a guest at the Stokes home. Anson Phelps Stokes, Junior, brother of Graham Stokes, a minister and chaplain at Yale University, stated in a letter to Ralph Bunche that the Stokes children had foregone ice cream during Lent in order to help educate an Indian student at Hampton Institute. Several of Graham Stokes' sisters, including the baroness Sarah Halkett, professed to be sympathetic to socialism. But Rose had reservations about the strength of their convictions, especially those of the baroness.

Graham Stokes requested that a copy of the interview be submitted to him before publication, and Rose sent it. Apparently he liked what she said about him, because he brought the article back himself during her absence, approving it, and clearly showed his disappointment at not finding her in. Her office friends teased her about it. From this beginning grew a friendship that brought her frequently to his apartment at the University Settlement, where gathered some of the brilliant intellectuals and radicals of the time, including Emma Goldman,[17] William English Walling, Leroy Scott, and others. Their conversation inhibited her. "What was there I could say to all those learned gentlemen and brilliant ladies?" she admitted, conscious of her shortcomings.

Soon she and Graham Stokes were seen together on all kinds

of occasions. It embarrassed her to go with him in a coach
and she explained that it was "for no other reason than that I
was compelled to do so...." By then Rose knew Graham
Stokes wanted to marry her, for, she says, "he talked of his
dreams of the future, in which I was to share...." "I contemplated the man," she says, "likened him to the young Buddha,
Siddartha. I sat in worship before him." But she insisted on
her own terms: "You will be coming to my world, not I to
yours ... we will have a flat somewhere on the East Side and
live and work among the people."

He must have been struck by her terrible intensity and drive
which all who knew her recognized and remarked about. She
generated excitement. An exotic, dark-eyed young woman with
magnificent hair and a good figure, she had a distinctive flair
of her own. To some people, however, she appeared to be
neurotic and theatrical. Her friend, the writer Anzia Yezierska,
who came from the same background as Rose Pastor, is supposed to have based her story *Salome of the Tenements* on the
love affair and marriage of Rose Pastor to Graham Stokes.[18]
The author describes the heroine, Sonya Vrunsky, who is also
an interviewer for a ghetto paper, as a "blazing comet," an
"electric radiance," a "tragedy queen," with "the driving force
that will carry her anywhere." But the millionaire philanthropist
John Manning[19] is a stuffed shirt, very tall, distinguished for
his "cultured elegance," "his finished grooming," his "high-bred
aloofness." But while Miss Yezierska's heroine sounds illiterate,
Rose Pastor Stokes's autobiography and letters reveal no trace
of careless grammar or solecisms of any kind.

"The luckiest girl in America," as the papers referred to
her, when they did not speak of her as "The Cinderella of the
Sweatshops," or the "Israelitish maiden," was married in 1905
on her birthday at the Stokes family estate, "Brick House" at
Noroton in Connecticut, by her husband's brother, the Reverend
Anson Phelps Stokes, Junior.

The Stokes family seems to have treated her with the respect
due a wife of a Stokes, but what some of them may have
thought of the marriage is unknown. Letters from Helen Stokes,
sister of Graham Stokes, indicate that she was devoted to Rose.
Later when trouble broke out between Rose and Graham Stokes,

Helen Stokes wrote to her: "I sincerely care about your future as I think you must know," and during Rose's final illness sent money to her, which Rose apparently accepted.

Very likely Rose felt uncomfortable with the Stokes family. She tells that before the wedding she was moved to tears watching "a corps of workers making a paradise for the few."[20] She realized anew that she belonged "to the gardeners, the servants, the stablemen, the mechanics; they who live insecure lives, saving what miserable little they can against the day when sickness or unemployment leaves them helpless."[21] Unquestionably her sympathy with the "helpless" was very real and it never left her.

Soon after their return from a sumptuous honeymoon in London, where she visited her old home, and in Paris and Italy, where a picture by Donatello reminded her that "Life lies bleeding and Art smiles," Stokes was drawn into politics. The Municipal Ownership League endorsed John Randolph for mayor and Graham Stokes for president of the board of aldermen. He "barely escaped" getting into office and his wife professed to be greatly relieved about it without saying why. Later he was told he was being considered for the governorship of New York State if he remained tied to the Municipal Ownership League. Joining the Socialist party with his wife seemed to have been his answer to them. Up to then Rose had been merely flirting with political panaceas; she had never endorsed a political solution. But Graham Stokes, who considered himself a radical, would never take a more radical stance than that of a member of the Socialist party.

The early years after their marriage were their best years. Like the young Francis Scott Fitzgerald, both would never feel so hopeful again. Living at 88 Grove Street and at "Caritas Island," where Graham Stokes built a cottage with his own hands, their homes became centers where their friends and fellow workers gathered. As one reads, it becomes clear that they were surrounded by exciting friends who made good conversation. At Grove Street, Maxim Gorky, who had so outraged America's conservatives (because he had dared to bring a woman with him who was not his wife), visited the Stokeses, and Miriam Finn Scott, wife of Leroy Scott, a "regular" of the Stokes circle, acted as interpreter. Another friend, William English Walling, had married one of the Strunsky sisters, who was a radical and a supporter of Emma Goldman. Mr. and Mrs. Stokes worked "with enthusiasm" for the University Settlement and she for the Charity Organization Society. But she was not happy visiting people dependent on charity, because she realized that "the ladies were putting gay if half-faded frills around the festering sores of the working class." Between 1906 and 1910 she spoke at organization meetings for the Women's Trade Union League, she helped in organizing new workers in a variety of trades and attended meetings of the Executive Board[22] of the WTUL. She also attended committee meetings of cigar makers to organize workers in cigar factories, attended hearings in City Hall on tenement conditions, and fulfilled lecture and speaking engagements. A persuasive speaker, she drew large crowds. She was also invited to join the "Heterodoxy Society" which included many prominent women and was not limited to radicals.

But it was not like her to be submissive. She met some of the well-known public figures—Andrew Carnegie, Mr. and Mrs. Oswald Garrison Villard, Dr. Charles William Eliot, president of Harvard University, among others, and it must have made her aware that she was straddling two worlds, the very rich, who liked to think of themselves as benevolent supporters of the poor, and the working class whom she could not forget. It put her in an anomalous position. She relates that when she went on a special train with her husband to attend a meeting of the Board of Directors of Tuskegee Institute on its twenty-fifth anniversary (1906), the conversation of the "liberals" who were present caused her many distressing moments. At a luncheon for Carnegie to which she and her husband were invited, she walked out in high dudgeon when she realized that Negroes were not welcome, her husband following her.

Both went on speaking tours on behalf of socialist candidates. She was invited by "all the conservative organizations of America—the D.A.R., The Women's Temperance Union, church societies, patriotic clubs—to talk on socialism."[23] Between strike activities and mass meetings (in 1912 she was active in the New York restaurant and hotel workers' strike), she toured the country on behalf of the Intercollegiate Socialist Society, of which Graham Stokes, Jack London, Upton Sinclair, and others had been the founders. By 1913, Mr. and Mrs. Stokes had opened sixty to seventy chapters in American colleges. But she was beginning to be suspicious of his real feelings toward the people. She admits, "I thought I detected a look of contempt as he looked upon some of them. He couldn't have dealt me a more personal blow that would have hurt more."[24] She seems to have been completely sincere.

After 1910 she began to turn her attention to writing articles on social and political themes, which were published in *Century, Everybody's*, and in Max Eastman's *The Masses*. She also began to involve herself in birth control activities with Emma Goldman. In 1914 she published a translation of Morris Rosenfeld's poems and in 1916 a play, *The Woman Who Wouldn't*.

Her translation with Helen Frank of Morris Rosenfeld's poems, which she called "Songs of Labor," brought her much appreciation and at least one devoted friend, Olive Tilford Dargan, who wrote under the pen name Fielding Burke. The effect of Rosenfeld's plaintive poetry on the Jewish workers of New York merits a short digression. His poems were to the exploited Jewish workers what Heinrich Heine's poems were to the romantic youth of Western Europe during the early nineteenth century. The philo-semitic Lincoln Steffens was also impressed with Rosenfeld's vigor and personality.[25] People undergoing the privations of the immigrant existence devoured his melancholy lines, because they so accurately portrayed the feeling of these people and the world in which they were living. Who could resist the pathos of a poem that wailed:

> Oh, here in the shop the machines roar so wildly,
> That oft, unaware that I am, or have been,
> I sink and am lost in the terrible tumult,
> And void is my soul—I am but a machine,
> I work and I work, and I work, never ceasing,
> Create and create things from morning till e'en;
> For what? and for whom? Oh, I know not! Oh, ask not!
> Whoever has heard of a conscious machine.

Her play, *The Woman Who Wouldn't*,[26] appeared in 1916. It seems amateurish in contrast to Gerhart Hauptmann's genuinely

convincing proletarian play, *Die Weber,* which appeared in
1892 and of which it is faintly reminiscent. It is filled with the
baldest propaganda: "Is the boss o' the mills ever arrested for
cripplin' in th' work?—for killin' them outright even? Don't
they wring th' sweat an' blood out of us an' buy laws with it t'
protect themselves?"

The outbreak of World War I marked a turning point in
the lives of Rose Pastor and Graham Stokes, because from
then on, she asserts, instead of "friends," as they had been
for the larger part of their married life, they became "friendly
enemies." At first both supported the war. As she explains,
she considered "the defeat of the German Kaiser and German
imperialism as the same thing in my mind as the victory of
the working class revolution." The first requirement, therefore,
was that the German people rid themselves of the Kaiser. In
this mood both left the Socialist party, which had repudiated
the war. But her eyes were soon opened to the truth that it
was an imperialist war and wrong in principle. In 1918 she
and her husband rejoined the Socialist party. Graham Stokes
had attempted unsuccessfully to form a National party in
Chicago, but to his wife it was "no genuine labor party, but a
labor party with labor left out." From then on she began to
veer sharply left and to make speeches against the war and
against conscription. In 1918 she was convicted for opposing
the draft, but on appeal the court reversed itself and the government dropped the case.

Also her marriage began to deteriorate steadily. In a letter
to her friend Olive Dargan she admitted that a certain "solemn-
faced puritanical person" told her that what she was doing was
"most unlady-like and hazardous" and that she was "utterly
crazy."[27] Until the split in the Socialist party in 1919 between
the leftists and the conservative elements, she might have been
considered merely a rebel. After 1919 she became frankly
partisan to the Communist group. It was impossible for her
to go back to bourgeois values. In 1922 she was a delegate to
the Fourth Congress of the Communist International in Moscow
and while there was elected to the central executive committee
of the Workers' Party, which later became the Communist

Party of the United States. She also began to write for *Pravda* and *The Workers*, which later became the *Daily Worker*.

In 1925 Graham Stokes brought suit for divorce which she did not contest. Despite her lawyer's counsel she refused "even to apply for any form of allowance." All she wanted was "secrecy—not publicity." Nevertheless she saw her story blazoned forth in all the newspapers. In replying to her lawyer's letter[28] urging that Graham Stokes be asked to make a settlement for her and her mother (whom he seems to have supported), she wrote: "Since Mr. Stokes does not see fit to provide for our simple needs from the ample means at his disposal I will not fight in the courts to compel him to do so."

Thus began the darkest days of her life. Her illness had first manifested itself in 1924. She tried to sell her drawings and poetry to magazines and attempted to get speaking engagements, but could not create a steady source of income. She had only one regular assignment with the *Daily Worker* to furnish a story and drawing twice a month for which she received $20 monthly. In 1926 an article entitled "There are Few Bad Divorces" appeared in *Collier's*.[29] In it she asserted she believed in "free marriage" and suggested that the state should "enforce the separation of those no longer in love."

From then on she was frequently in real need. She had a little cottage in Westport, Connecticut, and she admitted she had to go to the "woods" to cut her own firewood even though she was ill, because she did not have the money to buy it. In 1927 she married Jerome Isaac Romaine, who legally changed his name to Victor J. Jerome. She called herself Mrs. Romaine when she resided in New York City, but in Westport she was Rose Pastor Stokes. Victor Romaine was an impecunious communist who eked out a scant living as a language teacher and as editor of the communist magazine *Political Affairs*.

In 1931 she was very ill and in such desperate straits that the League for Mutual Aid, an organization founded to help indigent radicals, raised money for her in addition to promoting the sale of her engravings.[30] In March, 1933, she sailed to Germany to put herself under the care of the Roentgen Institute in Frankfurt am Main. There she kept a diary which is painful to read. "Am sinking daily," she wrote in a handwriting so spidery that it testified eloquently how much she must have suffered.[31]

Friends and acquaintances sent money to her regularly to pay for her hospital expenses and held mass meetings in Webster Hall in New York City to raise funds for her use.

She died in June of 1933. Her ashes were returned to New York.

The most convincing explanation for the breakup of the Stokes marriage was offered by one of Rose's friends who wrote in a letter: "Two natures with a superficial affinity, but in their deepest layers antagonistic. The war cut down to their foundations and exposed their roots springing from opposite poles."[32]

Olive Tilford Dargan also spoke of a difference in "socialistic ideals" between Rose and her husband. Another letter expresses the regret over the end of this beautiful romance: "I have always thought of him as such an earnest thinker and he did love you ... he idolized you. ..."[33]

It is obvious that they were ideologically incompatible. When Graham Stokes married Rose Pastor he had undoubtedly gone as far as he could in his radical stand; possibly her admiration helped to convince him that he was a real radical. For her marriage and freedom from economic worries made it possible to begin shopping around among advanced radical ideas and to decide on communism. In Louis Untermeyer's words the memory of "the bitter ballad of the slums" remained so fresh in her mind, she felt guilty at accepting comforts from which "her class" was excluded. She was both tempted and revolted by luxury. Envisioning herself as an instrument for the alleviation of the struggles she had witnessed and experienced, she plunged on where he could not follow. After 1919 it was impossible for her to be a compromiser.

CHAPTER 11

Foreign-born Physicians and Scientists

"FORGET YOU ARE WOMEN. . . . REMEMBER YOU ARE PHYSICIANS," was the advice of Dr. Joseph Longshore to female medical students. Women desiring to become doctors of medicine would have been very willing to forget that they were women and happy to assume the role of physicians if the men belonging to the medical profession had permitted it. The struggle of women to become doctors in America was a long and difficult one, but in Europe it took even longer and was accompanied by greater resistance. In Edinburgh, for instance, in the 1870s when women were admitted to medical school—to be taught in separate classes—there was rioting among the male students; the women were pelted with mud and rotten eggs and earned distinctions were withheld from them.[1] A repetition of this occurred in Kingston, Ontario, and thus furnished the proof that a medical school for women was needed. As a consequence the Kingston Woman's Medical College was founded, which was affiliated with Queens University.[2]

In American schools rioting seems not to have occurred, but women medical students were sneered at, insulted, snubbed by respectable folk who could not understand why "hens should want to crow."[3] Women doctors were refused as tenants; consequently they had no place in which to receive patients. Though some men—doctors and ministers—were willing to be helpful, those who did constituted a very small nucleus. Daughters and wives of ministers wishing to train as missionary physicians were among the first groups of women trainees.

Women did not begin to invade the male world of medicine until shortly before the midpoint of the nineteenth century. The attempt to gain admission into this male enclave may be classed as an extension of the women's emancipation movement. A great deal of support came from Quakers, who offered women

186

not only encouragement but financial help and in many instances became these despised physicians' first patients.

Men accepted women as midwives and nurses and even encouraged them to take up midwifery. What they objected to was to give them equal status as physicians. In the 1760s, Doctors John Morgan, who later became physician in charge of the American armies, and William Shippen, both of Philadelphia, opened a school in midwifery, but they are not on record for having aided women to enter the College of Philadelphia, the first medical school in colonial America. Physicians were apt to feel economically threatened by women doctors who would be invading one of the most lucrative fields in medicine, obstetrics, and admitted it. Others were probably sincere when they claimed their opposition to be based on the conviction that the woman doctor was bound to lose her modesty and become "unsexed." There were also those who were sure women lacked the required ability to become doctors. The acerb doctor, Mary Corinne Putnam, the first American woman to hold a medical degree from l'Ecole de Médecin in Paris, remarked:

The admission of women to the profession of medicine has been widely opposed because of the disbelief in their intellectual capacity. In America it is less often permitted to doubt—out loud—the intellectual capacity of women. The controversy has therefore been shifted to the entirely different ground of decorum.[4]

A male member of the "modesty-school" of opposition to women doctors raised this question: "May not habit so change that fine organization, that sensitive nature of women as to render her [sic] dead to those higher feelings of love and sympathy which now make our homes so happy, so blessed?"[5]

A variant of this theme is expressed in a remark by a professor of a German university who even during the early twentieth century had reservations about women physicians. His assertion was: "Women are either sex animals without a brain or brain animals without sex."[6]

European medical schools and hospitals were in existence during the Middle Ages, and in Italy, where the first medical schools were located, women were permitted to teach and practice.[7] European schools for midwives were famous throughout the world. Paris was the location of La Maternité, in existence since the seventeenth century. In Berlin the Royal Hospital Charité had been turning out well-trained midwives since 1735.[8] Vienna's school for midwives was part of Das Allgemeine Krankenhaus, which the Empress Maria Theresa founded in the eighteenth century. Foreigners were admitted there, as was Emma Goldman, when she decided to make midwifery and nursing her profession.

In the colonies the first midwives were English women who were among the first settlers. They were skilled, trustworthy, and hard-working. From inscriptions on their tombstones it is known that some women brought hundreds, if not thousands, of children into the world. But as for institutions to teach the healing crafts, there was none until the first medical school appeared in Philadelphia in 1765 as the medical department of the College of Philadelphia. By then a hospital was in existence that Dr. Thomas Bond and Benjamin Franklin had organized.[9]

By 1800 four more medical schools were in operation: King's College in New York; the medical school of Harvard University; Dartmouth College; and Transylvania University in Lexington, Kentucky, which had been established in 1792, seven years after Kentucky became a state. Between 1800 and the Civil War, twenty-seven more medical schools came into existence, and by the end of the nineteenth century there were more than a hundred.[10] Most of them were "proprietary schools," that is, privately owned corporations founded by physicians and surgeons. In the 1900s Abraham Flexner made a survey of medical schools for the Carnegie Foundation which resulted in the elimination of many inferior schools.

Young men wishing to train as doctors (as well as those early pioneer women who managed to sneak through) had to apprentice themselves to "preceptors" for whom they performed a variety of tasks, some menial, and in return were permitted to observe and in some cases to tend the patients of their preceptors. After two years of apprenticeship they could apply to the so-called medical colleges, where the instruction generally consisted of two or three college terms ranging from three to seven months each, the second term repeating what had been taught during the first term, so that those who had not mastered the material had another opportunity to learn it during the second term. The subjects taught were anatomy, a model of pâpier maché serving for demonstration, physics, surgery, medicine, obstetrics, chemistry, and materia medica. At the end of two terms an oral examination and a thesis were required. The graduates were then doctors of medicine, eligible to practice.

The intellectual ferment during the antebellum decades, which gave rise to many reforms, including greater legal rights for women, made it inevitable that women should demand the right to become physicians. It was a time when often there was no choice but to accept the services of male midwives, which outraged their sensibilities and their husbands' as well. Because the existing medical schools remained unresponsive to the demand to open the medical field to women, separate schools for women were started.

Dr. Elizabeth Blackwell, a nonnative and the first American woman to receive a recognized medical degree in the United States and the world, applied to twenty-nine schools before gaining acceptance through a fortuitous accident.[11] Her situation had seemed so hopeless to Dr. Joseph Warrington, a Quaker and her preceptor, that he advised her to go to Paris, don male attire and seek admission as a man.[12]

Her sister Emily, applying five years later, made nine applications, including one to Geneva College from which her sister Elizabeth had graduated with the highest honors, all in vain. The tenth application brought an acceptance from Rush Medical College in Chicago, but the Illinois Medical Society protested,[13] and after the first year she was not permitted to return. She had to start knocking on doors all over again before Cleveland College allowed her in.

Often the medical students, who were apt to be a rowdy lot, would dictate to the faculty whether to reject or admit a female applicant. For instance, in 1847 when Harvard University Medical School was disposed to permit Miss Harriott Hunt to attend medical lectures with no commitment to give her the degree she sought, the student body was so outraged that they offered an indignant resolution stating:

Resolved, That no woman of true delicacy would be willing in the presence of men to listen to the discussion of the subjects that necessarily come under consideration of the student of medicine.

Resolved, That we object to having the company of any female forced upon us who is disposed to unsex herself, and to sacrifice her modesty by appearing with men in the medical lecture room.[14]

Conversely, when the Dean of Geneva Medical College submitted to the students the application of Elizabeth Blackwell together with the recommendation from Dr. Joseph Warrington and told them she would not be accepted unless the entire student body voted affirmatively, the students resolved:

That one of the radical principles of a Republican government is the universal education of both sexes; that to every branch of scientific education the door should be open equally to all; that the application of Miss Elizabeth Blackwell to become a member of our class meets our entire approbation; and in extending our unanimous invitation we pledge ourselves that no conduct of ours shall cause her to regret her attendance at this institution.[15]

In spite of the admirable content of the resolution, it was supposed to have been a huge joke to the students and a surprise to the dean who had expected them to sound the death knell to Miss Blackwell's aspirations. The dean was amazed how well the students behaved when the future "doctress," a Quakerishly attired young woman, bowed to the applause she received when she entered the lecture room and that from then on she was treated with respect and decorum. Nevertheless, women applicants were henceforth kept out of Geneva Medical School, which lasted only until 1872 when it was taken over by Syracuse University. Soon thereafter it burned down.

The degree represented only the tip of the iceberg. The problem was where to get practical experience. There was the Blockley Almshouse in Philadelphia, a part of the Philadelphia Hospital, but women could sneak in only by serving as nurses. Miss Blackwell spent a summer in the syphilitic ward for women. To gather experience at the bedside of patients, men as well as women were compelled to go to Europe for further study.

The decade of the 1850s marked a breakthrough in the annals of progress for women doctors. Dr. Elizabeth Blackwell graduated in 1849, her sister Emily was to receive her degree in 1854, and Dr. Marie E. Zakrzewska (called Dr. Zak) in 1856. All three women, each foreign-born, became the first women doctors in America and in Europe as well. They were to play seminal roles in medicine in that they founded hospitals for women and children and schools to train women physicians. A student of Dr. Zak's, Dr. Susan Dimock, organized the first school of nursing. From this school graduated Linda Richards, "America's first trained nurse."[16] In the late 1870s Miss Richards created a nursing school at Massachusetts General Hospital in Boston.[17]

Nineteen medical schools for women were in existence before the institutions training male physicians began to open their doors to women at the end of the nineteenth century. The longest unbroken record for training women physicians is held by the Female Medical College of Pennsylvania, now called the Medical College of Pennsylvania. Since 1970 it has been admitting men. The school had serious difficulties at first. The woman who is credited with saving the institution when it was in its infancy is Dr. Ann Preston, a Quaker. More than two thousand women have received medical degrees from this school, among whom were outstanding native and foreign-born doctors of various races and religions, many of whom became medical missionaries.[18] In the 1900s when many medical schools were weeded out, the Medical College of Pennsylvania received a grade "A" rating by the American Medical Association.[19]

In New York Dr. Elizabeth Blackwell started the New York Infirmary for Women in 1853 and fifteen years later, in 1868, added the Medical College of the New York Infirmary. Both are inseparable from the careers of Doctors Elizabeth and Emily Blackwell. In 1899 when Cornell University promised to admit all the students attending the Medical College of the New York Infirmary, the school closed down. It had graduated 364 doctors.[20]

By 1880 the census showed more than 2,400 women engaged in medical practice in the United States. In 1893, when Johns Hopkins opened as a coeducational institution, having accepted an endowment somewhere between $400,000 and $500,000[21] from Mary Garrett, it was a signal to most of the prestigious schools to follow suit. But not all; even in 1934 28 percent had never graduated a woman; in 1939 the number had fallen to 19 percent, and in 1944 it was 9 percent.[22] The ratio of women to men in medicine is held to be from 4 to 8 percent. Only after World War II the number rose temporarily to 12 percent.[23]

Around the turn of the century a new bottleneck developed— internships for women. Dr. Emily Dunning Barringer tells us that when she received an appointment as an intern at Gouverneur Hospital in New York, it was not only considered a newsworthy item, but was announced as an "Extra." At first she was not on ambulance service, but when she finally achieved the privilege of being sent out on a horse-drawn ambulance, the neighborhood boys ran after her, yelling, "Get a man. Get a man."[24]

Foreign birth seems to have been no special handicap in gaining admission to medical schools or in being accepted by the medical profession. Up to a certain time in the nation's history no opposition was encountered—not even on the basis of religion, which became a significant hindrance after the 1920s when medical schools began to reject Jews. For instance, in 1910 Selman Waksman, who held a certificate from a Russian Gymnasium, though an "extern" (one privately educated, but who passes equivalency exams satisfactorily), was accepted at the College of Physicians and Surgeons in New York before he decided to make bacteriology his life's work. In the early 1850s Dr. Abraham Jacobi, a pathfinder in pediatrics, was surprised how little prejudice he encountered. His statement:

... from the first I was accepted, I was made welcome by the profession, although I brought nothing with me save my ignorance. ... All I could offer was a willingness to work hard and be grateful; and a desire to bridge the gap between American and European medicine, at that time closed books to one another.[25]

ose empty days she busied herself
lectures on the physical education
siderable interest among Quakers
ngs of a private practice. Later her
book form. It was the first of a
write on social questions.

mpting to gain a foothold in New
to medical schools. She, too, had
rder to accumulate the money for
h she was well aware of the diffi-
icine, it did not diminish her desire
s a lucky strike for Emily to be
ical College in Chicago and then
eveland Medical College. Elizabeth
for her "to walk the wards" of
eth had not been able to secure
beth would not be excluded from
doctors considered embarrassing
bsented herself when Dr. Willard
ic patients.
ed herself after her older sister,
es between them. Emily did not
ained shy and isolated as long as
ons, dreamt dreams and promoted
through," declares a medical his-
m Europe Emily brought back a
impson, Queen Victoria's obstetri-
firmly believe that it would be
nd anyone better qualified than

as again rejected for a dispensary
her own small dispensary in order
and eventually for other women
st step was very modest, a one-
the slum district of New York.
e to her she went to them, day
the midst of the most unsanitary
ker friends contributed financial
other necessary articles. In 1855

Dr. Stephen Smith, a classmate of Elizabeth Blackwell's at Geneva, who later became commissioner of health in New York City, befriended Dr. Jacobi by encouraging the newcomer to translate a series of German articles for his *Journal of Medicine*.[26] However, Dr. Marie E. Zakrzewska, who was professor of obstetrics and diseases of women at the newly founded New England Female Medical College, was supposed to have been called a foreigner[27] by Dr. Samuel Gregory, the dean, who avowedly did not like her. But there may have been other reasons for his antipathy.

If women comprised 4 to 8 percent of physicians in America,[28] the number of those of foreign birth can be at most a small fraction of the total. The majority of women applicants seem mostly to have been native Americans and women from families of good standing. A medical historian states: "In general the women who graduated from these schools [the women's medical schools] were of middle or upper-class background...many were daughters or wives of physicians; also in order to work as missionaries."[29]

As previously stated, the first woman to receive the degree of medicine from an American or European school was Elizabeth Blackwell (1821–1910). The time was 1849; five years later her sister Emily (1826–1910) earned her degree. Both women were born near Bristol in England into a cultured, well-to-do family. The father, a dissident in religion and a Whig in politics, owned a sugar refinery. In 1832 it caught fire and though Samuel Blackwell's friends offered him money with which to rebuild it, he preferred emigration. Elizabeth was eleven and Emily six when the family, accompanied by servants, four aunts and the children's governess, departed for the United States. There were eventually nine children in the family, of whom the last one was born in the United States.

Samuel Blackwell might have been successful with the new sugar refinery he established in New York if not for the Panic of 1837, which caused widespread economic havoc and forced him out of business. Having heard that Cincinnati was a blooming commercial and cultural center, the father decided to try his fortune there. But the refinery he started failed to flourish and he soon fell victim to the variant of the ague, so destructive of Europeans. When he died, he left his family nothing but the house in which they lived.

Elizabeth was twenty-two when she left for the South and a teaching job in the heart of the tobacco country and the slave system. There her sense of justice was continuously outraged at the treatment of slaves. For instance, one Sunday morning she watched a Negro in dirty rags standing beneath a veranda and imploring his mistress for a clean shirt. She sent him away. At the same time the planter's daughter appeared in all her Sunday finery to ride off to church. But in her awareness that critical remarks could serve no purpose but to antagonize, Elizabeth remained bland and calm, no matter what unfairness she witnessed. Her self-control proved a valuable asset, for in later years her ability to avoid provoking her male colleagues became a conspicuous characteristic. Dignity was another of her outstanding features; it was said that "dignity sat on her like a crown."

Her idealistic nature, reinforced by a reformer's instincts, suggested a career in medicine. She admitted she had always hated everything connected with the body and that the very thought of treating ailments filled her with disgust.[30] But the more difficult a medical career appeared, the more she was tempted. The idea that the study of medicine would involve a struggle to overcome prejudice against women and also make it possible for women to be able to consult physicians of their own sex determined her to go ahead.

When she entered the Geneva Medical College in 1847 she was too preoccupied with her studies to care about being stared at and avoided by the townspeople. When the professor of anatomy suggested that she absent herself from the session on the organs of reproduction, because it would embarrass her and would divert his attention and that of the others, she replied by letter:

> . . . it was a great mystery to her that a profound student of science and especially a teacher of the wonderful mechanism of the human body, could have his mind diverted from a subject so absorbingly interesting by the mere presence of a student in a woman's dress.[31]

Medical College. During th with preparing a course of of girls, which created co and brought her the beginn lectures were published in number of books she was t

While Elizabeth was atte York, Emily was applying had a stint of teaching in her medical training. Thoug culties facing women in med to become a doctor. It wa accepted first at Rush Med to be allowed to finish at Cl was able to gain admission Bellevue, a privilege Elizab for herself. But while Eliza any lecture or demonstration to women, Emily tactfully a Parker exhibited his syphili

While she clearly pattern there were distinct differenc make friends easily and rem she lived. "Elizabeth had vis projects; Emily carried them torian.[35] Upon her return fr testimonial from Dr. James S cian, in which he stated: "I difficult or impossible to fi yourself."[36]

In 1853, when Elizabeth w position, she decided to open to create an outlet for hersel doctors and students. Her fi room facility in the heart of When patients could not con or night, delivering babies in surroundings. Again her Qua support as well as linens and she had to close it for lack of funds, but she knew it would only be temporary. By then she had made the acquaintance of a young German woman, Marie E. Zakrzewska, who had made a spectacular start in Berlin, but had lost her post as professor of obstetrics at the Royal Hospital in Berlin through the jealousy and ill will of the male staff. Dr. Blackwell advised Marie Zakrzewska to seek a medical degree in the United States, then secured acceptance for her at the Cleveland Medical College.

What she foresaw was a triumvirate of women physicians working in an expanded dispensary. Emily was due to return from Europe soon and if Marie could gain a medical degree, there would be a staff of three doctors.

Two years later in 1856 Marie Zakrzewska returned with a medical degree to find the infirmary project bogged down for lack of money. But surprisingly "Dr. Zak" proved such a good fund raiser in Boston that a house on Bleecker Street was purchased and converted for use as a hospital. Dr. Emily was the surgeon, Dr. Marie the resident physician, and Dr. Elizabeth the director. During the first seven months the Infirmary cared for almost a thousand cases,[37] and during 1858 over 3,000 patients were treated.[38]

By 1858 the Infirmary was doing so well that Dr. Elizabeth felt she could leave for England to secure accreditation to the Medical Register of Great Britain, from which she would have been excluded after 1858 because of a recent change in the law.

When she returned she found that Dr. Zak had accepted a post as professor of obstetrics at the New England Female Medical College in Boston. Also the Infirmary had grown so rapidly that the purchase of an enlarged hospital was being contemplated.

Before such plans could crystallize the Civil War broke out. The matter of instructing nurses became a most urgent project. At a meeting called by the Doctors Blackwell, a Women's Central Relief Association was set up and from it developed the United States Sanitary Aid Association. Dr. Elizabeth selected the nurses who were to be trained at the Infirmary, at Bellevue and at New York Hospital, before being sent on to Dorothy

Dix, whom President Lincoln had appointed Matron General. Emily wrote a monograph, "The Selection and Training of Nurses," which was followed by thousands of Sanitary Commission Auxiliaries through the country.[39] When the Draft Riots broke out in New York City in 1863, only a miracle prevented an attack on the Infirmary, where Negro patients were being treated. In 1868 the Women's Medical College of the New York Infirmary opened with fifteen students.[40] The new medical school embodied many advances in the training of physicians, which put it ahead of many of the schools for males. The training period was extended to three years and the annual term was lengthened. Entrance examinations were required, ten years before they became compulsory by state law. A special examining board of physicians from the outside passed on the qualifications of the students. Above all, ample clinical experience was provided.

The school got off to such a good start that in 1869 Elizabeth Blackwell left for England, never again to return to professional work in America. This is why the question is sometimes raised whether she is to be considered English or American. But the claim that her contribution to American medicine was most noteworthy has never been impugned. As for Emily Blackwell, America was "home" to her. Elizabeth continued to see patients in England, but her main value was in opening the medical profession to the women of England.

The last time Elizabeth Blackwell returned to America was in 1906 when she was eighty-five. By then Emily Blackwell, too, had retired. Their legacy is the New York Infirmary, in existence to this day, rather than the Women's Medical College, which lasted for thirty-one years until Cornell University agreed to make the study of medicine coeducational.

Despite her ties to her family in America, Elizabeth Blackwell returned to her home in Hastings by the Sea, attended by a daughter she had adopted as a five-year-old. She died at eighty-nine in her native land.

Though it was Elizabeth Blackwell who began the Infirmary and the College, it was Emily who gave forty-three years of her life to the Infirmary and thirty-one to the Women's Medical

College as teacher, administrator, member of the Board of Trustees, and dean. The physicians she trained developed unusual careers in the United States and as missionaries in various corners of the world. One eminent physician was Elise Strang L'Esperance, daughter of Dr. Albert Strang, professor of anatomy at the College. She was responsible for establishing the first cancer prevention clinic in the world at the Women's Infirmary.

Dr. Emily did not possess the tact that was an outstanding characteristic of her sister, and consequently was not always easy to work with. For instance, when Dr. Mary Corinne Putnam, the first woman to graduate from L'Ecole de Médecin in Paris, assumed her teaching duties at the Women's Medical College in accordance to a promise she had made to Elizabeth Blackwell, she immediately had a disagreement with Dr. Emily. Dr. Putnam, who soon thereafter married Dr. Abraham Jacobi, appears to have been no more malleable than Emily Blackwell, but Elizabeth was able to mollify both of them. "She [Emily] had the misfortune of being Dr. Elizabeth's sister,"[41] remarks Dr. Lovejoy. Emily was aware that her sister outshone her—not as a physician—and that she aroused more affection. It is significant that when Emily retired, she clung to a friend who had been a colleague. In 1908 Emily wrote to Elizabeth: "The Infirmary is thriving. It now has 100 beds, a large out practice and quite a staff of women connected with it. Your work has borne fruit in many ways."[42] Not "our work," but "your work."

Emily always accepted changes more willingly and was far more inclined to move forward with the times than Elizabeth, who had always objected to vaccination, vivisection, hence to medical research based on animal experimentation. To the end of her life Elizabeth would vaccinate children only on request and remained a rabid anti-vivisectionist, even withholding her approval of Pasteur's work, because she considered his research "ethically unjustifiable." Emily, on the other hand, accepted vivisection as necessary and even defended it against her sister.

The two sisters, who had worked to make women physicians acceptable throughout the world, died in 1910, Emily preceding Elizabeth by three months.

Among the four women who are considered pioneers in American medicine, Doctors Elizabeth and Emily Blackwell and Dr. Marie E. Zakrzewska were foreign-born; the fourth, Dr. Ann Preston, who founded and developed the Woman's Medical College of Philadelphia, was an American of long lineage and Quaker antecedents.

Dr. Marie E. Zakrzewska, "Dr. Zak" for short (1829–1902), was born in Prussia, but was of Polish background. Her mother had trained as a midwife at the renowned Royal Hospital Charité in Berlin. Marie, who had assisted her mother since her teens, registered at the age of twenty for the same two-year course. She was considered so able that upon graduation at twenty-two she was appointed chief accoucheuse at the Royal Hospital and professor of midwifery, in charge of training students.

But when Dr. Joseph Schmidt, the director of the school for midwives and her protector, died, the jealousy and the intrigues of the male staff forced her to resign. Remembering the first report of a woman's medical college in Philadelphia which Dr. Schmidt had shown her—she had no idea of the difficulties by which the new little school was beset—she concluded there was a good chance she could arouse an interest in a hospital for women. Against the wishes of her father she decided on emigration.

America proved a severe disappointment to her. She found that "doctresses" or "she-doctors" were considered of the "lowest rank," no better than abortionists. After putting out a sign and finding herself completely ignored, she realized she would not be able to support herself. Her sister, who had accompanied her to America, took a job as a seamstress, while she was forced to subsist on homework, producing knitted articles she then tried to sell to the Broadway stores.

Without Elizabeth Blackwell's help Marie Zakrzewska might never have been enabled to enter a medical school in the United States. Elizabeth became her preceptor, taught her English, then secured admission for her at Cleveland Medical College, as well as credit for tuition fees for an indefinite time and monetary help from a group of women dedicated to easing the path of women preparing to become doctors.

At the Cleveland Medical College, which she entered in 1854 at the age of twenty-five, she found herself one of four women among forty-two male students, who made no secret of not liking the presence of women. "Some of the professors," she noted, "acted as if we did not exist." The male students petitioned the college to expel the women after the first term, but this the authorities refused to do. However, in 1856 a new policy of exclusion went into effect.

The opening in 1850 of the Women's Medical College of Pennsylvania had been the signal for male physicians to intensify their efforts to keep women out of medicine. The Philadelphia County Medical Society not only barred women from membership, but forbade their male members to teach at the newly founded school for women, or to consult with women physicians, or with any male members teaching there.[43] Even ministers supported the boycott, because they refused to participate at commencement exercises.

In 1856, having received the degree of M.D., the newly minted doctor returned to New York to keep her promise to Dr. Elizabeth Blackwell to work for two years without remuneration at the dispensary for which Dr. Blackwell had secured a charter from the State Legislature. Dr. Zak became resident physician, housekeeper, and instructor to students who came to gather bedside experience.

It was while Dr. Elizabeth was in England that Dr. Zak received an offer to organize a clinical department and to become professor of obstetrics at the New England Female Medical College in Boston where midwives, nurses, and women physicians were to be trained.

In this new post she was confronted by new problems. She found herself obstructed in trying to elevate the standards for medical students. Her refusal to certify those whose work she considered unsatisfactory made enemies for her and she was forced to resign.

By then she had influential friends and in 1862 a new plan was proposed to found the New England Hospital for Women, later known as the New England Hospital. Its purpose was to train physicians and nurses. Again Dr. Zak became the moving spirit; she gathered around her a corps of dedicated assistants who became outstanding physicians.

In addition she developed such a flourishing practice that she had to get a horse and buggy to make her calls. That she was a gifted practitioner was recognized by Dr. Elizabeth Blackwell, who wrote to her: "You are a natural doctor and your best work will always be in the full exercise of direct medical work. . . ." She also admitted: "You know I am different from you, not being a natural doctor. . . ."[44]

By 1872 a new and much enlarged hospital was erected. Male physicians, including Dr. Henry I. Bowditch, always a supporter of women physicians, accepted posts as consulting physicians. By the time Dr. Zak died in her seventy-third year the hospital had become a large institution with surgical, maternity, and dispensary wings. By mid-twentieth century it was still staffed exclusively by women. Men were to be found only on the consulting staff.[45]

A pupil of Dr. Zak's at the Female Medical College of Boston who had interned at the New York Infirmary for Women was Dr. Mary Harris Thompson, a former schoolteacher. In 1870 she established the Women's Medical College of Chicago. From this school another outstanding pioneer physician, Maria Josepha Mergler (1851–1901), graduated in 1879. Born in Bavaria, she was brought to Illinois as a child. Her father, a physician, encouraged his growing daughter to assist him. She became a high school teacher first, but did not find the work sufficiently absorbing. She entered the Women's Medical College of Chicago.

Upon graduation she found the path still obstructed and decided on postgraduate work in Zurich. Upon her return she was appointed to the faculty of the school from which she had graduated, was soon placed in charge of gynecology, and invited to join several other hospital staffs. Upon the death of Mary Harris Thompson she was appointed head physician and surgeon at the Chicago Women's Medical College.[46] Later she became dean of faculty. When she died of pernicious anemia in 1901, she was a well-known and highly regarded physician who had contributed many articles on medical subjects. A French medical journal remarked after her death that "in all Europe no comparable woman surgeon could be found."[47]

The changed pattern of immigration after 1882 that brought a huge influx of Eastern and Southern Europeans can also be seen, though not as a mirror image, in the ethnic composition of those who in the next two decades sought admission to America's medical schools. The largest number of arrivals in the late nineteenth and early twentieth centuries were agricultural laborers from Southern Italy and Sicily; people from the various Balkan states; Jews from Russia, Poland, Austria-Hungary, most of them so poor that they were close to destitution. Among Italians from the North there were said to have been several women physicians; one who had received a medical degree from the University of Rome; another from the University of Vienna. There were also several of the immigrant generation who entered American medical schools. But accurate records are unavailable.[48]

The majority of the Slavs consisted of peasants, shepherds, and day laborers; predictably their daughters were not likely to have entertained the ambition to become doctors. But the Jews belonged to a different category of immigrants. Among them were the most ambitious, tenacious, and culture-hungry people to be found anywhere. Though the exclusionary practices in Russia and in Poland had been harsh and deliberately intended to keep the Jews in subservient positions (policies toward Jews in Austria-Hungary were more lenient), it had not been possible to exclude all from existing educational benefits. Consequently some young men and fewer young women had received the beginnings of a classical education before emigrating, making it possible to dream of continuing their studies in America. Even those who had received no public schooling in their natal countries, once they reached American soil and realized there were no impediments that could not be overcome, began to make astoundingly ambitious plans.

Because the study of medicine required lengthy preparation before admission to medical school and a long period of financial dependence, it was undoubtedly a deterrent, especially for women. Parents and relatives were more likely to be willing to make sacrifices for sons than for daughters. The woman who had set her sights on a medical career had to be prepared to make all manner of sacrifices, including marriage. We know that hundreds of men achieved the goal of an M.D. for within less than thirty years—between 1882 and 1910—the number of Jewish doctors on New York's East Side is said to have doubled. Undoubtedly it was a rocky road for most. Not everyone who required financial help was fortunate to enlist outside support as did Doctor Anna Kleegman who was helped by a subsidy from the Upjohn Company (manufacturers of pharmaceutical products).[49]

Among the early women physicians many turned to obstetrics, a field in which the midwife was regnant, or to gynecology which, like all other specialties, was dominated by male physicians. But they also began to turn to new specialties—pediatrics, for instance, which the "Forty-Eighter" Dr. Abraham Jacobi had developed into a new field during the second half of the nineteenth century. According to a recent study pediatrics attracts the greatest number of women physicians and obstetrics and gynecology appears next to the lowest.[50] The M.D.s of the first decades of the twentieth century also began to turn to problems in public health and social hygiene. By 1969, 14.3 percent of all women M.D.s were engaged in activities not involving direct patient care—such as education, research, and administration, in contrast to male physicians of whom only 10.3 percent are similarly occupied.[51]

Two physicians who arrived in America in the 1880s as immigrants and received their M.D.s at the turn of the century may be considered "role-models" for their time. Dr. Marie K. Formad (1867–1941)[52] and Dr. Rachel Slobodensky Yarros (1869–1945)[53] were both born in Russia. Marie Formad came with her mother and a younger brother in 1883 at the suggestion of an older brother who had preceded them. He had studied medicine and became professor of pathology at the University of Pennsylvania. She entered the Woman's Medical College of Pennsylvania within a month after arrival, which means she must have had a Gymnasium education or the equivalent. Dr. Formad is said to have learned English concurrently with her freshman medical subjects and is supposed to have studied with the aid of a dictionary. She practiced as a surgeon and gynecologist in Philadelphia for fifty-two years before her career came to an end.

In advancing the frontiers of medicine for women, Dr. Rachel Slobodensky Yarros took a large leap forward. Enrolling at the Women's Medical College of Philadelphia at twenty-four, she interned at the New England Hospital for Women which Dr. Zakrzewska had founded, then enrolled for graduate study in pediatrics at the New York Infirmary for Women and at the Reese Hospital in Chicago.

She served as professor of obstetrics at the University of Illinois for twenty years before she received an appointment as professor of social hygiene. She pioneered in offering the first premarital consultation service in Chicago. Later she became associated with the United States Public Health Service. She traveled widely throughout the world to study health and welfare conditions and found time to write *The Modern Woman and Sex*.

A third foreign-born physician of whom it can be said that she further enlarged the trail for others to follow was Dr. Sophie Rabinoff (1889–1957).[54] She was a native of Poland. Graduating in 1913 from Woman's Medical College of Pennsylvania, she went overseas in 1917 to Palestine with a Hadassah unit that was attached to the British forces under Field Marshal Allenby. Upon her return she practiced general medicine and for a time was attached to the Health Center of the ILGWU, where she was considered a "very good doctor."[55] In 1934 Dr. Rabinoff turned to public health. Subsequently she became health officer of the Tremont-Fordham-Riverdale districts of the Bronx. In 1944 she received the degree of M.S. in Public Health from the School of Public Health and Administration at Columbia University. A teaching post followed. When she retired in 1956, a year before her death, it was as professor of Public Health at the New York Medical College.

The careers of two physicians who were sisters illustrate the pull the medical profession was apt to exert on the foreign-born. It was not unusual for several sons of one family to become doctors. Two sisters who did were Anna[56] and Sophie Kleegman[57] Born in the Ukraine, both girls were brought to America in 1905—Anna when she was twelve and Sophie when she was five. Anna (1893–1970) had been exposed briefly to a Russian school, but since early childhood had always dreamed of being able to attend school in America, where, she was told, no hindrances would be put in her path.

It took her only five years to catch up and to finish high school and three more years to graduate from Cornell University, where she was elected to Phi Beta Kappa in the junior year. Within another three years she had earned the M.D. degree from Cornell University Medical School. During World War I she became a surgeon for the American Army.[58]

In addition to practicing as a gynecologist and obstetrician, she was one of the first physicians to do marriage counseling and to become interested in planned parenthood and in voluntary sterilization. When she was seventy, she started to treat drug addicts.[59] She also found time to write—*The Mature Woman* and *It's Never Too Late for Love.*

Her sister, Dr. Sophie Kleegman (1900–1971), was from beginning to end a product of American schools. After graduating from New York University Medical School in 1924, she became within five years a member of the faculty of the New York University School of Medicine and the staff of Bellevue Hospital. There she worked with Dr. Papanicolau in perfecting the test for cervical cancer.[60] She also directed the infertility clinic at Bellevue for many years.[61]

She has the distinction of having been the first woman president of the New York University Medical Alumni Association, the president of New York City's Medical Women's Association, and of having been elected to membership in the New York Academy of Medicine.

During the pre-World War II decades, particularly during the thirties when Europe was being converted into a charnel house and emigration became the only means by which to escape certain death, the United States received a large inflow of physicians and scientists, some of whom had achieved world renown. Among them were practitioners in all the recognized

medical specialties as well as a new category of physicians—
the psychiatrists and psychoanalysts.

The influx of these new specialists encouraged an ever increasing tendency to apply psychiatric techniques to a variety
of somatic diseases. As Dr. Helene Deutsch, a graduate of the
University of Vienna and one of Freud's earliest disciples,
admits: "With the flight to the United States of great numbers
of refugees . . . the application of psychoanalysis to educational
and social problems found a much larger field of operation in
America."[62] She herself had been analyzed by Freud, had
been a member of the "Vienna Psychoanalytic Society" and the
"Vienna Training Institute" and had always had Freud's backing. While Freud chose to resettle in London, she and her
husband, Felix Deutsch, emigrated to Boston. There both became members of the Boston Psychoanalytical Institute. The
Felix and Helene Deutsch Prize, established by the institute in
their honor, attests to their reputation in the field of psychoanalysis.

An individual of immense impact on the field of psychoanalysis
was Dr. Karen Horney.[63] A graduate of the University of
Berlin, she came to the United States in 1932 at the age of
forty-seven on the invitation of Dr. Franz Alexander, head
of the Institute for Psychoanalysis in Chicago, to become its
assistant director. After two years in Chicago, she transferred
to New York where she taught at the New York Psychoanalytical
Institute from 1934–1941 and then founded the American Institute for Psychoanalysis. She is the author of several books,
including *The Neurotic Personality of Our Time* (1937) and
New Ways in Psychoanalysis (1939). When she died twenty
years after she had begun her work in America, the institute had
become one of the most outstanding centers in the United States.

A somewhat different contribution was made by Dr. Frieda
Fromm-Reichman (1890–1957),[64] former wife of Erich Fromm.
An expert on schizophrenia, she had been on the staff of the
Königsberg Hospital for brain-injured soldiers during World
War I. She also worked with brain-injured soldiers in Frankfurt
and taught at the Frankfurt Psychoanalytical Institute.

When she came to the United States in 1934 in her mid-forties, she became connected with the Chestnut Lodge Sanatorium in Rockville, Maryland, where she was consultant and supervisor of psychotherapy. She remained there for the rest of her life, serving at the same time as chairman of the faculty of the Washington School of Psychiatry.

Dr. Catherine Lodyjensky was one of the later refugees of World War II and one whose family broke its ties with its homeland twice. The first time they escaped, it was from Russia. After being imprisoned by the Bolsheviks, the father, who had been a member of the municipal government of the city of Leningrad and a liberal who favored democratic reforms rather than communism, was exiled to Siberia. Leaving his family behind, he managed in 1922 to flee to Paris. Two years later his wife, a practicing physician in Leningrad, followed him with their two young daughters.

In Paris the father established connections with some of his former Menshevik friends through whom he secured employment. The mother could not practice medicine, because in France medical practitioners had to be French citizens and between 1928 and World War II French citizenship was particularly hard to achieve.[65] The girls were brought up as French rather than as Russian children. After finishing at the lycée Catherine entered the medical school of the Sorbonne.

In 1940 when Catherine Lodyjensky was within a year of receiving the medical degree, a new danger crystallized, the imminent takeover of Paris by the German army. The father was aware that he was on the German blacklist. Though the family was not Jewish, he was able to get the Jewish Labor Committee to help in securing an emergency visa for the United States. Two days after they departed the Germans entered Paris.

In America Catherine Lodyjensky managed to secure admission to Montreal University Medical School, but she could not immediately accept, because she had only an emergency visa which would not have permitted her to reenter the United States on completion of her medical training. It took her two years to secure a permanent visa, during which time she worked as a substitute intern at Beekman Hospital.

At the University of Montreal she was fortunate to enlist the help of the Association of University Women of Montreal. After graduation she returned to New York to intern at Willard Parker Hospital, a center for contagious diseases in which she was interested. She fulfilled residency requirements at the New York Infirmary, where she rose quickly to become Director of the Pediatric Service.

Dr. Lodyjensky considered returning to France, but she is happy that she did not. A bouncy, cheerful woman with a reassuring smile, she characterizes herself as a "good foot soldier" in medicine. She is connected with St. Luke's Hospital, which is affiliated with the Columbia Medical Center. At St. Luke's she does bedside teaching in addition to treating patients.

Comparing her career with those of her French classmates, she asserts she has reason to feel that her career has developed more satisfactorily in the United States than it could have in France. She is glad she made the decision to live and work in the United States.

Before the onset of the twentieth century most women would probably have been willing to concede that women are less interested than men in abstract studies and that science might therefore be better left to men. When interest in the various branches of science began to accelerate at the beginning of the nineteenth century, it was universally accepted that superior mental equipment was the sine qua non for a career in science. What chance then for the "weaker sex"? The universities were in accord with this thinking, for when women scientists began to appear on the scene—women as thoroughly trained as men—they were, as we shall see, taken on in positions subordinate to men, if they were taken on at all. Today no one would dare say aloud that science should be left to males, or that women are not likely to come up to the accomplishments of men. Their outstanding success in the various fields of pure and applied science has put to rest the shibboleth that science is best served by males.

In the latter half of the present century the number of

women in all branches of science has increased immensely. There has been a sharp rise in college-trained women everywhere, and in America are included women of native as well as of foreign birth. Two women who secured their education in Europe, but developed their careers in America, have received Nobel prizes. With thousands of women working in research laboratories throughout the nation, it is not rash to predict that there will be others.

Among the earliest women scientists who arrived in America fully trained was Dr. Lydia Rabinowitch-Kempner (1871–1935).[66] A bacteriologist and a biologist, she was a younger contemporary of Marie Sklodovska Curie. As the daughter of a Jewish family in Kovno, Lithuania, she undoubtedly experienced a type of discrimination similar to the harassment practiced on Marie Sklodovska, whose family were Polish patriots resisting Russification. Both attended government gymnasia. While Marie Sklodovska's inclinations were toward mathematics and physics, Lydia Rabinowitch's were toward the biological sciences.

She had studied at the universities of Zurich and Berne in Switzerland, receiving the Ph.D. degree in 1894. After working at the Institute of Infectious Diseases in Berlin under Robert Koch, who was a physician, bacteriologist, and would receive the Nobel Prize in 1905, she came to America and gave the very first course in bacteriology at the Woman's Medical College of Pennsylvania. She also taught biochemistry. Eventually she returned to the Koch Institute. She was a pioneer in the study of plague, human and animal, TB, sleeping sickness, and other parasitic diseases.

A woman who as part of a husband and wife team made a contribution of the greatest significance to the understanding of the processes in the human body is Dr. Gerty Theresa Cori (1896–1957).[67] She is the second woman Nobel Prize winner and the first naturalized American citizen to receive this recognition. The first husband and wife team to be so honored were Marie and Pierre Curie. Doctors Carl and Gerty Cori received the Nobel Prize in medicine and physiology in 1947, sharing it with Dr. A. B. Houssay of Buenos Aires, whose independent researches on metabolism had meshed with those of the Cori team.[68]

Since their student days Gerty and Carl Cori had worked together at the medical school of the University of Prague, where both were medical students. In her first year of medical school she became attracted to biochemistry and began collaborating with her future husband. Their marriage took place when they received M.D. degrees, whereupon she spent a year at the Children's Hospital in Vienna and he as an assistant in pharmacology at the University of Graz in Austria. Their determination to devote themselves to medical research led to the decision to emigrate to America.

Dr. Carl Cori left Austria in 1922 to take up a position as biochemist at the Institute for the Study of Malignant Diseases in Buffalo. He went alone, but he soon found a job for his wife as assistant pathologist and she followed him.

In Buffalo they concentrated on finding a relationship between cancer and carbohydrate metabolism. While this work led to no final solutions, it yielded some new observations. In 1931 both transferred to Washington University in St. Louis. He was appointed full professor of pharmacology; she, research assistant in pharmacology. Eventually she would be appointed associate professor and finally full professor.

At Washington University they continued their concentration on carbohydrate metabolism, the chemical process by which the body burns sugar and starches. It involved the study of enzymes which are the catalyzers inducing chemical changes in the body. In the process of their work they discovered two new enzymes and isolated the enzyme that acts on glycogen and which is essential for the conversion of glycogen into glucose. The discovery of this enzyme, called phosphorylase, brought them the Nobel Prize in 1947.

Many honors and awards followed—the Squibb award in endocrinology in 1947, the Garvan Gold Medal in 1948, which is given only to women, the sugar research prize of the National Academy of Science in 1950, and honorary degrees.

With her husband she was the author of 150 to 200 scientific papers. She remained at work even after she was stricken by fatal illness.

The second naturalized American woman to be chosen for the Nobel Prize was Dr. Maria Goeppert-Mayer (1906–1972),[69] a theoretical physicist; she was also the second woman to receive recognition for her work in physics, exactly sixty years after Madame Curie received the award for isolating radium. Dr. Goeppert-Mayer's award was in recognition of her work on the structure of the atomic nucleus. In addition, she was known for her work in quantum electrodynamics, spectroscopy, statistical mechanics, and crystal physics.

She was born in Kattowitz, before the region became Polish territory, to a family distinguished for a long line of university professors. In Göttingen, where she enrolled for graduate studies, the influence of Max Born, Nobel Laureate, drew her into the field of physics. After a period in Cambridge, England, she received the Ph.D. from Göttingen in 1930.

An American Rockefeller fellow, Edward Joseph Mayer, was also studying at Göttingen. After marrying him in 1930, she went with him to America, where he was to join the faculty of Johns Hopkins. But not she, for in those days the chance that a wife of a faculty member would also receive an appointment was remote. But she was permitted to work in the laboratory, for which she received the title of volunteer associate. In 1939 her husband became assistant professor at Columbia University and she a lecturer at Columbia and at Sarah Lawrence. During this period she also did wartime research under the Laureate Harold Urey.

In 1946, when Edward Mayer was called to the University of Chicago, she received an appointment as professor in the physics department of the University of Chicago, also at the Enrico Fermi Institute for Nuclear Studies and as senior physicist at the Argonne National Laboratory. From 1948 on, she worked on what is described as a "new concept of the basic structure of the [atomic] nucleus"—that protons which are positive charges, and neutrons which are electrically neutral, are grouped in concentric shells.[70] The theory was that the nucleus consisted of layers.

Dr. Mayer shared the Nobel Prize with two other scientists:

Dr. Eugene Wigner of Princeton, the Hungarian-born mathematical physicist, who received half of the award. The other half was shared by Dr. Maria Goeppert-Mayer and Dr. J. Hans D. Jensen of the University of Heidelberg, who had arrived at the same conclusions as Dr. Mayer. They met in 1950 and wrote a book jointly on their theories.

In 1960 Doctors Edward Mayer and Maria Goeppert-Mayer joined the University of California at San Diego, he in chemistry, she in physics. When she died at La Jolla in 1972 of a heart attack, she was the author of several textbooks for graduate students and coauthor of many scientific articles and monographs.

That the immigrant experience could be no less difficult for trained professionals than for the most unskilled of immigrants is proved by the situation in which Dr. Valentina Suntzeff (1891–   ),[71] a physician trained in Moscow, and her husband, a mechanical engineer, found themselves upon their arrival in the United States in 1923. They had fled the Bolshevik revolution and had lived in Harbin, China, for two years. They had found Chinese culture "too alien."

When they arrived in San Francisco they had twelve dollars between them and could speak no English. Because of their "acquired habit of eating," as she puts it, both were forced to accept the first jobs they could find. She went into a factory manufacturing coats and for two weeks pulled basting threads for eight hours each day. After two weeks she was promoted to a sewing machine which a "kind" Italian girl taught her to operate. Her husband became an unskilled laborer. Later he found a job as a mechanical engineer in St. Louis. His brother, who had been a medical student in Russia, had a similar experience when he was forced to work as a longshoreman before returning to medical studies and earning the M.D. from Northwestern University.

Dr. Valentina Suntzeff, who was born in Kazan, knew at the age of nine that she wanted to be a doctor like her father, but when she was ready for medical school women were still banned from schools attended by men. (By then the study of medicine in the United States had been coeducational for more than two decades.) She entered a school for women, but within a few years medical schools in Russia also became coeducational. Otherwise, she states, there was no discrimination against women doctors. "Men came to women doctors as they would have come to men doctors." To her astonishment she noted that in America:

People do not trust the competence of women doctors, preferring men instead. Another surprise was the attitude of the women doctors. They were afraid to compete with men physicians. If a woman doctor married another physician, the woman would usually play a secondary role professionally. . . .

It also surprised her to learn that there was a separate medical association for women doctors. In Russia, she states flatly, "no such organization would have existed."

As a physician in Russia she had worked in a hospital connected with a big ammunition plant, had been the head of an isolation hospital during World War I, and during the civil war following the Revolution was placed in charge of an evacuation train making its way through Russia and Siberia. In China she worked in a railroad hospital. Undoubtedly she would have been able to reenter her profession in America, if not for her inability to pick up the English language. She admits, "I was generally quick to understand the principles of physics, math or biological sciences . . . but learning a language was always a laborious chore."

When her husband found a job as mechanical engineer in St. Louis, she and their only child followed him. But though she applied for an internship and made various efforts to get back into her profession, she found herself consistently rejected. She never practiced medicine again, but found her way into medical research through serendipity. At a party she met three Russian scientists who were working as a research team at the University of Washington Medical School, and they invited her to join them. They were doing research on cancer.

She was so delighted with her job in the Pathology Department of the Washington University School of Medicine that when it became too hot for the mice in the laboratories of the university (there was no air conditioning then), she transferred the mice to the basement of her home, where they would be more comfortable and she could continue her research.

After the retirement of the chief of the Department of Pathology, she accepted an offer from the Anatomy Department, where they were studying cancer of the skin. In this job she developed a special technique she derived from working in the kitchen. The results were published in 1942. To a nonscientific individual who expects from scientists only nonunderstandable conclusions, her remarks on cancer research seem startlingly commonsensical. An example is the following: "Another different aspect of cancer research is learning that at times your findings are essentially negative—that your contribution is not a productive one."

Now past eighty, she has remained active in cancer research, though in a diminished way. She is now facing the "very hard decision" whether or not to abandon her research completely.

A woman very much concerned with the prejudices encountered by women in science is Dr. Ruth Weiner,[72] chemist and chairman of the Department of Chemistry at Florida International University at Miami. The awareness of "considerable discrimination against women in chemistry at the point of graduate school admission" did not strike her until she and her husband were in the graduate program at Johns Hopkins University. She explains she didn't think about it then, accepting it as "a normal state of affairs."

At the conclusion of their studies her husband received an appointment at the University of Denver, but she could find a position only as research associate at the University of Colorado Medical School, a job which carried no tenure and was paid out of grant funds. The excuses she received palpably smacked of sex discrimination. No patient Griselda, she was not willing to hover uncomplainingly in the background, biding her time until she and her special competence could no longer be ignored. Thus, when a position presented itself at a small women's college, she accepted with alacrity and was told she was "a great success" for having found a tenured teaching position, even though the college was not "first rate." It was a satisfaction

to her to be able to introduce the chemistry major for the first
time and to encourage girls who had never striven for more
than to become laboratory technicians to aspire to professional careers.

Dr. Weiner was born in Vienna of professional parents. Her
father was a physician and a zoologist; her mother, a trained
biologist. Both grandfathers had been physicians. Because she
speaks of their "forced emigration" (after Austria's Anschluss),
it may be assumed the family fled from the persecutions of the
Hitlerian era. Educated at the Baltimore public schools, she
chose graduate work at Johns Hopkins because it seemed
"difficult and challenging" and that was the kind of situation
in which she wanted to be. It was after she had completed
her graduate courses that, as she says, "the doors began to
close to me" and she became aware of "a very restrictive and
overt sex discrimination." An outspoken woman, she mentions
candidly what others, particularly women of a previous generation, might have felt, but preferred to gloss over or to leave
unsaid.

Though married since she was eighteen and mother of four
children, with considerable professional demands to fulfill, she
admits she felt "somewhat unfulfilled" in her work. Consequently
she became involved in the conservation movement. As a scientist she knew she could supply valuable help to people concerned with the preservation of the environment. The group
she founded became more and more important and she found
herself appearing before committees of the U.S. Congress, helping to write the Colorado Air Pollution Control Act, and going
on speaking tours for the Conservation Foundation. It was
after a luncheon for a clean air group at Miami that the Dean
of the College of the Arts and Sciences of Florida International
University offered her the chairmanship of the Department
of Chemistry.

A job in Miami when her husband had a satisfactory position
as professor of chemistry in Denver posed a new problem.
Was he to give up his job and by following her be placed
in the same position in which she had found herself when she
could not obtain a satisfactory connection in the area in which
her husband was located? The decision they made was to lead

separate lives—he would remain in Denver with two children and she would take the other two with her to Miami.

Dr. Weiner is still at the beginning of her career which she admits has become very satisfying to her. In her new field she has the opportunity to make a two-pronged contribution—in conservation and by continuing to break down prejudice against women in her particular professional field.

One point remains to be stressed. The number of foreign-born scientists cannot even be conjectured, because it is hard to ascertain places of birth. This indifference to an individual's origin proves, if proof is sought, that the disadvantage of foreign birth was at no time and in no field of endeavor a real obstacle to the realization of one's ambition. The only place from which the nonnative was automatically barred was the Presidency of the United States.

CHAPTER 12

The Joy of Making Music

No GROUP OF NEWCOMERS ILLUSTRATES MORE CLEARLY THAN
musical artists what a remarkable contribution was made by
the foreign-born to the cultural life of America. In this field
the accomplishments of women are no less significant than
those of men. So many women have captured unique places
as singers, virtuoso performers, and as teachers of the musical
arts (especially the piano), that if only the most important
were to be listed, it would still make a long catalogue of
names. While there are fewer women performers than men,
in terms of talent the women are fully equal to their male
colleagues. With the exception of Caruso, Toscanini, and a
few others, even greater veneration has been heaped on some
women artists than on men.

It is natural for musicians to become metamorphosed into
internationalists, at least temporarily, while their careers are
at zenith and invitations pour in from all parts of the civilized
world. Rushing about from one musical center to another, they
become accustomed to feeling at home in any of the musical
centers of Europe, the United States, or South America, though
"at home" may mean only the stages where they receive the
plaudits of the public. The pattern of their lives demands that
they gyrate between such geographically disparate places as
Copenhagen and Rome or Milan; Bayreuth, Salzburg or London;
New York, Chicago, San Francisco or Teatro de Colon in
Buenos Aires. But after spending many seasons or even a lifetime in the United States, many are drawn back to their natal
countries. Those who are only sojourners in America, accepting
the remuneration as well as the homage lavished on them year
after year, but who eventually return to the places they call
home, cannot be counted as Americans. But should they be

dismissed as merely temporary residents? Their enormous effect on the American cultural scene and the pleasure they brought to their listeners would seem to entitle them to some recognition of their contribution to the United States.

It cannot be said of all great musicians that they were "birds of passage." In addition to those who came here as fully trained, even famous performers, in expectation of larger financial benefits[1] or for reasons of prestige, there were some who were brought here by their immigrant parents, and who discovered their talents in America and started to develop them here. There are also those who came as guest performers, then sought American citizenship and spent the rest of their lives here. By becoming teachers and coaches or just enthusiastic naturalized Americans after their retirement, some artists made an especially noteworthy contribution to American life.

Let us begin by turning our attention to singers.

A notion frequently encountered is that great singers must be foreigners and that outstanding European performers will eventually be brought to the Metropolitan Opera Company in New York. Both are incorrect. Many outstanding singers were and are native Americans. Marcia Davenport mentions that Toscanini realized there are "some beautiful voices and some fine musicians (particularly, as the Maestro used to explain after he got over his surprise, those trained in the United States)."[2] Also, if one peruses a biographical dictionary[3] of musicians one notes that a large number of Europe's outstanding vocalists never came to America. They were either not invited to the "Met" or to the other opera companies (the Chicago, the San Francisco, the Manhattan)[4] or they preferred to remain in Europe. Arturo Toscanini, for example, originally turned down the invitation to transfer to the United States, but reconsidered when his friend Giulio Gatti Casazza accepted the managership of the Met. But the relationship between them was not entirely harmonious and in 1915 Toscanini resigned despite Otto H. Kahn's entreaties to remain.[5] (Kahn was Chairman of the Board.)

The earliest great singer to make an appearance in the United States was Jenny Lind. When brought here in 1850, she already had a phenomenal career in concert and opera.

Phineas Taylor Barnum, the bizarre exhibitionist of circus fame, who presented the dwarf "General Tom Thumb" to Europeans (and privately to Queen Victoria), risked a guarantee of $187,000 before the diva consented to cross the Atlantic under Barnum's management.[6] Her first performance in 1850 was in Castle Garden, where 4,000 people gathered to listen. She had an equally tumultuous reception in every other American city where she was scheduled to sing. In New York tickets were disposed of at auction and fetched as much as $225[7] a ticket. Americans were not behaving like unsophisticated yokels, for Clara Schumann, wife of the famous composer, said of her: "The Lind has a genius for song which might come to pass only once in many years . . . every tone she produces is sheer beauty."[8] Classical music was then all but unknown in America and she made her listeners swoon over arias from Donizetti, Rossini, von Weber, and such sentimental ditties as birdsongs, ballads, and folk songs. After marrying Otto Goldschmidt, a conductor and composer, she went to England to live. Though her residence in America was short, as the first singer to "make" the history books, she deserves more than passing mention.

One of the great early singers who might be considered a demi-American by virtue of the fact that as a child she lived in New York, where her father was *regisseur* of the Italian Opera Company, was Adelina Patti (1843–1919). Born in Madrid of Italian professional singer parents, she made her debut in New York at sixteen and after a tour through the United States found herself idolized in Europe as well. In 1892 she returned to sing at the Metropolitan Opera. Apparently a castle was what she desired, but America did not strike her as a suitable place for a castle, because she built one in Wales, where she died.

The Metropolitan Opera Company, founded in 1883, was an outgrowth of the Academy of Music on East 14th Street, in existence since 1849. Between 1883 and 1908, when Giulio Gatti Casazza was engaged by the Met's prime mover, Otto H. Kahn, to become its impresario, it had had several managers, the first of whom had been the musical entrepreneur, Henry E. Abbey. Two years later the company was bankrupt and James R. Roosevelt, then president of the board, invited Leopold Damrosch to organize a German Opera Company. Damrosch responded by introducing the first Wagnerian operas heard in America. Within months Damrosch died unexpectedly from pneumonia induced by overwork and was succeeded by Anton Seidl, who Germanized the company still further. It was Gatti Casazza, whose eyes were said to have been riveted on the cash register, who put the institution firmly on its feet and made it affluent until the Depression of the Thirties undermined its solvency.

However, since 1883 the Metropolitan proved a great attraction to foreign musicians and singers, male and female. Some of these foreign imports remained only a season or two, others for a decade or more, often returning to the famous footlights after a lapse of several years.

Among the "birds of passage" was the singer Johanna Gadski, who visited the United States for the first time in 1875 as a member of the Damrosch Opera Company, which Damrosch had formed. From 1907 to 1917 she was one of the great prima donnas at the Metropolitan, where she sang Wagner roles. But she was also given the role of Hester Prynne in Walter Damrosch's opera, "The Scarlet Letter," which he composed in response to the American experience. Because her husband was a member of the German military, she was forced to return to Europe in 1917. In 1928, however, she was back in the United States for a tour with the German Opera Company.

Among the other German-speaking singers were Frieda Hempel, the brilliant German coloratura who graced the Met between 1912–1920, and the glorious Maria Jeritza, an Austrian, who was one of the leading singers between 1921 and 1932. There were so many outstanding artists that only a small number can be mentioned. One not to be forgotten was the soprano Lilli Lehmann, who, after a triumph in New York, returned to Berlin and there taught many singers, among them Olive Fremstad and the native American Geraldine Farrar. At the age of eighty-four Lilli Lehmann is said to have given as many as fifteen lessons a day.[9] She is not to be confused with Lotte Lehmann, who was born forty years later.

The number of Italian prima donnas is also very large. Among the early ones was the beloved Luisa Tetrazzini who created a sensation in San Francisco in 1904. She also performed at the Manhattan and the Chicago opera companies, in concert tours, and opposite Caruso at the Metropolitan. To this day Italian singers are very well represented and greatly admired by American audiences.

The Scandinavian countries may claim to have sent us some outstanding Wagnerian singers. At the top of the list belongs the Norwegian Kirsten Flagstad who came to the Met "unknown and unheralded . . . no triumphant reputation trailing her,"[10] and remained until 1941 when she returned to Norway. She was accused of having collaborated with occupation authorities, but according to one opinion, the accusation was "entirely without reason."[11] It was her husband who was a Quisling. She came back to the Metropolitan in 1947–1948 to make her farewell appearance. She then returned to Norway, but her daughter settled permanently in the United States.[12] Today Birgitt Nilsson, dramatic soprano of Swedish birth, is considered a peerless Wagnerian singer.

Another birthplace of great singers is Spain. In addition to Adelina Patti, one who deserves to be remembered is Lucrezia Bori, born in Valencia, who was heard at the Met between 1912 and 1915 and again between 1921 and 1936. In 1929, when the Metropolitan was already feeling the effects of the Depression, Miss Bori helped to raise funds to keep the institution alive, and in 1935 was appointed a member of the Board of Directors. This was a rare tribute at a time when women were rarely, if ever, accorded such recognition. Among the present group of Spanish-born singers are a number of noted artists, one of whom is Monserrat Caballé.

The English-speaking countries have sent us Mary Garden of Scottish birth who returned to Scotland. Nellie Melba was Australian, and Frances Alda, born Frances Davies, was a New Zealander. Melba went back to Australia and Alda married the manager Giulio Gatti Casazza, later divorced him, and died in Venice.

Poland, Hungary, Czechoslovakia, Yugoslavia, even Turkey can point to some of their nationals who helped to enrich the musical life in America.

Let us now survey the careers of three women, all of whom accompanied their immigrant parents to the United States as children. The first, chronologically, was Olive Fremstad (1871–1951), who was born of Norwegian parents in Stockholm and brought to the United States at the age of six. At first the family lived in a small town in Minnesota, then in Minneapolis, and still later in Wisconsin. Jenny Lind was called "the Swedish nightingale"; Miss Fremstad was likened to a lark by Willa Cather, whose book, *Song of the Lark,* was said to have been inspired by Fremstad's life and career. As a young girl she studied the piano, but she also sang at revival meetings with her father, a self-styled preacher and a gospel singer. A vocal teacher who heard her was so impressed with her voice that she took her on as a pupil. In 1890 Olive Fremstad left for New York, where she supported herself by singing in churches. She was encouraged to go to Berlin for further study and became a pupil of Lilli Lehmann. After an engagement at the Munich Royal Opera House and at Covent Garden, she was engaged in 1903 to sing at the Metropolitan, where she spent eleven years justifying the hopes placed in her. Irving Kolodin says of her: "Fremstad's Isolde was . . . one of the loveliest in the Met's 'Wagnerian gallery.'"[13] She was also heard in Boston, Chicago, Minneapolis, and at Norwegian benefit concerts. After her farewell appearance in 1920 she taught singing in New York.

Besides furnishing the subject of Willa Cather's *Song of the Lark,* a story based on her life was written by her secretary, Mary Watkins Cushing, under the title *The Rainbow Bridge.* After Miss Fremstad's death in a rest home in Irvington-on-Hudson in New York, she was buried in a cemetery in Grantsburg, Wisconsin, alongside her parents, brother and sister.

Some singers were satisfied with supporting roles. One of those was Marie Sundelius (1884–1958),[14] who was brought to Boston at the age of ten by her Swedish immigrant parents. In 1916 she found a place at the Metropolitan and remained there until 1928. She also toured the United States with the Scotti Grand Opera Company and the Philadelphia Opera Company. After 1928 Miss Sundelius taught the vocal arts at Malbin Conservatory of Boston.

The third of the trio who began as immigrant children was Alma Gluck (1884–1938), about whom Kolodin says that she "provided an enchantment."[15] She had an exquisite voice, a lovely, appealing face, and she combined a short but fabulous singing career with the romantic role of a woman who was idolized by a famous husband. She was the mother of Marcia Davenport and of two other children by her second marriage to the violinist Efrem Zimbalist.

Miss Gluck was born in Bucharest, Rumania, as Reba Fiersohn and was brought to America at six. Her father had died just before immigration and the family depended upon the generosity of an aunt who began as a garment worker and succeeded in becoming the proprietor of a successful dressmaking establishment. As a young girl she experienced the full gamut of deprivation associated with the immigrant experience. After attending the public schools of New York City, she worked as a stenographer and in her teens married Bernard Gluck who was in the insurance business. She began voice study after her marriage. The story is told that her teacher invited Gatti Casazza and Toscanini for dinner and arranged for her to come for her lesson so that they could hear her. The trick worked. They were so struck by her musical aptitude that they offered her a contract. While the story may be apocryphal, it is a fact that she secured a contract from the Metropolitan very early in her career. Between 1909 and 1912 she sang in supporting roles, sometimes in the same cast with Olive Fremstad. Later she studied with Lilli Lehmann in Berlin and with Marcella Sembrich.

After 1913 she confined herself solely to singing in concert and at private musicales. Her career lasted only a little more than ten years,[16] because she retired in 1924. But she was such a hit that only Caruso's and John McCormack's record sales exceeded hers. She made about 140 records, some of which she refused to release.[17] Her repertory consisted of French, German, Russian, and American songs. "Carry Me Back to Old Virginny" was the song for which she was probably best known and best loved. Between 1914 and 1919 she received royalties amounting to $600,000 from the Victor Talking Machine.[18]

In 1914 she married Efrem Zimbalist and after her marriage

she appeared less and less frequently in public, stopping entirely in 1924. Her explanation was that she wanted to devote herself to her husband and children, but her daughter believes she lost her voice and that it was "the one great tragedy of her life."[19] She was too proud to admit it, says her daughter. A devoted wife, she accompanied her husband on many of his tours, despite the urgent need to guard her health.

However, though she relinquished her career as a performing artist, she kept up her connections with the musical world. She was active in the Musicians' Emergency Fund, the Yorkville Music School Settlement, and she was a founder of the American Guild of Musical Artists.[20]

The place at the head of the list of those who came to America as fully trained artists and remained here after retirement belongs to Marcella Sembrich (1858–1935),[21] not only because she possessed a beautiful voice, but also because of her character and her beneficent personality. Born in the Austrian part of Poland, she was the daughter of a talented but impoverished church organist. He began to teach her to play the piano at the age of four, and at six he started her on a toy violin he had fashioned for her himself. She was a very young girl when she began to help in the support of her family by playing the piano for children's dancing classes and at carnivals.

While studying in Vienna she played for Liszt, who recognized that she had "three pair of wings," but advised her to make singing her career because she had the voice of an angel. She followed his counsel, and when she made her debut in Athens at twenty-two she experienced a triumph. In London she sang for Queen Victoria, and in St. Petersburg for Alexander II one week before his assassination. He rewarded her with a gold bracelet set with diamonds.

In 1897 she began a long engagement at the Metropolitan, where she often sang with Caruso. She remained a Metropolitan diva for twelve years until her retirement in 1909 at fifty-one. But in 1933 she sang in a benefit performance to aid the hard-pressed company during the depression. It was not her only benefit concert. In 1906, following the earthquake in San

Francisco, she had given a concert to benefit musician-victims and had distributed almost $10,000 to those who had lost their instruments. When she sang, she delighted critics, composers, and audiences alike. Henry Edward Krehbiel, one of the outstanding music critics of the day, pronounced her immortal, and Puccini wrote in her album: "You ARE the Mimi." Brahms was so approving of the way she sang lieder that he said he trusted her "perfectly to render his intention." An anonymous admirer contributed the following canticle:

> When Sembrich sings it seems that heaven, intent
> On brightening this dull old earth had sent
> The rarest voice in all the angel throng
> To shower on man the blessing of its song.

After 1904 she remained permanently in the United States. Artists from all the world congregated at her home in Lake George. There she conducted classes and discussion groups. Her residence at Lake George is now a memorial, open to the public on specified days. She was also director of the Vocal Department at the Curtis Institute of Music in Philadelphia (which awarded her the degree of Doctor of Music), and a member of the teaching staff of the Juilliard Graduate School.

Her husband, who had been her teacher and coach since the days when she was a neophyte, was no longer alive when she died. An only son survived her. A funeral mass at St. Patrick's Cathedral preceded her burial on American soil.

No immigrant became a more enthusiastic, devoted American than Ernestine Schumann-Heink.[22] She was considered the most famous contralto of her time. Austrian by birth, she was the daughter of an impecunious army officer. When she arrived in Chicago in 1898, at the age of thirty-seven, she had behind her a series of outstanding successes. She opened at the Metropolitan singing Ortrud in "Lohengrin" when she was in the last stages of pregnancy. The management was apprehensive about it, but her debut went off magnificently and she was an instant hit.

By the time her child was born she was so happy in America

that she insisted on naming him George Washington, despite the disapproval of the German consular authorities she had consulted. Her own explanation:

> ...from the very first I liked America. It really seemed another homecoming to me. I don't know why, but I felt I had a place here. You see, for some time I'd thought a good deal about America and its opportunities, not only for my singing, but for the children. No military duty for them, and freedom for many things.[23]

On her trips she is supposed to have carried "a little American flag." During World War I, when many German singers felt so uncomfortable that they went back to Europe to sit out the war, Mme. Schumann-Heink sang for American soldiers everywhere—the American Legion, on the streets and in the hospitals. Her eldest, German-born, son fought and died with the German armies, but her other sons and her American-born son fought in the American army. She looked upon all fighting men as "sons" and she was proud that they called her "Mother Schumann-Heink." She received so many letters from soldiers who thanked her for the pleasure her singing had brought to them that she requested:

> ...all my letters I have from the soldiers...I want them to fill my coffin when I'm dead. They will be the softest pillow I could lie on.[24]

Once, when she was asked by a soldier's buddy to sing at his friend's funeral, she did, then kissed the dead boy's face and said, "Goodbye, son of mine! Carry my love to my own dear boy."[25]

Her long singing career—thirty-three years at the Metropolitan—was a continuous bravo. In 1932 she sang her farewell performance, again in a Wagnerian role. It marked her retirement from the Metropolitan, not from singing. She entertained President Franklin D. Roosevelt at the White House, and at seventy-four her voice was heard in the film "Here's to Romance."

Her feeling about America emerges from these words:

> Gratitude!—that's my very last word—gratitude to the American people who have so made my American career! For it is here in

America that my happiest years have been spent—it is here in America—please God that I shall end my days—marching on, "booted and spurred" as my father used to say, like an old soldier of fortune.[25]

One of the German-born singers who became an American citizen as rapidly as possible was Lotte Lehmann (1888–   ). The Grove Musical Directory lists her as an "American singer of German birth." She began to sing opera in 1910, but did not come to the Metropolitan until 1934 when she was forty-six, which she admitted was "very late." Marcia Davenport reveals that she came here in defiance of Goering's edict that she confine herself to singing on German stages.[26]

In her youth she had hoped to be a writer, but instead turned out to be a magnificent singer and one of Richard Strauss's favorite sopranos. She also sang Wagnerian roles opposite Lauritz Melchior and gave lieder concerts. In Marcia Davenport's opinion:

... she had the most moving voice in the world. It had splendor, but it was not forbidding like those of other Wagnerian sopranos ... tones came out ... that have never been equalled for me in beauty and emotional power.[27]

During her final concert in 1951 at Town Hall when she was sixty-three, she broke down and wept when she came to the phrase in Schubert's song "An die Musik."

Her attitude to the United States was worshipful. Receiving citizenship in 1938 elicited this statement:

... And I who was born a German and was bound to Austria with the deepest love—I stand now at the door of America. ... I am sure I shall find my third home here and that I shall not again need to wander.[28]

After her retirement she dedicated herself to fostering the careers of young artists. As the director of the Music Academy of the West in Santa Barbara, California, she taught singing and opera-staging. One of her most outstanding students was Grace Bumbry. During her seventies she continued to direct student productions of *Der Rosenkavalier, Die Fledermaus,* and

Figaro. In 1962 she was called back to the Metropolitan to become co-director of *Der Rosenkavalier.* In addition to writing poetry, an autobiography, and a novel, which was translated from the German, she began to paint. In 1950 her illustrations of the two Schubert cycles, "Winter Journey" and "Poet's Love," were exhibited at the Schaeffer Galleries in New York City.[29]

Another great artist who retired to California and died there was the Italian coloratura soprano Amelita Galli-Curci (1882–1963). Born in Milan to musician parents, she was taught the piano first. To Harold C. Schonberg, music critic of the New York *Times,* her voice was a "silvery organ."[30] She made her debut in the United States with the Chicago Opera Company, then went to the Met and was recalled sixty times.[30] By 1925 she had acquired such a reputation that when she sang at the Hollywood Bowl she received $5,000 for the performance. She became so popular that when Victor released two songs, the Bell Song from *Lakme* and Cara Nome from *Rigoletto,* $540,000 worth of records were sold within the first two months of issue.[31]

An operation on the larynx forced her to give up her singing career in 1936. She attempted a comeback, but when cautioned by her physician to avoid cold climates, she quit. From then on she was content to read, to paint, and to garden. When she died in 1963, the New York *Times* remarked about her "lifelong devotion to the United States, her adopted home."

A coloratura of a different stamp was Lily Pons (1904–). She has been called an American discovery because it was at the Metropolitan where her extraordinary voice was discovered. Besides, she was pretty and appealing. One critic called her "the trapeze artist of the Met."

She was born near Cannes and first studied at the Paris Conservatory. During World War I, when she was still a very young girl, she played for convalescent soldiers. A *poilu* asked her to sing for him and she discovered that she had a voice.

Her marriage at eighteen to a wealthy banker enabled her to train for a career as a singer. In 1928 she made her debut in *Lakme* and after appearing for several years in a French provincial opera house, she was advised to go to the United States. An audition with Gatti Casazza in 1930 during which she sang the Bell Song from *Lakme* brought her an immediate contract.

The next thirty years were an uninterrupted hurrah. Several hundred thousand crowded Chicago's Grant Park to hear her. She received ovations all over the world; in France she was made an officer of the Legion of Honor and given the Gold Medal of the City of Paris; in Belgium she received the Order of the Crown. Between 1935 and 1937 she appeared in Hollywood productions.

It was as an American citizen that she set out in 1944 on several tours for the U.S.O. She was then married to André Kostelanetz and with him she traveled in Iran, Egypt, Italy, Indochina, Burma, Belgium, and Germany to entertain the soldiers.[32]

She is now a legendary figure who divides her time between her various homes—all in the United States. Several seasons ago she made an appearance with the Philharmonic at one of the Promenade Concerts and was declared to be singing as well as ever.

The Viennese born Fritzi Scheff[33] was one of the first among foreign-born singers to acquire American citizenship. In 1908 she forswore allegiance to Austria and became an American citizen. When Miss Scheff first arrived in the United States at the age of thirty, she sang at the Metropolitan, but three years afterward she turned to the musical comedy stage and became one of the most celebrated operetta performers.

A pretty, vivacious-looking woman with a captivating smile, she enchanted her audiences. Victor Herbert wrote "Kiss Me Again" for her, which made such a hit that at the opening she was compelled to sing twenty-six encores. She sang it so often it became her identifying mark as a singer. As a result she grew to dislike the song intensely. She also performed in vaudeville and despite her other successful roles in operetta, audiences always clamored for "Kiss Me Again." She was so tired of it that she stipulated in her will it was not to be sung at her funeral. When she died in New York in 1954, she had been a naturalized citizen for close to fifty years.

A recent contribution to the musical life of America was and is being made by Maria Augusta von Trapp and the Trapp family members. She was born in Vienna and would have become a nun, but she was "loaned" to Baron Georg von Trapp to teach his seven children. She taught them to perform as a musical group with herself as participant. After her marriage to the baron they began to perform publicly. In 1938 they appeared in America for a concert tour. Shortly after their return to Austria, the Anschluss occurred. Feeling menaced by the Austrian Nazi party, they decided to escape. They now live in Stowe, Vermont, fulfilling their concert schedule during the winter and running a musical camp during the summer. Mrs. von Trapp makes a touching comment about the meaning of America to immigrants:

> The real America is not neon-sign language; it is a state of mind. It is warm, spontaneous generosity—full measure, pressed down and running over. . . . A refugee is not just someone lacking in money and everything else. A refugee is vulnerable to the slightest touch: he has lost his country, his friends. . . . He is a stranger, sick at heart. He is suspicious, he feels misunderstood. . . . He is a full-grown tree in the dangerous process of being transplanted, with the chance of possibly not being able to take root in the new soil. . . .[34]

Because the growth of musical development in America was fostered by many more individuals than can be listed here, the decision who is to be singled out for inclusion and who is to be omitted seems magisterial. In narrowing down a large circle to a small nucleus arbitrariness cannot be avoided. If the enormity of the collective achievement is recognized, the intent of this chapter will have been accomplished.

CHAPTER 13

Teaching Music: An Unselfish Joy

BY THE BEGINNING OF THE TWENTIETH CENTURY MUSICAL AUDI-
ences had grown more sophisticated and appreciative. It was
a concomitant of the influence of foreign-born conductors,
teachers, and performers. The story, told by Walter Damrosch,
about the cowboy in Fargo, North Dakota, who upon hearing
Beethoven, was heard exclaiming at intervals: "Goddamn it, but
I like that music,"[1] belongs to the American Middle Ages, as
does another anecdote about a cowboy in Lincoln, Nebraska.
While listening intently to a symphony concert, he amused
himself by spitting frequently and aiming for the bald head
of the bass player who had to duck to avoid it.[2]

When music schools came into existence the faculties were
originally composed of a majority of foreign-born teachers,
who were often specifically imported to fill those jobs. As the
century progressed music appreciation in America became equal
to, if it did not surpass, the interest Europeans have traditionally
lavished on music and the practitioners of the musical arts.

Let us now explore a different avenue that fed the broad
stream of musical development—the work of teachers and of
some instrumentalists.

Two New York music schools who owed their existence to
foreign-born individuals were the Institute of Musical Art,
established by Frank Damrosch, and the Mannes School of
Music, founded by Clara Damrosch Mannes and David Mannes.
David Mannes was a native American, but Clara Damrosch,
like her brothers Walter and Frank, was born in Germany.
The Institute of Musical Art merged with the Juilliard School
in 1925 and became its undergraduate division. The faculties
of these institutions trained some of the most gifted artists
and teachers of our time.

232

Of the German musicians who came to the United States during the end of the nineteenth century, the Damrosch family was most influential on America's musical growth. Leopold Damrosch had studied medicine in Berlin, had received his medical diploma, and was qualified to practice and to become an eye specialist, when he decided to chuck it all and to devote himself to music. When he landed in the United States in 1871, to be shortly followed by his family, it was at a time when American musical tastes were beginning to emerge from the Dark Ages, when any classical piece of music in order to be tolerated had to be sandwiched in between Yankee Doodle or any lively jig and "America the Beautiful." Dr. Damrosch, violinist and conductor, protégé of Liszt and friend of some of the most famous musicians of Germany, had received a call to direct a New York Sänger Verein, the Arion Society. It was his first step in the development of his American career; the New York Oratorio Society which he formed in 1878 was his second; his third was the establishment of the New York Symphony Society, and his last the direction of the Metropolitan Opera Company. In 1885 he died suddenly, leaving a wife and five children, three of them teen-age girls. His American career had lasted fourteen years.

Every member of the Damrosch family was to play some part in promoting musical activities in America—his wife, who upon her death was recognized as the "Queen Mother of New York's most musical family"[3]—his wife's sister, who lived with the family, and particularly his sons Frank and Walter and his daughter Clara. His wife, Helena von Heimburg, who had also been a protégée of Liszt, led the soprano section of the chorus; her sister, Marie von Heimburg, sang in the chorus and taught at the Spence School; the three Damrosch daughters, including the American-born Elizabeth, also sang in the chorus. More important roles awaited Walter, who was nine, Frank who was eleven, and Clara, who was two at the time of the family's arrival in the United States. The one destined to have the strongest influence on contemporary musical affairs was Walter; but in the long run his brother's and sister's legacies would be no less significant.

The importance of Walter Damrosch as a symphony conductor and in his use of radio for musical instruction does not lie within the scope of this book. The role of Frank Damrosch as a teacher has a greater bearing on the subject with which this book deals, because by establishing the Institute of Musical Art, he brought several foreign-born women instrumentalist-teachers into it.

The fourth offspring of Leopold Damrosch, his daughter Clara (1869–1948), married David Mannes, a violinist, and with him founded the Mannes School of Music which in 1956 became the Mannes College of Music. She was trained as a pianist. Because she was a skilled instrumentalist and teacher and because she was one of the two founders of a school of music, it seems proper to begin this survey of music teachers and performers with her.

Though she grew up in the United States, in a family which clung to European values, it would have been difficult to disregard, or even to tone down, the heritage associated with the Old World. In many ways Clara Damrosch remained a European traditionalist, despite the influence of the American environment.

As the prototypical daughter of a good family, she was sent to a private school conducted on lycée principles. She began the study of the piano at the age of six, practicing under the exacting supervision of her mother. When the family went abroad she received instruction from the most competent German teachers and as an adult studied with the famous Busoni in Berlin.[4] She was such an accomplished pianist that Pablo Casals chose her to accompany him in one of the first recitals he gave in this country.[5] She sang in the alto section of the New York Oratorio Society, and it was during a joint session of the New York Symphony and the Oratorio Society that David Mannes, leader of the first violins of the New York Symphony, noticed her. He admitted that from then on he looked forward to every oratorio rehearsal, without discovering for a long time that the ash-blond singer with the expressive eyes and the beautiful features was the sister of the conductor. She is said to have been an exceedingly romantic girl, shy, and not at all aware of her good looks.[6]

David Mannes (1866–1958), too, was handsome, tall, lean,

dark and romantic-looking. But when he presented himself at the Damrosch home, his reception by the matriarch was impersonal. As the son of a Polish immigrant baker, later the owner of a store which sold furniture, old china, and books, he was socially no match for the Damrosch clan, whose matriarch had come from a Junker family. When he discovered that Clara, her aunt, and the Frank Damrosches were leaving for Europe, David Mannes booked passage on the same boat. The family realized that the young people would not be separated and made no objections to the marriage. Clara Damrosch was repeating what her mother had done when she had married Leopold Damrosch.

Both Clara and David Mannes taught music; she at home, he in a study at Carnegie Hall. He also taught at the Third Street Settlement Music School, of which he ultimately became the head, and founded the Music School Settlement for Colored People. Later he was elected trustee of Fisk University in Nashville, Tennessee. He was very proud of the series of free symphony concerts which he conducted at the Metropolitan Museum for twenty years. Many aged New Yorkers still remember them with a great deal of appreciation. At the Metropolitan he played for audiences of 1,500 people.[7] In addition both performed in joint violin and piano ensembles in the United States and in England, earning such accolades as: "Mr. & Mrs. Mannes have attained a degree of finish which makes their work a delight."[8]

As music teachers they were irked by the low level of music instruction, which made them long for a small conservatory of their own, where they could put their ideas into operation. They had an example in Frank Damrosch, Clara's brother, who, after conducting the People's Choral Union, a chorus of wage-earners, had established the Institute of Musical Art in 1905. Their intention in starting their own music school was not only to foster the development of musically talented children, but to raise the standards of general musicianship.

Wealthy patrons advanced the money,[9] and in 1916 the plan to open a modest school materialized. David Mannes gave up his work in the Third Street Settlement, but they went on with their recital tours in order to augment their own salaries which were deliberately kept low. In addition to being "the mistress of household accounts," as her daughter puts it, Clara Mannes became the administrator of the school. A dreamer and a visionary, David Mannes, to whom money was both a mystery and anathema, was content to leave all practical matters to her, confining himself to teaching and producing a beneficent and soothing effect on teachers, students, and parents—according to his daughter one of his special talents.[10] The combination of David and Clara Mannes made for a successful school and a very good marriage.

The school grew quickly and within three years the location on 70th Street proved too small. New and enlarged quarters were created by purchasing three brownstone houses on East 74th Street and remodeling them into a beautiful colonial building which enhances the appearance of the neighborhood to this day.

In 1933 a provisional charter from the University of the State of New York turned the school into a tax-exempt, non-profit institution which was administered by a Board of Trustees with Mr. and Mrs. Mannes as co-directors. David Mannes wrote of his wife:

Clara was to find the fulfillment of her musical life, of her great talents and capacities of mind and heart, in directing the growing school. Without her, this important crux of her life would have been impossible. It needed her loyal adherence to the highest standards of art and spirit of music, and her clear judgment in the consideration of necessary details, to give unified expression to our combined vision. Alone neither of us could accomplish our destined work. What I lack in clarity and courage and decisiveness she provided. And I, perhaps, contribute a certain philosophical and a certain phantasy— which sometimes appears to be irrational if not downright mad— without which no vision could be sustained.[11]

Clara and David Mannes were the parents of two children, a son, Leopold, and a daughter, Marya. Marya Mannes continues as a trustee of the school and a member of its Executive Committee. Leopold, now dead, combined a conspicuous musical talent with a scientific mind. He was a physics major at Harvard and after nine years of work in the laboratories of Eastman

Kodak in Rochester he and his collaborator, Leopold Godowsky, the son of the pianist, perfected Kodachrome in 1935. After that, music won over physics, as music had won over medicine in the life of his grandfather, the first Leopold Damrosch. In Marya Mannes's words: "He turned over the greater part of his Kodachrome royalties to support his parents' school, returned to the piano and formed a trio in which he and the late Luigi Silva and Bronislaw Gimpel played both across the continent and in Europe."[12] He also composed music for the piano and the orchestra.

In 1940 he was appointed assistant director of the Mannes School and later served as its president. Under his administration the school began to offer instruction leading to a college degree and the school became the Mannes College of Music. In 1968 the school was authorized to award the degree of bachelor of music as well as the honorary degree of doctor of music.[13]

The school offers a full teaching curriculum which includes theory, ear training, the teaching of all orchestral instruments, and composition and conducting. It also conducts an opera workshop, provides special training for ghetto children, and courses for people who do not intend to make music their career. By arrangement the college also offers musical instruction to students of Marymount Manhattan College. In 1972 a new program was worked out between Mannes and Queens College of the City University, by which a master's degree in performing arts is awarded to qualified students by Queens College.[14] Famous Mannes students were David bar Illan, Eugene Istomin, Julius Rudel, Matiwilda Dobbs, and others. Many other graduates occupy important positions in a variety of musical organizations.

Clara Mannes was to be found at the school even during her seventies. But she also made time for drawing and painting. Her husband and she collaborated in writing on musical instruction and he contributed articles to musical journals.

As for David Mannes, his daughter discloses that he continued to play the violin when he was past ninety. Clara Mannes died at seventy-six of a heart attack. Their imprint on the musical development of America is in the school they founded.

The career of only one faculty member of the Mannes College will be discussed. She is Madame Nadia Reisenberg,[15] one of the outstanding virtuosi of the piano and a teacher of high repute who looks every inch a diva. She turned to teaching in 1955 after thirty years of intense concertizing in Europe, America, and Israel. It was Leopold Mannes, son of the founders, who brought her into Mannes College. Today she is connected with the teaching program which grants, in conjunction with Queens College, a master's degree in the performing arts. Her teaching experience has convinced her that an effective teacher must possess a certain kind of talent to be able to transfer knowledge to others; that some skilled artists make poor pedagogues; that teachers are born, not taught. She stresses the pleasure that comes from discovering talent and developing it. Her enthusiasm suggests that she must be an uncommonly successful teacher. She has conducted master classes in Tulsa, Oklahoma, at the University of Southern California, and at the Rubin Academy of Music in Jerusalem, and has been a judge in many competitions, including the Leventritt Award. Beginning with the 1974–1975 season she will be a member of the faculty of the Juilliard School.[16]

Born in Vilna in 1904, her family moved to Petrograd, where she became a pupil at the Imperial Conservatory and was taught by Leonid Nikolaeff, teacher of Shostakovich. But she did not graduate, because the revolution broke out and the family fled, abandoning home, possessions, and their means of livelihood. A stealthy border crossing brought them to Lithuania, and by following a circuitous route they reached Poland, where she played her first concert with the Warsaw Symphony under Artur Rodzinsky, whom she was to encounter again in America. Eventually they reached Germany. On their various stops she gave joint recitals with her sister, who was a violinist.

From Germany they proceeded to America, arriving in 1922 when she was eighteen. She became a pupil of Alexander Lambert, who had been a pupil of Liszt. He prepared her for the concert stage by arranging for her to play at musicales in private homes at a fee of $100 per concert. The next step was the Curtis Institute in Philadelphia where she studied under Josef Hoffmann and taught at the same time.

Her first public recital at Aeolian Hall in 1924 marked the beginning of a story book career. She played with all the major orchestras under the most celebrated conductors, performed with several renowned chamber groups, appeared on radio, and made a large number of recordings, covering an unusually diverse repertory. For instance, she appeared in weekly broadcasts over station WOR under the baton of Alfred Wallenstein, where she played all the Mozart concerti. She recorded all twenty Chopin nocturnes, fifty-six Chopin mazurkas and other Chopin works, seven Haydn sonatas, all of Kabalevskys' preludes, and as might be expected of an ardent Russophile, some Tschaikovsky, Moussorgsky, and Rachmaninoff, in addition to several chamber music works.

In America she traveled for many years with the Budapest String Quartet, also with the cellist Joseph Schuster and the violinist William Kroll, in addition to major concert tours in America and Europe. In 1955 she was glad to exchange traveling for teaching. Now she takes pride in the "incredible progress made by American students." She admits with obvious satisfaction that "many American students are now so good they stand out in the best European schools."

Madame Reisenberg still harbors a deep love for Russian culture. In addition to her identification with music, she has a strong affinity for painting, because as she pointed out, musicians are always surrounded by sound, whereas painting can be enjoyed in silence. Also, painting to her represents the same kind of poetry and rhythm as music.

She admits she was very lucky in that her husband, a European intellectual, gave her every support in the pursuit of her career. She has two sons, one who is an engineer, and another who is well known in music circles as the program director of the radio station WQXR in New York City. Though she still speaks Russian with family and friends, she insists she wants to live nowhere but in America.

The Juilliard School, as it has been called since 1969, is not only one of the nation's most prestigious music schools;

it is known all over the world. As of 1974 it had 700 enrolled students, 500 in the music department and 200 in the dance and drama divisions.[17]

The career of Frank Damrosch, "Doctor" Frank Damrosch by virtue of an honorary degree from Yale University in 1904, meshed during the last decade of his life with the Juilliard School of Music, which had been established in 1920 by a legacy from Augustus D. Juilliard, an industrialist from Ohio. Damrosch's Institute of Musical Arts had been in existence since 1905. Both institutions became the Juilliard School of Music with Dr. Frank Damrosch remaining as the dean of the undergraduate division until his death in 1933. Since 1926 the Institute of Musical Art and the Juilliard Graduate School have been operated under the title of the Juilliard School of Music and since 1969 as the Juilliard School.

During the first quarter of the twentieth century other music schools came into existence, notably the Curtis Institute of Music in Philadelphia and the Eastman School of Rochester, New York. All of them were first dependent on teachers trained in Europe, some of whom were: Alfred Cortot, Ernest Bloch (Mannes), Efrem Zimbalist, Marcella Sembrich, Josef Hoffman (Curtis), Isabella Vengerova, Jennie Tourel, Ilona Kabos (Juilliard), among others.

But this dependence was short-lived. Because of the instruction given in these music schools, more and more native Americans were able to take their places beside foreign musical educators, and today it is surprising to note how many faculty members of music colleges are native Americans trained in those self-same schools. This is perhaps the most significant achievement of foreign-born teachers of the musical arts. Because the piano has always had a special attraction for women and because the Juilliard School has a number of outstanding teachers of the piano, two of the women presented in these pages are pianists; the third faculty member, a performer of Renaissance and baroque music and a composer, represents a more esoteric type of musician.

Mme Rosina Lhevinne (1880–) has been connected with Juilliard since its inception. She has been called "the grande dame of music," the "matriarch of music," "the doyenne of the piano," "a tiny potentate," and one of the "greatest piano teachers of all time." Miss Suzanne Bloch, a colleague, calls her "incredible . . . a miracle . . . a unique personality who still has a wonderful freshness about her."[18] When she was ninety she taught twenty-two pupils with the aid of two assistants, and gave three lessons a day at home.[19] Today, at ninety-four, she still gives some master classes at home, but is no longer available for interviews, hence this résumé is drawn from printed sources and the impression of others.

Born in 1880 in Kiev, she was at the age of nine the youngest pupil of Vassily Safonov at the Moscow Conservatory. At that time Josef Lhevinne, aged fourteen, was also a pupil of the famed Russian teacher. When her regular teacher became ill, Josef Lhevinne, then seventeen, was assigned to teach her. Upon graduation at eighteen she was awarded the same gold medal he had won; a week later they were married. Since then she was linked to him as his partner in duo piano performances, as a teacher, but only rarely as a soloist.

Why did she only rarely perform as a soloist? Apparently she had been warned about marital disharmony between competing artists, so she vowed she would never appear as a soloist. Some people have said that she excelled him as a teacher. She still frowns on the competitive spirit in musicians, condemns rivalry among them, and discourages her students from allowing competitive feelings to dominate their musical judgments.

It was the cellist and composer Cesar Cui, a friend of both, who suggested that Rosina and Josef Lhevinne form a duo piano team. For forty-six years they played together, he as soloist, she as his partner in piano duets. Their appearances were billed as "concerts on one and two pianos."

She kept her vow not to play as a soloist for forty years, until in 1938 the Juilliard School decided to honor their fortieth anniversary with a concert at Carnegie Hall. It was Josef Lhevinne who announced he would play only if she played a solo. The program included the Tschaikovsky First Piano Concerto played by him, the Chopin First Piano Concerto played by her, and a Mozart Concerto for four hands.[20]

Josef Lhevinne died in 1944, but the next solo recital she

gave was not until 1955, when she was engaged by the Aspen Music School in Colorado and was informed it was taken for granted all members of the faculty would play with the orchestra as soloists. She chose to perform a Mozart concerto, one she had never taught nor ever played before.[21]

Between 1945 and 1955 she conducted summer master classes at Berkeley, California, and more recently at the University of Southern California in Los Angeles.

On her eightieth birthday she made another appearance with the Juilliard Orchestra under Jean Morel, playing the Mozart Piano Concerto No. 21 in C-major, which was recorded and for fifteen years has benefited the scholarship fund in the name of her husband. Her last appearance was with the Philharmonic Symphony at the age of eighty-two and created a sensation.

Mme Lhevinne and her husband were invited to teach at the Juilliard when it opened and she is now the only original faculty member left. She is said to typify the romantic school of piano playing by underlining sensuous tones. In this she follows the Russian school founded by Anton and Nicholas Rubinstein in 1850, which favors a romantic style and embodies an emotional as well as a technical approach. By stressing mood the piano becomes "a veritable expression of the artist's emotional make-up."[22] To Suzanne Bloch her "sense of musicality for the Romantics is extraordinary."[23]

Though she considers the communication of mood important in piano playing, she rejects meaningless emotionalism. She is said to have reminded male students, "Your best girl is a metronome."[24] Because she considers individuality of style to be an artist's signature, her advice to students is not to imitate the style of others, but to make their interpretations indicative of their own response to the music. She regards the artist as "the middleman between the music and the listener [who] reproduces the intention of the composer," and the role of the teacher as one who builds a bridge between the composer who may be of a past generation with the performer who is of the present."[25] Among the virtuosi she has trained are Van Cliburn, John Browning, Mischa Dichter, Daniel Pollock, and others. Though she admits that she does not care for many of the modern composers, she is quick to stress "it doesn't mean they're no good."[26]

She has lived in the United States for fifty years and has two children who reside in California, neither of whom is a musician. In spite of her advanced age, in some respects she has remained surprisingly young. Miss Suzanne Bloch tells a story of seeing her at a concert sitting beside Felix Salmond, a cellist, now dead. As they were listening to Schubert's Unfinished Symphony, they kept looking at each other, shaking their heads over the wonder of it, as if they were hearing it for the first time and were unable to believe that such beauty could be created.

In an interview with Harold C. Schonberg, music critic of the New York *Times,* she is supposed to have asserted: "America is my homeland and Juilliard my alma mater."[27]

Another outstanding woman pianist of Russian birth on the faculty of the Juilliard School is Mme Ania Dorfmann.[28] She is a comparative newcomer at Juilliard, having joined the faculty in 1966 after fifty years as concert pianist in Europe, North America, and South America. She also teaches master classes at Stephens College at Columbia, Missouri, where she appears twice a year in the spring and in the fall. The observation that it sounds like a strenuous assignment brought forth a smile and the quick rejoinder, "It's worth it." She has also conducted master classes in Europe, as she did in Sion, France, last year, where trained musicians from various places in Europe came to consult her.

Though her teaching career at Juilliard started relatively recently, she has been a resident of the United States since 1938 and a citizen since the early forties. She looks upon her life as consisting of three parts: the Russian period that came to an end in 1920 when she was lucky to escape on the last Italian boat sailing from Odessa; the middle part in Paris which she called home until 1938, and the third in the United States which began when she decided to bring her mother and her daughter to America. She admits she has been deeply thrilled by the United States ever since her first glance at the Statue of Liberty. "I had an incredible feeling of coming home," she explained, "of having found my own country again."

When urged to explain the instantaneous reaction to America, she spoke of the resemblance between Russians and Americans, which she is not the first to recognize, specifically the warmth and kindliness of the American people. "I've adored America ever since," she avers, "and nothing can move me from here." Her statement becomes meaningful when one learns that her only daughter, brought up as an American girl, and now a successful writer, lives in Switzerland. She admits she is often asked, "Why don't you live there too?" "But," she says, "I answer, NO. America is for me." Mme Dorfmann is a self-contained, reserved woman with a calm, contemplative outer surface but occasionally a gesture or a smile conveys there is more below the surface which is not for exploration.

Born in Odessa she began the study of the piano at the age of seven. After making her debut in Russia at eleven, she was taken by her mother to Paris to study with the great Isador Philip. Summers were spent in Russia, where the outbreak of World War I caught them.

The following six years were a time of terrible hardship. Government broke down; people starved and froze; they had to burn paper to heat a little water and were forced to chop up perfectly good furniture to provide a little heat occasionally. She played with frozen fingers on lorries on an upright piano "in order to earn a piece of bread," as she puts it.

In 1920 after escaping with her mother to Paris, Isadore Philip passed a few students on to her, and she began to work again. Within two years she was able to give a recital in Belgium, followed by concerts in Paris and London.

Her first American tour was in 1936, where she was booked to perform in New York, Boston, and Chicago. The reviews were so encouraging that the following year her contract called for thirty concerts.

In 1938 when she was again in America, the political situation in Europe had become so ominous and war so imminent that she decided to transplant her family to America.

Until 1966, when she was invited to join the faculty of the Juilliard School, she kept touring the United States and South

America, and after the war went back for regular engagements throughout Europe. Her repertory consisted of classical and romantic music, including Rachmaninoff. Virgil Thomson, for instance, spoke of a "new approach," and described her playing as "subtle and delicious, sound and sensible, delicate and robust, in every way lovely."[29]

While Mme Dorfmann admits she looked upon performing as such a pleasure that she used to wonder why she was being paid for doing something she enjoyed so much, she now stresses the satisfaction she derives from teaching. With a smile that was like a glimpse into a sealed chamber, she confessed she sometimes feels "drunk with the joy of being able to bring out the potentialities of students." "Teaching," she remarked, "is like watching flowers grow—they unfold before your eyes." To shape the careers of others, without having to impose one's own personality on them, as the teacher does, she now feels, is more rewarding than bringing pleasure to listeners.

Mme Dorfmann has made many records of Chopin, Schumann, Beethoven, and all the Romantics—and three times under the direction of Toscanini. She played under the famous maestro on the NBC Symphony broadcasts and with the Boston under Munch and with many of the great conductors of Europe and America. She has also recorded a piano work by Gian Carlo Menotti which he dedicated to her.[30] She has not been back to Russia, but she knows her records are being played there. "I am happy to be a teacher in America," she repeated with unbelievable modesty, "and I am grateful for the satisfaction I get from it."

Suzanne Bloch (1907–   ),[31] Mrs. Paul H. Smith, is the third of a trio of Juilliard faculty members, and an individual of different mettle. Ebullient and overflowing with joie de vivre, she is teacher, performing artist whose concerts send audiences into transports of delight, and composer as well. Her music, the kind with which Anne Boleyn entertained Henry VIII, is played on a variety of Renaissance instruments and has the effect of making a listener forget time and place.

She is one of three children of the composer Ernest Bloch

and was born in Switzerland. It was not her father who discovered her musical talent, but a teacher in a Geneva primary school who observed her singing along with other children and sent word to her mother during one of her father's absences that she ought to have musical instruction. When she was ten she was brought to New York where she was entered in the Hunter College Model School. Because she attended only one year of high school, she refers to herself as a "dropout."

Her first instruction was in the harp. One year later she played in the Salzedo Ensemble and began to compose for the harp. By 1921 when the family moved to Cleveland, where Ernest Bloch was to be director of the Cleveland Conservatory of Music, she was studying counterpoint and composition with him, was teaching younger pupils, playing in a string orchestra, even trying her hand at conducting.

The strongest effect on her musical development was supplied by Nadia Boulanger, under whose influence she came in 1925 when her father left the conservatory and she was sent to Paris to study. She explains that it was beneficial to be away from her father's domination because his strong parental pressures restrained her from developing freely. After three years of study with Nadia Boulanger she won the Prix aux Femmes in 1928 for her Suite for Flute and Piano.

In 1928 she was exposed to lute music at the home of Albert Einstein and, overcome by enthusiasm, she began to concentrate on the lute. While teaching privately and in progressive schools she made it her goal to save enough money to purchase a lute that would cost about $350. The only lutemaker of that day was Arnold Dolmetsch, whose project was the Haslemere Festival of Music. It was a proud day for her when she was able to acquire a lute restored by the master. In 1934 she gave a recital at Haslemere and impressed a famous critic who heard her. The next step was to master the recorder and the virginal.

After her first concert at Town Hall, where she played the lute, virginal and recorder and sang at the same time, she acquired a manager. Erminie Kahn was the kind of agent who put a protective mantle around her clients. Between Miss Kahn and her husband, Paul H. Smith, a professor of mathematics at Columbia University, who encouraged her to follow her bent, Miss Bloch's music-making expanded fully. She taught the recorder to her husband (who had had some musical training) with such success that he became a soloist in her New York concerts and in her words "stole the show." At first she took short tours, then when her two boys were old enough to be left at home with their father and a helper who was often one of her students, she set out for longer tours through the South, Canada, and as far West as Hawaii.

Miss Bloch's repertory consists of Elizabethan songs and music of the sixteenth and seventeenth centuries and the baroque period. For example, at a concert at King's College in Canada in 1969, her program included music for lute of the early sixteenth century; recorder music from the thirteenth to the seventeenth centuries; and music for the virginal from 1529 to the seventeenth century. On occasion she played the lute as solo instrument with orchestra, as in St. John's Passion and in the Ode to St. Cecilia's Day by Handel. She was also the first to start and direct an ensemble of students and talented amateurs, using early instruments. These concerts, which were given in the recital hall of the New York *Times,* were a great hit. Her most recent project is to give a free recital annually to benefit an old church in Vermont near where she maintains a summer home, in order to provide the church with the money for maintenance and needed additions.

Her teaching career at Juilliard began in 1942 when she was engaged to teach composition to young people, seven to thirteen years of age. She taught them by encouraging them to make music in response to fairy tales. ("The Little Mermaid" proved a very fruitful source.) The next was the regular school where she taught solfeggio basic ear training (the attempt to apply the tones of the scale—do-re-mi-fa-sol-la-ti-do—to singing exercises), making up her own drills for ear and sightreading training. Between 1955 and 1965 she concertized so extensively in America and Europe that she could not teach. But in 1965 she returned to the Juilliard School to teach Renaissance music in the graduate school, where her classes included students of the caliber of Van Cliburn and John Browning.

Some of the music she played and composed was recorded, but very little is extant. In 1965 Vox Records brought out a disc, "The Art of Suzanne Bloch," which features music for virginal, lute, recorder, and songs. It has been presented over various FM stations.

A startling composition is her "Lachrymae for Strings." She explains that she composed it in 1945 because she had a "terrible feeling" about the war. The League of Composers had called upon their members to compose music on war subjects. These compositions seemed so trite that it awakened in her the desire to do something to focus attention on the plight of children in wartime. This affecting and beautiful piece was performed by several orchestras.

Today she looks upon two tasks as most important to her, the biography of Ernest Bloch which she is writing and the "organic" contribution she feels she can make through contact with young people. It has been her habit to find daily quotations from great people—musicians, philosophers, thinkers—which she then displays on a special bulletin board. She does not identify them as coming from her, yet the students know them as "Miss Bloch's quotations." They are, she feels, a counter effect to some of the angry statements one sees plastered in many public places.

As for her feeling about America, she asserts she is proud to call herself an American and feels that in America "bad weeds can grow, but they cannot thrive." She is happy that what is best in America is being preserved.

The instrument that seems to hold the greatest attraction for women is the piano. Because it is a basic instrument, musical instruction is generally begun on the piano, and while some students proceed from the piano to other instruments, many remain lifetime devotees.

Since the proliferation in the twentieth century of excellent music schools and music departments in the colleges, women have been concentrating on all instruments. The violin, viola, cello, and flute have been attracting more and more women who play in symphonies, chamber groups, and as soloists in concert. Though the violin in particular has been exerting a strong pull on young women, the number of outstanding women violinists is small and those of foreign birth still smaller.

(1875–1910).[3] Born in Dublin, she was brought to the United States by her father, a physician, who settled on the East Side and soon established a good practice. She was sent to convent schools and then to Teachers' College. With her newly earned diploma she went off to teach in a public school on the lower East Side, where most of the children were immigrants from Jewish homes. She taught there two years.

Young, pretty, dainty, and immensely empathetic, Miss Kelly lavished kindness and understanding on her charges. These children, who had come from a world which distrusted Christians, were disarmed by her personality. She was able to tame wild boys, to resolve feuds among the children, even to disarm the parents.

Miss Kelly was so impressed by the potential she saw in these little aliens that she wanted to tell the world about them. Under the pen name of "Miss Bailey" she began to turn out sentimental stories stressing attractive qualities in these children. Her first story, *A Christmas Present for a Lady*, was about a boy too poor to buy his teacher a Christmas gift of soap, so he decided to bring her something his father had given his mother which had made his mother appear very happy. He took this to mean that it was a proper gift for a lady. The soiled ink paper he placed in her hand was a receipt for a month's rent for their home.

Her stories appeared first in magazines, then were issued in book form. Long after she left school and until her untimely death she kept writing about the children she had taught, producing volume after volume titled *Little Citizens, The Isle of Dreams, Little Aliens, Wards of Liberty*, and others.

Was Miss Kelly a professional writer? The characters she used were stereotypes which very often strike one as unreal. Yet Miss Bailey, her alter ego, became such a respected character that President Theodore Roosevelt wrote to the author:

While I was Police Commissioner I quite often went to the Street Public School and was immensely interested and by what I saw there. I thought there were a good many there, and the work they were doing among their who were so largely of Russian-Jewish parentage like the

---

The author was fortunate to meet a young woman of Polish birth who has been fascinated with the violin since the age of eight. She is Hanna Lachert,[32] one of two women occupying chairs in the string section of the Philharmonic Symphony Society of New York. Born in Warsaw in 1944, she began piano practice at three and gave her first public concert at five. At eight she discovered the violin and it has never lost its hold on her.

She comes from a family of talented musicians. Her mother is a pianist and teacher; her brother is a pianist and composer. She is a graduate of the Warsaw Academy of Music and of several European conservatories, specifically in Hanover and Brussels. She has played with orchestras, chamber groups, as soloist, and has given over three hundred recitals throughout Europe, including on radio and television. In 1969 she accepted a graduate assistantship at the University of Connecticut to teach the violin, which included the opportunity for further study with Bronislaw Gimpel. At the end of two years she had earned the master of arts degree and additional experience in playing with several American orchestras. She then auditioned at the Philharmonic Symphony and was taken on as a member of the orchestra.

Miss Lachert has been a protégée of the Jeunesses Musicales Association of Warsaw, which has a branch in the United States. Under its sponsorship she made a debut at Carnegie Recital Hall and fulfilled engagements in Washington (at the Smithsonian Institution), in Mexico and elsewhere, receiving appreciative notices.

She stresses the fact that she came to the United States of her own volition, because she is convinced that the United States is now the capital of music. She feels she has a better chance to succeed here. Whether she remains a performer or eventually returns to an academic job, she is convinced that her future can best develop in the United States.

There must be a limitation on the number of individuals who can be brought forward, because there are so many performers and instrumental teachers of distinction. Whether they deserve to be honored more for their achievement in having created a

new generation of American musicians equal to any in the
world, or for their individual contributions as gifted performers
who have enriched the American musical scene, the author
gladly leaves to the judgment of others.

CHAPTER 14

Immigrant Women Writers:
Real Truth versus Artistic Truth

WITH THE TRIUMPHANT STATEMENT "MINE IS THE SHINING FUTUP
America's best known woman immigrant concluded the perso
story of a girl (herself) who had been hurtled from a Rus
speck of a village into the American environment, to be t
formed within the space of eight years into an American pr
When Mary Antin wrote her life story, the brave words,
is the Shining Future," were a declaration of her f
America, where some marvelous things had happened
rather than an assertion of supreme self-confidence.
was not to have a "shining future." Before we proc
most lyrical autobiography extant, one which sold ne
copies[1] before the author's death, a general appr
writings which have come from the immigrant
in order.

While the experiences of immigrants in the Am
ment have made a considerable impact on Ar
the effect of immigrant writers themselves on t
has been a modest one. For one thing, there w
few of them. Furthermore, with the excepti
Rolvaag, Ludwig Lewisohn, and Abraham C
literary stature are lacking. Only in the fie
can the claim be upheld that foreign-b
made a considerable impress in terms of r
ness.[2] The force which emanates from
(autobiographies) of the foreign-born
the presentation of a new facet of /
on American soil, one with which nat'
also from the uncommon vigor which
One upon whom the new environ
impression as to compel her to writ

children you write of) was very much like what your Miss Bailey has done.[4]

Immigrants have had many chroniclers and their role in our society has not gone unnoticed. There exists a considerable corpus of fiction which illumines the habits and life styles of practically all ethnic groups—Italians, Irish, Jews, Greeks, and others in the cities and elsewhere; Germans, Russians, Scandinavians in the midst of their acres; Slavs and Balkanites in the mining districts, or in the wilderness "stitching away"[5] at the earth as they laid tracks for the railroads.

However, most of these writings do not come from the immigrant generation but rather from their posterity, and the number of men exceeds that of women. Clearly the imagination of their descendants was fired by what their parents or grandparents related to them, or perhaps by the contrast between their own assured lives and the difficulties the immigrant generation had endured. One wonders that these native writers should have been able to accomplish what the actual participants did not—to present these experiences realistically, yet in fictional terms. Was it because the writers were not themselves implicated in these struggles that they were able to fuse stark truth with the requirements of fiction? Would Rolvaag, the most powerful immigrant writer, have written as he did about the settling of the wilderness if he had himself participated in it, or Abraham Cahan about the grasping women's apparel manufacturer, David Levinsky, if he had not been able to view him at some remove from himself? Surely George Santayana's *Last Puritan* did not represent his own clash with the Calvinist heritage. Clearly, in creating such an extraordinary band of characters Rolvaag gave his imagination full play. *Giants in the Earth* is a persuasive example of what the artistic imagination can achieve in heightening the effect of unvarnished reality. His is artistic truth with no sacrifice of actual truth.

We know that many attempted to express their emotions through poetry. Morris Rosenfeld,[6] a sweatshop worker and one of the most melancholy singers in any language, had an immense following and stirred his readers to their depths. Among others who achieved recognition as poets were Carlos Bulosan,[7] a Filipino whom Harriet Monroe discovered, and Pascal d'Angelo,[8] an Italian laborer who won a poetry contest sponsored by the *Nation* and contributed an autobiography as well. What these poets dispensed was real truth, made more artistic by the gloss of poetry. But if the number of autobiographies extant tells us anything, it is that immigrants who felt the urge to write about their experiences preferred autobiography. They may have been "driven by private needs," as Mary Antin suggests, or in the words of Pascal d'Angelo, were "filled with the urge to cry out, to cry out disconnected words, expression of pain, anything to cry out."

The immigrant autobiography has a history as old as the North American continent. The earliest colonists, Captain Smith of Virginia and Governors Bradford and Winthrop of Plymouth and Massachusetts Bay, respectively, produced the earliest chronicles of an individual confronting a new way of life. These early autobiographers were followed by a steady trickle which kept pace with immigration. Several hundred autobiographies exist in published form and it is safe to conclude that many more were treated as family documents.

The immigrant autobiographer was only very rarely a professional writer. Most often he was either a businessman (Andrew Carnegie, Edward Bok), scientist (Michael Pupin), teacher (Morris R. Cohen, Ludwig Lewisohn), minister (Edward Steiner), doctor (Max Thorek), or journalist (Maurice Hindus). There were also many others. Among women many were factory workers who rose to become union leaders or labor organizers and felt they had a vital story to tell. But we also find personal stories by women who were in different fields of work—doctors (Marie E. Zakrzewska), musicians (Lotte Lehmann), or social workers (Elizabeth G. Stern)—who may have felt that it was incumbent upon them to leave a record of their work. For some, autobiography marked the beginning of a writing career, as it did for Ludwig Lewisohn and Louis Adamic, among others. Autobiography proved such a satisfactory outlet that some wrote two memoirs at different times of their lives. Examples are Ludwig Lewisohn[9] and George Santayana.[10]

While the personal story may consciously or unconsciously adumbrate, change or omit facts touching on certain aspects of one's life, the actual facts of an individual's life can rarely be disguised. It is well known that immigrants of both sexes were apt to be wildly ambitious. Women young enough to proceed along the educational route found in teaching and social work the quickest route to security and respect. To become a writer, however, called not only for a long-term effort, but it was an ambition that carried a high risk of disappointment. People who led precarious lives would understandably hesitate to take risks. Even those women who may have had a strong desire to express themselves through writing may have been held back by the will-of-the-wisp aspect of success as writers.

While language difficulties may have been a deterrent to some, for young people of intelligence it could not have been a decisive factor. The apparently uncomplicated grammar of the English language made it easy to master the language, particularly for those who had had a secondary education, or part of it, which very frequently included Latin. One of the most surprising facts was the ease with which so many learned to speak English well. Anyone capable of writing an autobiography was sufficiently well equipped to essay any other kind of writing. Yet most of those who produced an effective biography never attempted anything else and those who did were often unable to equal the impact they had achieved with the personal story. There are, however, some exceptions. Ludwig Lewisohn was one; the philosopher George Santayana, the author of *The Last Puritan*, was another. But neither of Santayana's two autobiographies was as stirring as those of some immigrants of lesser intellectual distinction.

The dearth of imaginative writing by the immigrant generation is surprising when one considers that many carried around a "psychic wound" with its built-in predisposition toward making their experiences known. Heinrich Heine's ditty is applicable here: "Aus meinen grossen Schmerzen / mach ich die kleinen Lieder" (Out of my great pain I construct my little songs). Also, publishers were hospitable to foreign-born writers whose experiences were unique. Of course, it can never be known how many may have made a try at an American novel and given up. One must conclude that it was difficult to acquire the artistic distance needed to universalize an experience in which one's involvement was as total as that of an immigrant trying to find himself in the American world. When they wanted to write about it, as so many did, they turned to the autobiography, which was as dramatic as anything that could be invented; the fictive immigrant story had to wait for the more detached observer.

There is no better example of the effect of which the immigrant autobiography is capable than *The Promised Land* by Mary Antin (1881–1949). Her specific contribution is to have "dramatized for Americans the spiritual meaning of America from the point of view of the immigrant."[11] Hers is the classical autobiography, except that her story stops rather inconclusively at her twentieth year, eight years after her mother brought her and three other children to Boston to join their father. Although *The Promised Land* did not appear until 1912, more than ten years after she had concluded it, it was not brought up-to-date at the time of publication. She stopped at that particular point because, she explains, she felt she had by then fully been "made over." The person she had been no longer existed and it was time to draw up a balance sheet.

To Ellery Sedgwick, editor of the *Atlantic Monthly, The Promised Land* was the single rival to *Up From Slavery*.[12] It is typical of the immigrant autobiography in that Antin employs the usual pattern of sketching in the European background, followed by the experiences of the family in Boston. Life in Russia and later in the United States was just what one would expect, except for one difference. In Russia there had been poverty, insecurity, even persecution; in Boston they also suffered want due to a succession of economic failures, but she found the kind of unexpected, amazing personal success that few immigrants experienced. While other autobiographers are apt to be critical of some features of American life, she is worshipful throughout. She saw America not as a place where slums and exploitation existed, where people, as she observed of her father, "practice every form of drudgery" and yet could not earn enough to pay the rent of three and a half dollars a week and "buy a bone for the soup," but "as a blessed land" resting firmly on its professed ideals. It is a viewpoint of a very idealistic girl who is recompensed for the deprivations she suffers by her almost magical success in the spiritual realm. Petted, pampered by teachers, principals, librarians, and social workers, including the great Edward Everett Hale himself, she was enabled to scramble up rapidly in her climb toward recognition.

The tone of her book is lyric, though the contents are, except for one summer at the seashore, very somber. Her style must be attributable, at least in part, to the loving care the teachers at the Latin School for Girls expended on their most promising pupil. It was not surprising that she was the pet of her teachers, for she was a persuasive advertisement for the wonders of the public school and what it could achieve in educating aliens. No one could doubt her sincerity. She considered teachers "holy" and her faith in America was a "healing ointment." She believed in the potency of American ideals, because the treatment she received confirmed the existence of these ideals. Ludwig Lewisohn, for instance, who had, like her, received his education in America (though in the South), pronounced the vaunted American ideals sham and hypocrisy, because they had not been applied to him.

Her first teacher, Miss Dillingham, realized very soon that she had an uncommonly bright girl in her class. All the schooling Mary had received in Russia was what her Hebrew teacher had taught her. In Boston she learned so rapidly that after four months Miss Dillingham sent one of her first compositions to an educational magazine. It was printed. Before long her poems, paeans to America, began to appear in the Boston *Herald* and when she entered the Latin School for Girls four years after coming to America, one of the newspapers devoted half a column to the event. When she was in her late teens Miss Josephine Lazarus, a Jewish community leader, came upon letters Mary had written to an uncle in Russia describing the voyage to America and her early impressions. Miss Lazarus persuaded the *American Hebrew* to publish them. Then she encouraged her to make these letters the basis of *The Promised Land*. The book is dedicated to Miss Lazarus.

In an article published in 1914 two years after the appearance of her autobiography, she spoke of the debt she owed to those who helped "to keep her in school." "I was reared in the tenement district," she explained,

where the poor of many nations contend with one another for a scant living and the only reason I am no longer of the slums is because a hundred heroes and heroines among my neighbors fought for my release.[13]

Among the chief "heroines" who aided in her escape from the slums was her sister, older by only a few years. She was sent to work while Mary and the younger children were taken to school. Whether or not a young person of foreign birth went to an American school or not made an essential difference. When the sister married at seventeen and her father could not find work, their only source of income was what her brother earned selling newspapers. Others who "helped" keep her in school were the humble tradesmen of the neighborhood, the grocer who extended credit, the druggist who replenished her cough medicine without insisting on payment, and others. They basked in her achievements. Only the landlady, intent on her rent, shouted at her that foreigners who were poor had no right to an education, that geometry was not for her, that she ought to go to work to enable the family to pay the rent instead of prattling of going to college.

Though everyone expected that she would proceed from the Latin School to Radcliffe College, she did not. Fate intervened. She fell in love and married a non-Jew she had met on a botanical field trip. He was William A. Grabau, a graduate of the Massachusetts Institute of Technology and a graduate student at Harvard University and for him she gave up college. Her autobiography makes no mention of the young man, except for a hazy reference to field trips. After her husband was called to teach at Columbia University she studied at Teachers' College and at Barnard, but by then she had a child and she never acquired the college degree.

One would have expected that a young woman who had been subjected to such a multiplicity of experiences and could express herself as vividly as she did, would have turned to writing. But nothing appeared between 1914 and 1941. In 1914 *American Magazine* carried a series of her articles which condemned the attempt at exclusion of immigrants. She sounded as passionate, as moving as ever. In 1941, eight years before her death, *Common Ground* published *The House of One Father,* which seems more like a persuasive article on ecumenicism rather than as a renewed commitment to her people as it is said to have been. The ability to express herself well and forcefully was very evident, but there was no spectacular message. When she died after a succession of various illnesses, all that could be said was that she had had a shining past.

Among foreign-born playwrights there are also more men than women, but we can point to at least one and possibly another, if she will be accepted as a dramatist. Bella Cohen Spewack (1899–) was exclusively a playwright and screen writer and with her husband Samuel Spewack turned out some very successful plays. About the other—Vicki Baum—there is some question whether she should be classed with dramatists. She is a novelist, but had one spectacular play to her credit, *Grand Hotel.* It was not written as a play, but she asserts that she herself turned it into a play[14] when she found that the first act the dramatist in Germany submitted to her did not please her.

In 1931 when Vicki Baum arrived in America to arrange for the film version of *Grand Hotel,* she was a well-known author of ten novels. As for Bella and Samuel Spewack, in 1931 they were still in the fledgling state and were yet to write their first successful play. Later, when Bella Spewack was lured to Hollywood as a scenario writer, her career ran parallel to that of Vicki Baum, who then lived in Hollywood and for a time also wrote for the screen.

Bella Cohen's marriage in 1928 to Samuel Spewack, who had been a reporter and foreign correspondent in Moscow and Berlin, marked the emergence of a new writing team that would produce more than a dozen plays. Their first play had no East Side characters in it. But the second play, *Poppa,* and the third, *Spring Song,* were plays about people who still adhered to their European shibboleths, or were still in the transition stage

between the traditions of the Russian Pale and the mores of
the lower East Side.

Poppa has for its main character an insurance agent who
neglects his job, which we suspect he does not like, for an
activity he finds more soul-satisfying—that of being active in
the district's Republican Club. He stills his conscience, which
reminds him that he ought to be about trying to make a living,
with the comforting notion that by helping people he is doing
"what he can for his country free of charge."

Spring Song, a tragedy, is more of an immigrant story than
Poppa because Mrs. Solomon, the main character, is completely
bound up in the old customs. A widow, she is the mother of
two daughters, one of whom is as dependable as the younger
is flighty and frivolous. Mrs. Solomon is the prototype of the
Jewish mother who slaves away at her newspaper stand selling
newspapers, candy and cigarettes with only one thought in
mind, how to insure the happiness of her daughters.

Mrs. Solomon's reaction to the news that her younger daughter
is pregnant, after having seduced the older girl's sweetheart,
is to insist she must marry the young man, even though he
does not care for her, nor she for him, and she knows that the
older girl's happiness is irretrievably ruined. The "wages of
sin" concept prevails, the marriage takes place, and the girl
dies in childbirth.

To the surprise of Max Gordon, who produced the play, it
was unsuccessful. Mrs. Solomon's solution was not one that
even theater-goers not too far removed from the immigrant
generation could easily accept.

After that Bella and Samuel Spewack had enough of writing
about unassimilated foreigners. They went on to such successes
as *Boy Meets Girl* and the musical, *Leave It to Me,* to which
Cole Porter contributed the lyrics.

Vicki Baum (1882–1960) was born in Vienna and there had
studied the harp at the Konservatorium. Though she played for
some years in various orchestras, she seemed to have felt that
the harp was a "stupid instrument."

She began writing at the age of fourteen. Despite the "something like thirty novels" she claims to have written, her reputa-

tion rests on *Grand Hotel*. Some of her other novels were also turned into plays, but the success of *Grand Hotel* did not repeat itself. Could she therefore be considered a dramatist? It has always been very hard to write both novels and plays. We need only to recall Henry James's struggles with the stage to realize how difficult it is to be both novelist and dramatist.

Her novel, *Menschen im Hotel*, was being serialized in the *Berliner Illustrierte* when an astute theatrical agent in Berlin recognized its dramatic possibilities. The play, produced by Max Reinhardt in 1928 in Berlin, became *Grand Hotel*.

Menschen im Hotel was the first of her writings to be translated into English. Her English publisher sold it to Nelson Doubleday in New York, who turned it into a best-seller.[15] Metro-Goldwyn-Mayer invested $35,000 in the production to secure the movie rights and Henry Shumlin produced it in New York. The play, in which the characters touch but for a moment, was such a huge success that it grossed more than $1,250,000 and ran for thirteen months.[16] Yet her share is supposed to have been altogether $30,000, the greatest part of which came from the serial rights ($10,000) and $3,600 for the movie rights.[17]

Miss Baum was brought to New York to assist in the making of the film which was produced by the legendary Irving Thalberg with an all-star cast, and was paid $2,500 a week for more than six months. When her contract expired she returned to her family, consisting of husband and two sons, and to her job at Ullstein Verlag. In Germany she found that the Nazi Party was "visibly expanding" and that Germany was "desperado-filled." Her decision to leave Germany was "by instinct."

She worked for Metro-Goldwyn-Mayer for several years before she realized that she had no talent for movie writing and "withdrew from it." The years in the United States were productive years, for according to her statement she produced about twenty novels. But she could never duplicate the success of *Grand Hotel* though she employed the same formula in a novel, *Hotel Berlin*.

As a writer in America she either could not or did not want to write about life in the American setting, although some of her novels have American characters in them. In her autobiography, *It Was All Quite Different,* she allots one-sixth of the book to the thirty years she spent in the United States. America apparently made little impression on her. She is an example of the mature immigrant who merely transferred her domicile from Germany to California. She continued to write as if she were insulated against American influences. A guide to how seriously she is to be considered is supplied by her own estimate of herself: "I know what I'm worth; I'm a first-rate second-rate author."[18]

No greater antithesis between two writers can be imagined than between Martha Ostenso, Norwegian, and Anzia Yezierska, Polish-Jewish. The contrast lies in the locale in which their fiction is placed, the people they write about, and in the personalities of the authors, which are stamped on their writings. Miss Ostenso gives the impression of being contemplative, inclined to considered judgment; Miss Yezierska is explosive and her emotional response is instantaneous.

Martha Ostenso (1900–1963) was born in Norway and brought to the Northwest when she was a child. Reared in South Dakota and Minnesota thirty years after the Northwest had become "settled country," the people she encountered were the descendants of pioneers rather than the pioneers themselves.

She began to write while attending the University of Manitoba and in 1924 her first novel, *A Far Land,* was published. It made no splash but a year later she won a prize of $13,500 for her novel *Wild Geese.* It was serialized and turned into a movie which won her instant acclaim.

Miss Ostenso taught in the Midwest and she also tried being a social worker in New York's East Side,[19] which seems to have had the effect of strengthening her identification with the people with whom she had grown up. Over the years she became the author of numerous novels, an anthology of verse, and many short stories. She also collaborated with the Australian nurse, Sister Kenny, on a book, *They Shall Walk,* which became an outstanding movie with Rosalind Russell.

A regional writer, her settings are the plains of the Midwest and Northwest, where many Scandinavians and middle Europeans settled. Characters in an Ostenso novel are generally the descendants of those who "made the prairie bloom." While one of her best novels is built around Norwegians and Irish, others may have at most one or two foreign characters and most center around people so thoroughly assimilated that their ethnic backgrounds cannot even be guessed at.

One of the most brutish of her male characters is the farmer Caleb Gore in *Wild Geese*. It is a harsh, but vivid farm novel, a tour de force, in which Caleb Gore holds the whip over his family by means of a secret he knows his wife wants to conceal at all costs—that she is the mother of an illegitimate son who does not suspect his relationship to her. A feeling of terror hangs over the story as one observes Caleb in his deceptively soft-spoken manner driving his wife and children to the breaking point. He denies to one daughter the glasses she requires, ignoring the irritated condition of her eyes. The other children are worked like farm animals. His long-suffering wife accepts her servitude, but the daughter Judith harbors a murderous hatred for him. When Caleb comes to the end he deserves one can only feel relieved that Judith has not murdered him.

In another, less consequential, story, a father ruins the lives of all his children, save the youngest one, not by deliberate or fiendish cruelty, but by exercising a lethal control over them that makes them unable to act on their own. One after another is drained of initiative and will. His weapon is a miasmic religiosity which holds them with tentacles from which they cannot escape. Also a soft-spoken man, who is an economic failure, he seems to be spreading a creeping disease.[20]

Not all villains in Miss Ostenso's fiction are male, and some of her males can be admirable. Such a man is the Norwegian Ivar Vinge in *O River, Remember,* who has a mystical love for the earth he tends. He saw the land as providing:

> . . . work for the idle, food for the hungry, peaceful sleep at night for the worn in heart; here was dark, living gold. His eyes saw the blue of the empty northern horizon cleave the sea of spring grass, but he knew only the strong velvet of the earth in his hand; it was more than a feeling in his hands, it was almost a taste in his mouth.

The book carries the author's philosophy of the relation between man and the earth from which he draws sustenance. To take one's living from the earth is right, but to hoard land, to hold it for profit as Magdali Vinge and her brother do, is morally wrong. Here the woman is cast in the role of villain because she sees the earth, not as the supplier of life, but in terms of "cloudy future dollars and cents." But Ivar cannot prevail against his wife, who goes on accumulating all the land she can, selling and buying and exchanging until she and her brother are rich, owning the bank, the mill, the hotel, the lumber yard, the branch railroad, while he wants only as much land as he can cultivate.

The handicap with which Miss Ostenso and probably any writer drawing his theme from the Northwest have to contend with is the shadow of Ole Edvart Rolvaag, beside whose monumental *Giants in the Earth* any story set in the Northwest is apt to seem pallid in comparison.

The word "pallid" cannot be used in any connection with Anzia Yezierska (1885–1973). She was a readhead with disillusioned eyes but a determined look and well-cut features. In a sketch by the artist Willy Pogany she resembles a handsome unsmiling Polish girl rather than a Jewess from Eastern Europe. The intensity of her writings is reminiscent of Mary Antin whose autobiography also sounds as if she had "dipped her pen in her heart." But while Mary Antin wrote one autobiography, Miss Yezierska presented the experiences of her life in America in a dozen different autobiographical guises. She is the Sophie, Sarah, Rachel, Yetta of her stories. Even the story of a shopgirl who marries a millionaire,[21] supposed to be drawn after Rose Pastor Stokes, represents a certain aspect of the author—not in the wish to be the wife of a millionaire, but in the striving to improve herself, in her desire to make herself worthy of a man who "lives only for learning and thinking" (Miss Yezierska's categorization of a man with intellectual leanings), and above all else in her sympathy for the poor and the disadvantaged which she fully shared with Rose Pastor Stokes. She has only partially transmuted real truth into artistic truth.

Although Anzia Yezierska wrote about seven so-called "novels" and one autobiography,[22] all harped on the same theme—hunger and loneliness. She is the Everyman of the Russian and Polish immigration of the turn of the century and speaks for all, men who worked as machine operators or pressers, or hawked comestibles from pushcarts, or did not work at all, like the author's father who, having chosen to "have his portion in the next world," worked for "God and his Torah," letting daughters or sons support themselves as best they could. She also embodies every immigrant woman who had to feed her family and pay the rent somehow, who struggled with dirt and vermin, who worried about young children in school and palpitated over the fate of marriageable daughters. Like Walt Whitman, one can say of every one of her books: "Camerado! This is no book; / Who touches this, touches a man [human being]."

She was born in the Russian part of Poland and if the various "I's" of her stories are to be taken as autobiographical embodiments of herself, she was old enough upon coming to America to be sent to work—at least in her early teens or late pre-teens. She sewed buttons, made artificial flowers, sewed shirts, rolled cigars, worked in laundries. Unlike Mary Antin, who in her love for America had no word of condemnation for the sweatshop system to which her sister (and others) were exposed, Anzia Yezierska's barbaric yawp communicates her outrage at the conditions under which immigrants were compelled to slave for subsistence, and that it was so difficult "to work yourself up for a somebody." Her "I's" are no cringing little people; they make demands: "Ain't everything possible in the new world?" she asks. "Why is [exists] America, but to give me the chance to lift up my head with everybody alike?"[23]

Her first conflation was *Hungry Hearts*, and all the stories in it are of one kind—what the immigrant existence was like. It is autobiographical because all of the outrages she describes could (and might) have happened to her. But it can also lay claim to being fiction because some situations she herself would not have experienced. For instance, a woman scraping together every cent for a can of paint with which to transform her kitchen for the son who is returning from military service, finds that the landlord raises her rent because the apartment is now worth more. Another is that of a mother of young children who is sent by a charitable institution for a vacation and finds the experience humiliating.

Hungry Hearts was turned into a silent movie and she was transported to Hollywood and treated like Cinderella. But the opulence of the environment affected her ability to work and she returned to New York. Her autobiography discloses very little of her early experiences and this makes it impossible to tell whether she, like one of her heroines, managed by dint of the grimmest efforts to go to college. She was so hungry for education that an unexpectedly earned fifty cents went to the janitor's daughter to teach her everything that she was being taught at school. What her autobiography discloses is that after her return from Hollywood she lost everything she had saved in the crash, that she could not find work and was compelled to join the Writer's Project of the W.P.A. At first she was put on the Creative Project which meant she could work at home and report only once a week, but when the office was reorganized, she was put on a project to create a new "Guidebook," to which she and everyone had to contribute two thousand words daily. Her assignment was to catalogue trees in Central Park. When she wrote up her W.P.A. experience, Orville Prescott declared it "a vivid picture of quixotic good intentions, hysterical folly, pitiful bungling, and general bedlam."[24]

She was able to leave the W.P.A. when one of her old East Side friends, a fish peddler, bequeathed his lodge money of nearly eight hundred dollars to her. She remained a productive writer until shortly before her death, turning out stories, articles, and occasional book reviews.[25]

She realized that there was too much "I . . . I . . . I" in her stories, too much self-analysis and introspection.[26] It was because she was forced to live alone so much, she explains. She was also aware that essentially she had only one story to tell. "My one story," she says, "is hunger. Hunger driven by loneliness."[27] In her autobiography we come upon this admission: "When I stopped turning it out [the life she knew], I saw my own funeral procession go by."[28]

She was intense, passionate, unrestrained. Her stories are sordid to the point of being repugnant, and her style, according to Orville Prescott, is "effusive." She is repetitive in her expressions ad nauseam. "God from the world" and similar expletives appear several times in each story, if not on each page. Her dialogue is lame. But she can stir one powerfully, because what she presents is lived life in all its horrors. To read her stories is to experience the hammer on the anvil and one is grateful that the time when people lived like that in America belongs to our unlamented past.

CHAPTER 15

In the Business World

IN THEIR DESIRE TO BECOME SUCCESSFUL IN BUSINESS, WOMEN were not "diverse" from men. Like men, women, though fewer than men, have prospered in commerce since colonial days. That a large number of men of the first generation in the northern, middle and southern colonies became affluent during colonial days and the early national period through the fur trade, the "triangular trade," shipping, and other enterprises requires no corroboration. A forerunner of the plutocrats whose number would increase considerably during and after the Civil War, was John Jacob Astor. He came from Germany in 1783, and when he died in 1848, leaving an estate of more than $20,000,000, he was the richest man in America. Though the new crop of post-Civil War millionaires consisted mostly of natives and men, a large number of non-natives (and men) of diverse national backgrounds were able to participate in the national plunder. Emulating the example set by native businessmen, some immigrants managed to amass large fortunes by becoming bankers and railroad builders, by producing iron and steel, dealing in lumber and in a variety of food products from German delicatessen to Italian olives and olive oils, in meat processing, the production of wines, the manufacture of apparel for men and women and in a variety of other enterprises.

There were Dutch female traders in New York and Albany long before the Dutch colony of "Nieuw Amsterdam" was taken over by the Duke of York in 1664. From the beginning they carried on a lively commerce with the Indians, dispatching furs to Holland, acting as supercargo, importing goods from the mother country, which were then sold in their own trading centers. Not all were widows continuing what their husbands had started; some seemed to have liked business activity; others wanted to release their husbands for other work while they "tended the store."

One of the earliest women whose eye was on business was Margaret Hardenbroek van Vries, who was already affluent when she married her second husband, Frederick Philipse, a carpenter who worked for Governor Stuyvesant. It was said that she made her husband the richest man in the colony of Nieuw Amsterdam.[1]

Another was Elizabeth van Es, the daughter of a magistrate in Albany. After her husband's death she removed to New York, opened a store, and when she died left a considerable estate. The wife of the German-born Jakob Leisler, who occupies a permanent niche in colonial history for rising against the royal government following the revolution of 1688, was also a trader.[2] And there were others.

But by comparison with men, the total number of foreign-born women who won success in the world of business is infinitesimal. Immigrant women who distinguished themselves in business before the twentieth century were extremely rare, first, because women were restricted to their homes; also there was no demand for those specialties they could supply.

When President Franklin D. Roosevelt appointed Frances Perkins to his cabinet in 1932 it represented an unprecedented breakdown in prejudice against women. President Truman went further when he appointed the foreign-born Anna M. Rosenberg Assistant Secretary of Defense during the Korean War. By then women were thoroughly entrenched in the business world and some were keeping pace with men. In 1959, for instance, during the Eisenhower administration when Richard Nixon was Vice-President, the establishment of Helena Rubenstein was so well-known that the State Department asked her to represent the United States cosmetic industry at the American National Exhibition in Moscow.[3] Her rival, Elizabeth Arden, foreign-born too, had by that time also reached a prominent position in the world of business. Several other women whose stories follow were by then recognized as pathbreakers in their areas of business.

The spheres of activity in which immigrant women were active were those based on "woman's work," as Helena Rubinstein's male secretary, Patrick O'Higgins, referred to the cosmetics industry. In scanning the lives and achievement of women who showed a talent for business the conclusion seems inescapable that these women were more richly endowed with unusually good judgment, even canniness and, above all, courage, than women in other fields or professions.

Let us begin with a woman who became extremely successful, not because she possessed a conspicuous kind of competence, but by feeling her way step by step in a situation in which she accidentally found herself. Her abilities were latent and they grew as her business expanded. She was Jennie Grossinger (1892–1972).

However, she did not accomplish it entirely by herself. Her husband, her mother, and father separately contributed their efforts. But she participated actively in turning a dilapidated farmhouse in the Catskills into a glittering hostelry which acquired the appellation "Waldorf in the Catskills." Begun in 1914, it was enlarged in 1917, and in 1932 it was named The Grossinger Hotel and Country Club. By 1950 the hotel occupied 1,300 acres and was able to accommodate 150,000 people annually.[4]

Among the socially prominent who visited Grossinger's were Eleanor Roosevelt, Vice-President Alben W. Barkley, Governor Rockefeller, Robert F. Kennedy, Cardinal Spellman, Ralph Bunche, Chaim Weitzmann of Israel, King Baudouin of Belgium, and others. Their guests include prominent people in the sports and entertainment worlds, with a sprinkling of artists, authors, and well-known professors. While the majority are Jews, Christians come with their Jewish friends and form 25 to 33 percent of the total number of vacationers.[5]

Jennie Grossinger was born in the Polish part of Austria and was brought to America as a child. Her father started as a presser of pants and in 1914 opened a little restaurant where his wife was the cook, he the waiter, and Jennie the cashier, when she did not help him wait on table. She attended school only until she was thirteen, then worked as a buttonhole maker while going to school at night. The restaurant prospered modestly until the father collapsed from overwork. Her father's nephew of the same name, whom Jennie had married when she was twenty, purchased a primitive farm without electricity, where it was hoped "Pop" and "Mom" Grossinger could do their own farming and maintain themselves.

It was Jennie who suggested that they take boarders. Harry, Jennie's husband, solicited vacationers and did the heavy work outside. While "Pop" did the lighter work, "Mom" Grossinger cooked Jewish delicacies, and Jennie scrubbed, helped with the cooking, washed dishes and kept books in addition to taking care of her baby. Not until 1916, when they had a profit of $81, did they acquire a chambermaid and a secondhand car in which "Pop" met incoming guests. By the time Jennie Grossinger died the initial profit of $81 had multiplied into an intake of $7,000,000 a year.[6]

The essential reasons for the spectacular growth of the hotel were the managerial abilities of Harry and Jennie Grossinger. She was not content to be an ornament. Her contribution was her personal quality that made friends of employees and guests alike. He proved an entrepreneur of vision who recognized the need for a huge pool, an airport and the many extensions of the original property. The hotel became known for its superb food. Even the breads that were served were considered superior, which the General Baking Company recognized when they arranged to distribute rye and pumpernickel breads made from recipes used at the Grossinger Hotel. The hotel was managed like a family business and Jennie made the help and the guests feel that they were part of one big family.[7] Until 1950 the hotel never had a union or a strike.[8]

Jennie, an attractive, slim, blond, warm, cheerful and well-dressed woman, proved to be a born hostess who, according to the statement in the New York *Times*, "ruled with real dignity." She liked hotel keeping so much that after a religious service on one of the Jewish High Holy Days she said she hoped God would make her a hotel keeper when she reached heaven.[9]

She was also the speechmaker for the management and at the end of many an entertainment was apt to rise, elegantly gowned as she always was, to thank her guests in her simple, utterly sincere manner, for coming to Grossinger's.

The whole family has always been celebrated for its aid in behalf of various philanthropies of all denominations and for its patriotic backing of World War II. Its support of the hospital in nearby Liberty was so generous that a clinic bears the name of the family.[10] In 1932 at the height of the Depression a large benefit performance was arranged in behalf of the Christmas Fund sponsored by the New York *American*. George Jessel, master of ceremonies, collected more than $50,000. Such diverse charities as the Red Cross, the March of Dimes, the Boy Scouts, the Damon Runyon Cancer Fund, the Jewish War Veterans and the Albert Einstein School of Medicine have benefited from charity drives initiated at Grossinger's. Jennie personally endowed a clinic and a convalescent home in Israel.

During the war a "Canteen-by-Mail" service dispatched food, cigarettes, and games to servicemen who had been on the staff or guests at the hotel. To promote the sale of War Bonds special entertainments with Eddie Cantor were arranged, to which only purchasers of bonds were admitted. They never sold less than $25,000 at the conclusion of each Saturday night show.[11] Millions of dollars of War Bonds were disposed of. At her death Jennie Grossinger was the sole owner, her husband having died in 1964. The hotel was turned into a corporation of which the son, Paul, a graduate of the Cornell School of Hotel Management, is the president.

Jennie Grossinger is a concrete illustration of the effect of the American environment on some individuals who would otherwise have had no expectations of fame or fortune.

The restaurant business has always attracted the foreign-born and some of them were women, but no one, man or woman, has experienced a more spectacular business and personal success than Patricia Murphy (1912?–   ) of candlelight and popover fame. "A born gambler ready to shoot the works on a business venture or a purely personal decision," as she describes herself in her autobiography,[12] she gambled her entire fortune of sixty dollars on a tearoom in a Brooklyn basement and worked it into a million-dollar business, which includes one restaurant in

Westchester serving a million meals a year[13] and another near Fort Lauderdale in Florida, serving 2,000 daily. In addition she owned a supper club in London which she bought over a weekend. She also has a reputation as a horticulturist of distinction who has won many awards for her floral exhibitions. She combined the management of her restaurants with the art and science of horticulture; her estate in Florida was considered a showcase for flowers and blooms of the most exotic varieties; her Westchester restaurant is known for its flowers; her penthouse on upper Fifth Avenue in New York housed a greenhouse where 100,000 orchids were grown.

She explained her success [as] "due to instinct and to such intangibles as hard work and painstaking attention to details." Her "green thumb," which she inherited from her mother, she explained as "nine-tenths muscle." Her husband, the late Captain James E. Kiernan, considered her a "real Horatio Alger character." But, she admitted, she had to work like a "stevedore."

She was born in a small fishing village in Newfoundland, where everything "from a needle to an anchor" was sold at her father's general store. She studied music at a nearby convent and when she left for New York in 1929 it was with the intention of studying music. But once she was in New York and had set aside sixty dollars—the fare back home if she failed—she decided to get a job. She found one playing the piano in a student cafeteria near Columbia University and was soon dishing out food and working as a cashier.

When she lost her cashier's job she moved to Brooklyn Heights. A few doors from the subway she came upon a basement tearoom that had failed several times during that year. As she stood talking to the most recent owner, she remembered her nest egg of sixty dollars. The temptation seized her to gamble it all on candlelight and popovers.

With twenty cups and saucers, a maximum of thirty-six settings, and some student helpers, she prepared to serve her first meal. All she hoped for was "to break a little better than even," so that she would have a chance for a second night. She used candles because the electric lights were unshaded and she offered popovers because she considered them "slightly exotic and easy to make." Her dinners were priced at sixty-five and

eighty-five cents and included a profit of ten cents each. At the
end of the month she found she had made a profit of $500.

Of course she succeeded, first in Brooklyn, then in her second
restaurant on 60th Street in Manhattan, and in her third restaurant in Manhasset, Long Island, which grossed $1,500,000 during
its first year.[14] By then she was married to Captain Kiernan,
a naval architect, who gave her every help and encouragement.
But running three restaurants proved too much of a workload
and she disposed of all three to concentrate on one, in Westchester, which opened in 1954. More than a million was spent on
it and $169,000 was put into landscaping. By then she had a
showpiece of a home in Florida, to which she would bring
flowers from her greenhouse in Westchester to transplant, and
from which she took back Florida hibiscus, camellias, and
orchids. In the Westchester restaurant one could buy "orchids,
plants, and bouquets for a song."[15]

After her husband's death in 1959 she opened the Bahia Mar
restaurant in Fort Lauderdale, on which she spent $75,000 for
landscaping. It served 2,000 meals daily.[16] She would commute
from Westchester to Florida by flying her own two-engine plane.

Her triumphs as a horticulturist reached a high after the
death of her husband. Her gardens and penthouse terraces
were thrown open for annual spring showings which provided
scholarships to promote the study of natural science. Above the
streets of New York City an old-fashioned garden, an herb
garden, miniature apple trees, and beds of strawberries, in
addition to orchids, delighted the viewers.[17] She received more
than a dozen citations, prizes, and awards. For instance, in 1961
she won first prize at the International Flower Show and in
the same year the trophy of the Horticulture Society.

Mrs. Kiernan describes herself as "restaurantrice and businesswoman, horticulturist, horsewoman, aviatrix, hostess, and world
traveler." She succeeded because of a canny business sense
which told her that if she adhered to the motto, "food and
atmosphere at reasonable prices," she would not fail. Also because she was not frightened of taking chances.

In the field of women's fashions the name of Hattie Carnegie
(1889–1956)[18] brings up recollections of New York's most famous

couturieres and fashion dictators. It was said she never could or did sew anything, but that she had an "instinctive knowledge about good clothes." She made "the little black dress" fashionable and educated women into regarding it as an indispensable part of their wardrobes. According to Pauline Trigere, who worked for Hattie Carnegie as a designer, she was "a fabulous woman," who had "great taste" and made elegant clothes available for women of all stations.

One of seven children of an artist and designer in Vienna, Henriette Kanengeiser was brought to America as a child after the family home in the suburbs of Vienna burned down. In the United States the family name was changed to "Carnegie," as if in foreknowledge of the distinction that would come to a member of the family. Her father died when she was thirteen and she was forced to go to work. Her first job was that of cash girl in Macy's.

She began by trimming hats and at twenty was ready to start her own shop, which she called "Carnegie–Ladies' Hatter." It was a time when hats were a stand-by for the well-groomed woman. She had a partner who offered custom-made dresses, while Miss Carnegie took charge, designed hats and modeled clothes.

The shop was immediately successful. The next step was to buy out her partner and to start what today would be called a boutique. It was called "Hattie Carnegie, Incorporated," at 42 East 49th Street, a most fashionable address.

In 1919 she took her first buying trip to Paris and thereafter went several times a year in order to be able to present to her customers the latest in Parisian models. Her customers were society women and actresses and her dresses cost several hundred dollars each. Even chiffon handkerchiefs were priced at ten dollars apiece.

Less wealthy women discovered Hattie Carnegie's shop when the Depression made her aware that people were "broke," as the *New Yorker* put it. She opened a ready-to-wear department and it brought her more money than any other branch of her business. What she offered was simple elegance at prices the average woman could afford. All her designs, declared the *New*

Yorker,[19] "breathe[d] the French spirit." For herself she preferred
clothes designed by Schiaparelli and Vionnet.

Miss Carnegie did not limit herself to the retail trade. In her
wholesale department she showed French models adapted to
American tastes. She sold cosmetics, perfume, and jewelry in
addition to apparel, but only to one store in a city.

The epitome of the stylish sophisticate, she raised livestock on
her farm in New Jersey, but filled her home in New York
with French antique furniture, modern paintings, and Chinese
porcelains.

A brisk, breezy woman, Pauline Trigère's personality[20] seems
reflected in the clothes she designs, which are striking, elegant
yet understated, serviceable, and what she calls "ageless" (can
be worn a long time). Cutting must always have come easy
to her, because she reveals that she had wanted to be a surgeon.
"No, not a doctor," she insisted, "a *surgeon.* Now I cut fabrics."
On one of her wrists she wore a kind of identifying mark, a
magnet fashioned like a wristwatch, that served as a nest for
pins. "I'm always covered with pins," she remarked.

Her mother was a dressmaker in Paris; her father had a
tailoring establishment; and she grew up learning to sew and
design fashions in her parents' atelier while she attended the
College of Victor Hugo in Paris. In 1937 the threat of war
forced the family to think of emigrating, not to the United States,
but to Chile. However, a short stopover in the United States
convinced them that they ought to make their home in America.
She fell in love with the "tempo of New York," the "openness
of people," "democracy at work." In 1944 she became an
American citizen.

For a short while she worked as a designer and in 1942
was ready to strike out for herself, with her brother as partner.
It was risky, for she had responsibility for her two young sons.
But, never short on courage, she pawned a diamond brooch
and got started modestly with a collection of eleven models,
which her brother took on the road to show to prospective
buyers. Today her collections consist of a hundred and twenty-
five pieces and appear four to five times a year. She is said to
be a genius with fabrics and is able to drape and cut fabrics

on live models without making canvas patterns. Sometimes she can cut a garment in ten minutes.

Now she creates jewelry, men's ties as well, and has launched a new perfume called "trigère." In jewelry she likes animal motifs, especially the turtle, which also adorns the packaging of her perfume. As for her jewelry, it is often intended to complement a specific garment and sometimes a necklace is found attached to a dress. For a black chiffon model, for instance, she said she would choose rhinestones if diamonds are out of one's reach. "They can be very pretty," with a characteristic wave of her hand, "if that's the best you can afford."[21]

When questioned if she has a formula for success, she said, "You've got to have it in you." She considers it essential to work hard, to persevere and not to give up. She says she works harder now than she did twenty years ago.

Miss Trigère has won several of the most prestigious prizes. She is a three-time winner of the Coty Fashion Critics' Award and in 1959 received the fashion world's highest honor, the Coty Hall of Fame Award. She is also a recipient of the Neiman-Marcus Award, the National Cotton Award, and in 1972 the Silver Medal of the City of Paris, which she wears as an ornament.

Of all foreign-born women Helena Rubenstein (1882–1964) is best known. She is considered the "Queen of Successful Businesswomen" by virtue of the size of her business which she founded and built up. Though she has been widely imitated, it is she who opened the first beauty salon in the western world. She seems to have possessed an innate talent for business and a sixth sense for divining the right time and place for embarking on new ventures. An extraordinarily hard worker, she spent the day before she died in her office.[22]

Her American business in the early fifties is said to have grossed about twenty-two million a year.[23] She employed more than 30,000 people,[24] of whom two hundred were engaged in the manufacture of her products in her factory in Long Island City, where she claimed to have "worked" with chemists.[25] At her death her business is said to have grossed nearly $100 million throughout the world.[26] She maintained five homes and left a fabulous collection of jewelry, furniture, African art (to which, she claims, Jacob Epstein, the famous sculptor, had introduced her) and pictures by such esteemed painters as Dali, Picasso, Renoir, and others. She was painted by some of the most famous artists of the world, all portraying her arrayed in glittering clothes and jewels.

She made her sisters and several other members of her family rich running her various salons in Australia, London, Paris, Milan, Rome, Vienna, Canada, Tokio, and in cities of South America and Israel, as well as in the United States. She was married twice, the first time to a chemist, the second time to a Russian prince. She loved to be called "Princess Gourielli," but mostly she was known as "Madame." She seemed to have been inordinately vain, contradictory, superficial, and shallow. Patrick O'Higgins, who accompanied her everywhere and knew her well, thought her "shy, imperious, but somehow also on the defensive."

Madame Rubenstein was born in Cracow, Austria, now Poland. At eighteen she was ready for greener pastures and set off for Australia where an uncle, who was an oculist, had settled. She had taken along a dozen jars of special facial cream for her own use. When she noticed the dry, rough skin of Australian women, she smelled a business opportunity. She borrowed money from some of the women she had met on board ship and wrote to the man who had created the formula for the face cream she was using, to send her all the cream he could. The Australian women, including Nellie Melba, the opera singer, proved so responsive that at the end of two years she had earned twelve thousand pounds.[27]

This was a signal to expand. Leaving the Australian business to a sister she imported from Berlin where she was studying chemistry, Madame departed for England. There in 1908 she started a new salon in what used to be Lord Salisbury's home with a capital of $100,000. The warning that Englishwomen were conservative did not inhibit her; she knew better. In record time she acquired more than one thousand clients, most of them prominent socialites.

In 1912 she proceeded from London to Paris, leaving another

sister in charge of the London salon. Madame seems always to have wanted to be thought of as a "lady scientist," to judge by her allusions to the professors of dermatology with whom she says she studied in Vienna, Berlin, and Paris. But she also believed in effective packaging and advertising stunts, such as floating balloons in the air.

In Paris, where the writer known as Colette became one of her clients, she proved not only successful but socially popular. She began to collect art, becoming as the *New Yorker* puts it in a "profile," "the fairy godmother of all artists." However, in 1914 the political situation upset her plans. Her husband, an American citizen, urged that they and their two sons betake themselves to the United States. She realized immediately that she could look forward to a "huge new market." Within three years she had not only a *salon de beauté* in New York, but also branches in San Francisco, Boston, Philadelphia, Washington, and Toronto.

She was also reaching out to retail stores, eventually acquiring 3,000 accounts.[28] She and another sister she had again imported (there were eight sisters) trained saleswomen personally to counsel customers as to the right preparations for their particular needs. In the late twenties she sold her American business to Lehman Brothers for $8,000,000, but right after the crash she was able to buy back the controlling interest for $2,000,000.

A year after her divorce she became a princess by marriage. From then on it was "Madame" in business, and "Princess" after six in the evening. Her second marriage led to a new venture—a "Gourielli specialty shop" for men under the management of the prince. What she hoped to accomplish was to make men more "beautiful." When the prince died suddenly in 1956, the shop was given up.

In 1959 she made an official visit to Moscow as the American representative of the cosmetic industry. Her response to Khrushchev and Nixon, both of whom she met in Moscow, was expressive of her shrewdness, for Patrick O'Higgins, who accompanied her, reports she said she preferred the "Russian" because he was much more direct, but would not trust either one or the other, because "both were out for themselves."[29]

Another "priestess" serving at the altar of feminine beauty, to whom Helena Rubenstein was apt to refer as "The Other One," was Florence Nightingale Graham (1884–1966). Born in Toronto of Scottish parents, she was inspired by Tennyson's *Enoch Arden* to call herself "Elizabeth Arden" when she entered the cosmetic business in New York. However, when she became a horse-breeder and acquired a large racing stable, she wanted to be known as Mrs. Elizabeth N. Graham.

A lively rivalry existed between her and Helena Rubenstein and they were supposed to have constantly practiced the game of putting something over on one another. In the end Madame triumphed when she took on Miss Arden's ex-husband as manager, five years after Miss Arden had divorced him and he was no longer constrained by an agreement that bound him not to work for any of Miss Arden's competitors. Like Helena Rubenstein, Miss Arden married for the second time a Russian prince, but divorced him within two years. Also like her competitor, Miss Arden collected paintings, albeit by different artists.

The young Canadian started as a student nurse in Toronto, but soon decided that she was unsuited for the nursing profession. Her American career began in 1908 with a secretarial job. Two years later she entered into partnership with Elizabeth Hubbard, another cosmetician. The arrangement proved unsuccessful, and Miss Graham, by then Miss Arden, decided to open her own establishment. She borrowed money to outfit her own salon, but was able to pay it back within four months.[30]

By 1914 when Madame appeared on the American scene, Miss Arden's business had taken root and she had begun to expand. In 1915 she became a citizen automatically by marriage. By the end of World War I there were Arden establishments in Washington, Boston, San Francisco, Palm Beach, and Newport. Eventually she established one hundred and fifty salons throughout the world.[31]

Helped by her husband, who was her sales manager, she began to develop a wholesale business which jumped in one decade from $20,000 in 1920 to $4,000,000 in 1930. In the 1950s she opened a shop where men's toiletries were sold, and for the convenience of men, a line of gifts for women. Also her New

York establishment featured a complete floor of fashions for women.

Her spectacular rise seems less startling than her success as the owner of a racing stable. Having inherited a love of horses from her father, she bought a farm in Mount Vernon, Maine, which she called "Maine Chance" Stables. There she raised and trained racehorses. She is said to have picked her own yearlings with the help of a turf adviser. Some of her horses won the most highly coveted prizes—the Kentucky Derby in 1947 and the Santa Anita Derby in 1946—and brought her enormous winnings. She was so fond of her horses that she would massage them herself with her own unguents.[32]

Later she transferred her stable, and her farmhouse in Maine became a health center for women. She also opened another in Phoenix, Arizona, where women were subjected to a regimen consisting of a mixture of athletics (to music), beauty treatments, and diet.

Elizabeth Arden was a recipient of a type of recognition which might have made any competitor jealous. She received an honorary degree from Syracuse University in 1940. Another trophy was a "Great Lady Award" in Los Angeles, for having brought beauty to all women. She was also honored by the Canadian Women's Press Club of Toronto on their fiftieth anniversary. One wonders how Madame escaped being given an honory Doctor of Cosmetics. There is no record extant of Madame's reactions to the honors bestowed on her competitor.

A woman whose qualifications differ uniquely from the business talents of the individuals in these pages is Anna M[arie] Rosenberg (1900–). Without doubt she is one of the most outstanding business executives to be found anywhere. In 1938 the *New Yorker* called her "a sort of middlewoman in ideas, a kind of switchboard through which enemies can make connections."[33] In a 1943 article in the *Saturday Evening Post*, she was referred to as "Mrs. Fix-It." Considered a dynamo of human energy, she has worked with and for some of the most prominent men of our time—Presidents Franklin D. Roosevelt and Truman, Fiorello La Guardia, mayor of New York City, Governor Rockefeller, Secretary Marshall, Hugh Johnson, Nathan Strauss, Jr.,

Bernard Baruch, and officials of the most important labor unions. She was born in Budapest, Hungary, to educated parents and into a well-to-do home. Her father, a dealer in antiques, furnished some of Emperor Franz Joseph's palaces. When the emperor cancelled an order, it bankrupted her father, and he emigrated to the United States.

She was eight when the mother and the two daughters of the family joined the father after some lapse of time. Life in America struck them as very different from what they had imagined. They had brought a Hungarian maid with them, but found her superfluous in the Bronx. With the need to build roots again, their whole outlook on life changed. It was part of her father's teachings that the foreign-born had the obligation to perform whatever services they could for the country which had accepted them.[34] To judge by her services to the nation during the Thirties, Forties, and Fifties, her father's principles had made a deep impression.

She went to public school, then to Wadleigh High School, and even as a schoolgirl demonstrated a startling talent for leadership. She started a political club and led a student delegation to the Board of Aldermen to request a shorter school day and less crowded classrooms. After the United States entered World War I she sold Liberty Bonds and thrift stamps from a booth at 145th Street and Broadway.

Her marriage at nineteen to a serviceman ended the expectation of going to college. She had a child soon after and settled into being a housewife. But it was not long before she began to interest herself in politics, and helped to elect several "small-time" politicians. A stint of settlement work brought her into contact with Mrs. Belle Moskowitz, the doyenne of settlement workers, who had groomed Alfred E. Smith to become Governor of New York State. Mrs. Moskowitz taught Mrs. Rosenberg a bit of practical wisdom she still remembers. After performing what she had thought of as a volunteer assignment, Mrs. Moskowitz pointed out that anyone undervaluing her own work would be worth no more to anyone else.

She was in her early twenties when she opened an office as a personnel consultant and labor mediator. Before long she was known as an efficient troubleshooter in industrial relations.

It was in this role that she came to the attention of the then Governor Franklin D. Roosevelt.

In 1934 she received the first federal appointment as assistant to Nathan Straus, Jr., who was regional director of the National Recovery Administration (NRA). A year later he resigned and she was appointed head of the NRA in New York State. After the NRA was declared unconstitutional, she was made director of the Social Security Board in New York, where she supervised twenty-three field offices.[35] A succession of jobs followed. Among the various posts she held was that of secretary of the combined War Labor Board, member of Mayor La Guardia's Business Advisory Committee, and federal defense coordinator for New York State. In this job she was entrusted with training defense workers, assigning them to jobs, and providing recreational facilities for them.[36] At the same time she retained her private practice in labor relations, where she earned as much as $60,000 a year in addition to her government salary.[37]

She relinquished her private business when Paul V. McNutt appointed her in April, 1942, to the War Manpower Commission of the State of New York, where she allocated workers to plants and industries engaged in war production. She shipped workers to the Pacific Coast, to upstate defense areas and elsewhere, and was instrumental in breaking down prejudice to Negro labor by labor unions and employers. She was what someone called "the manpower czarina." She also provided New York State with Negro and migratory workers to help cope with farm problems. In 1944 she undertook a mission for President Roosevelt in Europe as his personal observer and a year later was sent by President Truman to study the problem of demobilization of troops.

Though she resigned in 1945 to return to private practice, she continued to serve on government and civic assignments. In 1950 President Truman and Secretary Marshall chose her to fill the highest job ever given to any woman in government, that of Assistant Secretary of Defense. Her responsibility was to coordinate the Defense Department's manpower needs. She prepared the Universal Military Service and Training Bill that created a force of 3,200,000 servicemen and specified the training of eighteen-year-olds.[38]

Honors were showered on her. In 1947 she received the U.S. Medal for Merit, the first woman to be so honored, and an honorary degree of Master of Humane Letters from Russell Sage College. In 1949 she was the recipient of the Horatio Alger Award presented by American schools and colleges.

In spite of a high degree of competence, she believes that "luck" cannot be ruled out of any career. "Success," she observed, "depends on getting the chance and then using it in the right way."

With the presentation of this group of businesswomen, the attempt to introduce female immigrants as they contended with the American way of life, comes to an end.

This book has a two-fold purpose: to tell a story of striking achievements, and to strengthen the claim that women, too, accomplished tremendous and unbelievable tasks. What is generally assumed is that the experiences of women immigrants were of little consequence. That, obviously, is untrue. A vague recollection may come to mind that some women made militant strikers, that wives must have had a hard time making ends meet and raising families, and, yes, they must have done pretty well at it, because most of their children became fine, even distinguished people.

Yes, and it's the magic of America that unexpected success was possible, but this magic worked for both men and women.

Like Henry James's statement that the whole of life can never be told in one volume, the whole story of immigrant women functioning in our culture cannot be compressed into one book. Though the number of women presented herein may seem to be forming a long queue, in reality they are a microcosmic group. Behind every woman mentioned in each category an unending line of others may be imagined lining up.

Samuel Johnson, hardly a great admirer of women, remarked about a woman's preaching: "Like a bear dancing, it need not be done well, it is remarkable that it is done at all." What is remarkable about these women is the contrary—that what they did, they did so well.

Notes and References

Chapter One

1. Margaret Winthrop to John Winthrop, junior, dated May or June 1631. *The History of New England*, ed. James Savage (Boston, 1825), p. 382.
2. Virginia was founded in 1607; Plymouth Plantation in 1620; Massachusetts Bay in 1630.
3. J.H.R. Yardley, *Before The Mayflower* (New York, 1931), p. 115.
4. Ibid., p. 89.
5. Alice Morse Earle, *Colonial Dames and Goodwives* (Boston, 1895), p. 4.
6. Ibid., p. 4.
7. *The Works of Anne Bradstreet*, ed. John Harvard Ellis (Charlestown, 1867), p. xxxi.
8. Edith Abbott, *Women in Industry*, (New York, 1913), p. 11.
9. John Demos, *A Little Commonwealth: Family Life in Plymouth* (New York, 1970), p. 131.
10. *The Diary of Samuel Sewall* (New York, 1963).
11. Edmund S. Morgan, *The Puritan Family* (The Trustees of the Public Library, Boston, 1944).
12. Ibid., p. 9.
13. John Winthrop, *The History of New England*, p. 10.
14. Alice Morse Earle, p. 23.
15. Ibid., p. 22.
16. They were the *Arbella, Talbot, Ambrose* and *Jewell*.
17. See John Demos, p. 29, for a description of a colonial home.
18. Alice Morse Earle, *Margaret Winthrop* (New York, 1895). pp. 101–2.
19. Ibid., p. 334.
20. *Some Old Puritan Letters*, ed. Joseph Hopkins Twichell (New York, 1893), p. 33.
21. Ibid., p. 53.
22. Ibid., p. 74.
23. John Winthrop, p. 216, II.
24. Edmund S. Morgan, p. 10.

25. *The Works of Anne Bradstreet*, LXII.

26. Alice Morse Earle, *Colonial Dames and Goodwives*, pp. 52–53.

27. *Notable American Women*, 1607–1950 (Cambridge, Mass., 1971), pp. 235–36, I.

28. Ibid., p. 236, I.

29. Ibid., pp. 61–62, III.

30. Ibid., pp. 69–71, III.

31. Ibid., p. 70, III.

32. Harriet Mory Ravenel, *Elizabeth Pinckney* (New York, 1896), p. 102.

33. Ibid., p. 56.

34. *Notable American Women*, pp. 584–85, I.

35. Perry Miller, *From Colony to Province* (Boston, 1953), p. 179.

36. *The Diary of Samuel Sewall*, Introduction.

37. Cotton Mather, *Magnalia Christi Americana* (Hartford, 1853), p. 80.

38. *Winthrop's Journal*, ed. James Kendall Hosmer (New York, 1908, p. 315, I.

39. Samuel Eliot Morison, *Builders of Bay Colony* (Boston, 1930), p. 93.

40. A definition of antinomianism: "Individuals in a state of grace could ignore moral laws." Henry Bamford Parkes, *The United States of America* (New York, 1957), p. 36.

41. Kate Campbell Hurd-Mead, *A History of Women in Medicine* (Haddam, Conn., 1938), p. 411.

42. *Antinomianism in the Colony of Massachusetts Bay*, ed. C. F. Adams (Boston, Prince Society: 1894), p. 329.

43. Perry Miller, *The New England Mind: The Seventeenth Century* (New York, 1973), p. 259.

44. The remark that the Quakers seemed to lust after hardships and that they sought "a crown of martyrdom," is in Daniel J. Boorstin's *The Americans* (New York, 1958), p. 36.

45. *The Works of Anne Bradstreet*, p. 102.

46. Cotton Mather, *Magnalia Christi Americana*, pp. 134–35, I.

47. *Notable American Women*, pp. 573–74, III.

Chapter Two

1. *Notable American Women*, pp. 47–48, II.

2. Ibid., pp. 688–90, III.

3. Papers and Addresses of the Lebanon County Historical Society, vol. III, No. 8 (1905–6), pp. 202–47.

4. Maldwyn Allen Jones, *American Immigration* (Chicago, 1960), p. 22.

Chapter Three

1. Ralph Waldo Emerson, *The Young American* (New York, 1934), p. 156.
2. *The Letters of Mrs. Adams,* Foreword by Charles Francis Adams (Boston, 1848).
3. Edith Abbott, *Women in Industry,* p. 33.
4. Frances Trollope, *Domestic Manners of the Americans* (New York, 1966), p. 52.
5. Alexis de Tocqueville, *Democracy in America* (New York, 1845), p. 55.
6. *The Letters of Mrs. Adams,* p. 76.
7. Eleanor Flexner, *Mary Wollstonecraft* (New York, 1972), p. 265.
8. Ibid., p. 265.
9. Elias Nason, *A Memoir of Mrs. Susanna Rowson* (Albany, New York, 1870), p. 34.
10. Ibid., p. 49.
11. Ibid., p. 85.
12. Frances Trollope, *Domestic Manners,* p. ix.
13. Frances Wright, *Views of Society and Manners in America* (London, 1821).
14. Una Pope-Henesy, *Three English Women in America* (London, 1929), p. 27.
15. Sally M. Miller, *The Radical Immigrant* (New York, 1974), p. 37.
16. McAlister Coleman, *Pioneers of Freedom* (New York, 1929).
17. Ibid.
18. Sally M. Miller, p. 57.
19. Yuri Suhl, *Ernestine L. Rose and the Battle for Human Rights* (New York, 1959), p. 10.
20. Ibid., pp. 57–64, *passim.*
21. Sara A. Underwood, *Heroines of Free Thought* (New York, 1876), p. 276.
22. Ibid., p. 277.
23. Yuri Suhl, p. 123.
24. Ibid., pp. 205–6.
25. Ibid., p. 49.
26. Aileen S. Kraditor, *Up From the Pedestal* (Chicago, 1968), p. 225.

27. Yuri Suhl, pp. 245–46.

28. Carl Schurz, *The Reminiscences of Carl Schurz* (New York, 1907), p. 197, I.

29. A. B. Faust, *Mathilde Franziska Giesler-Anneke*, German-American Annals, New Series, vol. XVI (1918), p. 76.

30. Anna Howard Shaw, *Story of a Pioneer* (New York, 1916).

31. *Notable American Women*, pp. 292–94, I.

32. Ibid., pp. 416–17, III.

33. William Morris, *Encyclopedia of American History* (New York, 1953), p. 44.

34. Edward Hunter, *In Many Voices* (Norman Park, Georgia, 1960), p. 75.

35. Ibid., p. 89.

36. Ibid., p. 89.

37. H. A. Ratterman, *Anna Ottendorfer* (Cincinnati, 1885).

38. Ibid.

39. *Zur Erinnerung an Anna Ottendorfer*, 1884.

40. Ibid.

41. Ibid.

42. Louise Hall Tharp, *Adventurous Alliance* (Boston, 1959), p. 338.

43. Ibid., p. 279.

44. Ibid., p. 279.

45. Pauline A. Shaw, *Tributes Paid Her Memory* (Boston, privately printed: 1917).

46. *Notable American Women*, pp. 278–80, III.

47. Ibid., pp. 246–49, III.

48. John D. Hicks, *The Federal Union* (Boston, 1952), p. 195, II.

49. The breakdown was as follows: from Italy, 959,763; Russia, 658,735; Austria-Hungary, 944,239; Germany, 176,995; Great Britain and Ireland, 385,469. Ricchard B. Morris, *Encyclopedia of American History*, p. 448.

50. Ibid., p. 448.

51. Henry Bamford Parkes, *The United States of America*, p. 467.

Chapter Four

1. Winthrop S. Hudson, *Religion in America* (New York, 1965), p. 10.

2. Ibid., p. 46.

3. Charles A. and Mary R. Beard, *History of the United States* (New York, 1949), p. 214.

4. *The Autobiography of Benjamin Franklin* (New York, 1956), p. 107.

5. Ibid., p. 109.

6. Winthrop S. Hudson, p. 346.

7. *Notable American Women* 623–24, I.

8. Ibid.,

9. F. W. Evans, *Ann Lee* (New Lebanon, 1858), p. 122.

10. Edward Deming Andrews, *The People Called Shakers* (New York, 1963), p. 196.

11. F. W. Evans, *Shakers* (New Lebanon, 1867), p. 22.

12. Ira V. Brown, "Watchers for the Second Coming: The Millenarian Tradition in America," *Mississippi Valley Historical Review*, vol. XXXIX, No. 3 (Dec., 1952), p. 452.

13. F. W. Evans, *Ann Lee*, p. 40.

14. Alvin Boyd Kuhn, *Theosophy, A Modern Revival of Ancient Wisdom* (New York, 1930), p. 22.

15. Marguerite Fellows Melcher, *The Shaker Adventure* (Princeton, 1941), pp. 112–15.

16. F. W. Evans, *The Shakers*, p. 128.

17. Marguerite Fellows Melcher, *The Shaker Adventure*, p. 115.

18. F. W. Evans, *Ann Lee*, p. 43.

19. Ibid., p. 50.

20. Ibid., p. 46.

21. Ibid., p. 49.

22. Marguerite Fellows Melcher, p. 112.

23. Edward Deming Andrews, p. 92.

24. Letter from Robert F. W. Meader, Director of the Shaker Museum, dated Oct 27, 1972.

25. Marguerite Fellows Melcher, p. 257.

26. Letter from Robert F. W. Meader.

27. Bertha M. H. Shambaugh, *Amana That Was and Amana That Is* (Iowa State Historical Society, 1932), p. 40.

28. Ibid., *passim*.

29. Ibid., p. 133.

30. Ibid., p. 61.

31. Ibid., p. 176.

32. Ibid., p. 121.

33. Richard T. Ely, "A Study of Religious Communism," *Harper's Monthly* (Oct., 1902), pp. 659–68.

34. Ibid., p. 666.

35. Ibid., p. 664.

36. Letter from Charles L. Selzer, president Amana Church Society, dated March 1, 1973.

37. Alice Leighton Cleather, *H. P. Blavatsky As I Knew Her* (Calcutta, 1923), p. 6.

38. Hartley Grattan, *The Three Jameses* (New York, 1962), p. 135.

39. Helena Petrovna Blavatsky, *The Secret Doctrine* (London, 1888), p. XIV.

40. G. Baseden Butt, *Madame Blavatsky* (London, 1925), p. 33.

41. Ibid., p. 37.

42. Ibid., p. 37.

43. Ibid., p. 104.

44. Ibid., p. 2.

45. Alice Leighton Cleather, p. 26.

46. *New York Times Book Review*, Feb. 4, 1973, p. 24.

Chapter Five

1. Pietro di Donato, *Immigrant Saint* (New York, 1960), p. 70.

2. Luciano J. Iorizzo and Salvatore Mondello, *The Italian-Americans* (New York, 1971), pp. 68–69.

3. Di Donato, pp. 110–11.

4. Ibid., p. 127.

5. *Notable American Women*, pp. 115–16, I.

6. Di Donato, p. 193.

7. Ibid., p. 216.

8. *Notable American Women*, pp. 524–26, I.

9. Ibid., pp. 647–48, II.

10. Information supplied by Professor George J. Prpic, John Carroll University, Cleveland, O.

11. *Notable American Women*, pp. 115–16, I.

12. Etling Nicolai Rolfsrud, *The Borrowed Sister* (Minneapolis, 1953).

13. Ibid., p. 32.

14. *Notable American Women*, p. 605, I.

15. Theodore C. Blegen, *Norwegian Migration to America* (Northfield, Minnesota: Norwegian-American Historical Association, 1959), p. 179.

16. Ibid., p. 134.

17. Rolfsrud, p. 31.

18. Ibid., pp. 72–73.

19. *Elisabeth Fedde's Diary, 1833–1838, Norwegian-American Studies and Records*, vol. XX, Norwegian-American Historical Association (Northfield, Minn., 1959), p. 179.

20. Rolfsrud, p. 85.

21. *Elisabeth Fedde's Diary*, p. 185.

22. A. N. Rygg, *Norwegians in New York* (Brooklyn, 1941), p. 90.

23. St. John Ervine, *God's Soldier, General William Booth of the Salvation Army* (New York, 1948), p. 82.

24. Philip Whitwell Wilson, *General Evangeline Booth of the Salvation Army* (New York, 1948), p. 82.

25. Interview with Brigadier-General Christine McMillan, Dec. 5, 1972.

26. Wilson, p. 46.

27. Ibid., p. 38.

28. Interview.

29. Wilson, p. 67.

30. New York *Times*, July 18, 1950.

31. Wilson, p. 148.

32. Ibid., p. 148.

33. Ibid., p. 185.

34. Interview.

Chapter Six

1. Harry Roskolenko, *When I Was Last on Cherry Street* (New York, 1965).

2. Edward Corsi, *In the Shadow of Liberty* (New York, 1934).

3. Samuel Gompers, *Seventy Years of Life and Labor* (New York, 1925).

4. *Life and Labor* (Nov., 1911), p. 329.

5. John Cournos, *Autobiography* (New York, 1935).

6. Corsi.

7. Leonard Covello, *The Heart is the Teacher* (New York, 1958).

8. Elizabeth Shepley Sergeant, "Toilers of the Tenements," Consumers' League of the City of New York, reprinted from *McClure's*, vol. XXXV, No. 3 (July, 1910), p. 232.

9. Ibid., p. 242.

10. Ibid., pp. 239–44, *passim*.

11. Victor Greene, *The Slavic Community on Strike* (Notre Dame. Ind., 1966), p. 49.

12. Henry Barnard, *Eagle Forgotten* (Indianapolis, 1938).

13. Edward W. Bok, *The Americanization of Edward Bok* (New York, 1937).

14. Andrew Carnegie, *The Autobiography of Andrew Carnegie* (Boston, 1920).

15. Morris R. Cohen, *A Dreamer's Journey* (Boston, 1949).

16. Jerre Mangione, *Mont Allegro* (Boston, 1943), p. 225.

17. Charles Angoff, *Something About My Father and Other People* (New York, 1956).

18. Jo Sinclair, *Wasteland* (New York, 1946).

19. John Palmer Gavit, *Americans by Choice* (New York, 1922).

20. Philip Roth, *Portnoy* (New York, 1964).

21. Daniel Greenburg, *How To Become a Jewish Mother* (New York, 1964).

22. Elisabeth Koren, *The Diary of Elisabeth Koren* (Northfield, Minn.: Norwegian-American Historical Association, 1955).

23. Louis Adamic, *Laughing In The Jungle* (New York, 1932).

24. Theodore C. Blegen, *Norwegian Migration to America* (Northfield, Minn.: Norwegian-American Historical Association, 1940), p. 38, II.

25. Ibid., p. 48, II.

26. Gro Svendsen, *Frontier Mother* (Northfield, Minn.: Norwegian-American Historical Association, 1955).

27. *The Diary of Elisabeth Koren* (Northfield, Minn.: Norwegian-American Historical Association, 1955).

28. Blegen, p. 64, II.

29. Mari Sandoz, *Old Jules* (Boston, 1935).

30. David Greenberg, *Land That Our Fathers Plowed* (Norman, 1969).

31. Sandoz, p. 66.

32. Milo Milton Quaife, ed., *A True Picture of Emigration* (Chicago, 1936).

33. Greenberg, p. 66.

34. Maureen Whipple, *The Giant Joshua* (Boston, 1941), p. 74.

35. Leonard J. Arrington, "The Economic Role of Pioneer Mormon Women," *The Western Humanities Review* (Spring, 1955), p. 145.

36. William Mulder, "Through Immigrant Eyes: Utah History at Grass Roots," *Utah History Quarterly*, vol. XXII (1954).

37. Veronique Pettit, *Plural Marriage* (Ithaca, 1885), p. 72.

38. Victor Greene, p. 34.

39. Emily Greene Balch, *Our Slavic Fellow Citizens* (New York: Charities Publication Committee, 1910), p. 349.

40. *Charities and the Commons*, vol. XXI (Jan. 2, 1909), pp. 570–80; (1910), p. 349.

41. Ibid., p. 576.

42. Ibid., p. 576.

43. Thomas Bell, *Out of This Furnace* (Boston, 1941), p. 55.

44. Lauren Gilfillen, *I Went to Pit College* (New York, 1934), p. 99.

45. Bessie Olga Pehotsky, *The Slavic Immigrant Woman* (Cincinnati, 1925), Preface.
46. Emily Greene Balch, p. 350.
47. Thomas Bell, p. 212.
48. Ibid., p. 209.
49. Told to the author by Professor George J. Prpic, John Carrol University, Cleveland.
50. The story of Maxo Vanka appears in Louis Adamic's *From Many Lands* (New York, 1938), pp. 156–71.
51. Victor Greene, p. 98; p. 143.
52. Ibid.
53. Ibid., p. 143.
54. Louis Adamic, pp. 55–68.
55. Information supplied by Professor George J. Prpic.
56. Hapgood Hutchins, *The Spirit of the Ghetto* (Allograph Press Corp., by arrangement with Harvard University Press, 1967).
57. Ibid., pp. 71–72.
58. President Lincoln rescinded the order within three weeks.
59. *Encyclopedia Judaica* (New York, 1971), vol. 15, p. 1596.
60. Ibid.
61. Ibid., p. 1596.
62. Ibid., p. 1607.
63. Ibid., p. 1608.
64. Ibid., p. 1615.
65. Maurice Hindus, *Green Worlds* (New York, 1935).
66. *Encyclopedia Judaica*, p. 1596.
67. Rose Schneiderman, *All For One* (New York, 1967).
68. Jo Sinclair, *Wasteland* p. 19.
69. Michael Gold, *Jews Without Money* (New York, 1930), p. 158.
70. Harry Roskolenko, *When I Was Lost on Cherry Street*, p. 92.
71. Alfred Kazin, *A Walker in the City* (New York, 1951), p. 67.
72. Alfred Kazin, *Starting Out in the Thirties* (Boston, 1962), pp. 40–41.
73. Alpheus Thomas Mason, *Brandeis: A Free Man's Life* (New York, 1946), p. 94.
74. Ibid., p. 582.
75. Told to the author by the daughter of Dr. Modell and Mrs. Anuta Modell, Jan., 1973.

Chapter Seven

1. *Notable American Women*, pp. 81–82, I.
2. Alexander C. Flick, *The History of the State of New York* (New York, 1933–37), pp. 405–6, II.

3. Edith Abbott, *Women in Industry* (New York, 1913), p. 37.
4. Ibid., p. 113.
5. *Notable American Women,* pp. 368–69, II.
6. Edith Abbott, p. 278.
7. Ibid., p. 81.
8. Gladys Boone, *The Women's Trade Union League* (New York, 1942), p. 48.
9. Ibid., p. 49.
10. Ibid., p. 42.
11. Alice Henry, *The Trade Union Woman* (New York, 1915), p. 37.
12. Gladys Boone, p. 53.
13. Ibid., p. 54.
14. Mary Jones, *Autobiography of Mother Jones* (Chicago 1925, reprinted by Arno Press, Inc., 1969), p. 188.
15. Ibid., pp. 12–13.
16. Ibid., p. 233.
17. Ibid., p. 201.
18. Ibid., pp. 19–20.
19. Ibid., p. 238.
20. Sheila Rowbotham, *Women, Resistance and Revolution* (New York, 1972), p. 99.
21. Mary Jones, *Autobiography,* p. 204.
22. Ibid., p. 204.
23. Ibid., p. 26.
24. See Agnes Nestor, *Woman's Labor Leader* (Rockford, Ill., 1954), pp. 71–72.
25. Figure given by Mary Jones.
26. Irving Werstein, *Labor's Defiant Lady* (New York, 1969), p. 135.
27. Maldwyn Allen Jones, *American Immigration* (Chicago, 1960), p. 179.
28. Ibid.
29. Alice Henry, *The Trade Union Woman* (New York, 1915), p. 41.
30. Gladys Boone, p. 62.
31. Benjamin Stolberg, *Tailor's Progress* (New York, 1944), p. 106.
32. Alice Henry, pp. 137–38.
33. E. J. Hutchinson, *Women's Wages* (New York, 1919), p. 154.
34. Gladys Boone, p. 62.
35. Mary Anderson, *Woman At Work* (Minneapolis, 1951), p. 37.
36. Alice Henry, *Memoirs of Alice Henry,* ed. Nettie Palmer (Melbourne, 1944), p. 37.

37. Mary Anderson, p. 37.

38. Mary E. Dreier, *Margaret Dreier Robins, Her Life, Letters and Work* (New York, 1950), p. 152.

39. Mary Anderson, p. 175.

40. Gladys Boone, p. 107.

41. Ibid., p. 107.

42. New York Department of Labor Library, WTUL file.

43. Mary E. Dreier, pp. 42–43.

44. Gladys Boone, p. 98.

45. Announcement in *Life and Labor*, Oct., 1921, Tamiment Library, New York University.

46. Gladys Boone, p. 117.

47. Rose Schneiderman and Lucy Goldthwaite, *All For One* (New York, 1967), p. 83.

48. Ibid., pp. 222–23.

49. Gladys Boone, p. 144.

50. WTUL Convention 1919, Proceedings, pp. 2–4.

51. This information was received from Miss Pauline Newman, who was chairman of the New York delegation.

52. Rose Schneiderman, *All For One*, p. 181.

53. Rose Schneiderman Collection, Tamiment Library, New York University.

54. Rose Schneiderman, *All For One*, p. 5.

Chapter Eight

1. New York *Times*, Editorial page, August 12, 1972.

2. Rose Schneiderman, *All For One*, p. 50.

3. In 1923 the Cloth Hat and Cap Makers' Union and the millinery workers became affiliated with the much more powerful Hatters' Union.

4. Gladys Boone, p. 83.

5. Benjamin Stolberg, *Tailor's Progress*, p. 64.

6. Ida M. Tarbell, *Carola Woerishoffer, Her Life and Work*, Class of 1910, Bryn Mawr College, 1912.

7. Alice Henry, *The Trade Union Woman*, p. 122.

8. Gladys Boone, p. 90.

9. Ibid., p. 99.

10. Leon Stein, *The Triangle Fire* (Philadelphia, 1962), p. 109; the number is given as 146.

11. Rose Schneiderman, *All For One*, pp.100–101.

12. Rose Schneiderman Collection, Tamiment Library, New York University.

13. Rose Schneiderman, *All For One*, p. 145.

14. *Life and Labor*, Dec., 1920, Tamiment Library, New York University.

15. Brookwood College file, Tamiment Library, New York University.

16. Rose Schneiderman, *All For One*, p. 162.

17. The Brookwood College file, Tamiment Library, New York University, supplied all the information in regard to the founding and dissolution of the school.

18. Rose Schneiderman, *All For One*, p. 162.

19. Letter from Thomas Lamont in the Rose Schneiderman Collection, Tamiment Library, New York University.

20. Frances Perkins, *The Roosevelts I Knew* (New York, 1946), pp. 31–32.

21. Rose Schneiderman, *All For One*, p. 156.

22. Ibid., p. 180.

23. Mary Anderson as told to Mary N. Winslow, *Woman At Work*, p. 85.

24. Ibid., p. 62.

25. Ibid., p. 49.

26. Ibid., p. 106.

27. Ibid., p. 104.

28. Ibid., p. 148.

29. New York *Times*, January 30, 1964, 29:3.

30. *Notable American Women*, pp. 413–15, III.

31. Frances Perkins, *The Roosevelts I Knew*, pp. 31–32.

Chapter Nine

1. *Life and Labor*, June 1921, Tamiment Library, New York University.

2. New York *Post*, Sunday, June 7, 1964.

3. Interview with Miss Newman, April, 1973.

4. Interview with Miss Newman, January, 1974.

5. Interview, 1973.

6. New York *Post*, June 7, 1964.

7. Interview, April, 1973.

8. Ibid.

9. Ibid.

10. Matthew Josephson, *Sidney H. Hillman, Statesman of American Labor* (New York, 1952), p. 49.

11. Joel Seidman, *The Needle Trades* (New York, 1942), p. 118.

12. Matthew Josephson, p. 100.

13. Interview with Mrs. Philoine Fried, daughter of Mr. & Mrs. Hillman, April, 1973. Information was also taken from *The Advance,* organ of the Amalgamated Clothing Workers' Union, vol. 57, No. 1 (Jan. 13, 1971).

14. Interview, April, 1930.

15. *Notable American Women,* pp. 124–26, I.

16. Ibid.

Chapter Ten

1. Emma Goldman, *Living My Life* (New York, 1931).

2. Ibid., p. 56.

3. Ibid., p. 594.

4. Ibid., p. 38.

5. Ibid., p. 123.

6. Ibid., p. 306.

7. Ibid., p. 613.

8. Justin Kaplan, *Lincoln Steffens* (New York, 1974), p. 250.

9. Richard Drinnon, *Rebel in Paradise* (Chicago, 1961).

10. Sources on Rose Pastor Stokes are the Rose Pastor Stokes Papers, Yale University Library, New Haven, Conn.

11. Taken from an unfinished and unpublished autobiography by Rose Pastor Stokes. "I Belong to the Working Class," Rose Pastor Stokes Papers, Yale University Library. All quotes are verbatim.

12. Autobiography, Rose Pastor Stokes Papers.

13. Ibid.

14. Rose Pastor Stokes and Helen Frank, *Songs of Labor* (Boston, 1914).

15. Ironically, Inspector Schmittberger was later demoted as the result of the Lexow Investigation into police corruption to "a lonely beat in Goatsville." Justin Kaplan, *Lincoln Steffens,* p. 89.

16. Emily Dunning Barringer, *Bowery to Bellevue* (New York, 1950), p. 159.

17. Graham Stokes received one mention in Emma Goldman's autobiography, *Living My Life,* as having been present with other members of the University Settlement at a gathering for the Russian revolutionary Catherine Breshkovskaya.

18. Anzia Yezierska, *Salome of the Tenements* (New York, 1923).

19. Anzia Yezierska refers to Graham Stokes, whom she does not mention by name, in her autobiography *Red Ribbon on a White Horse* as "a young millionaire who dreamed of becoming the new St. Francis of Assisi." *Red Ribbon on a White Horse* (New York, 1950).

20. Rose Pastor Stokes, Autobiography.
21. Ibid.
22. New York State Department of Labor, WTUL file.
23. Rose Pastor Stokes, Autobiography.
24. Ibid.
25. Justin Kaplan, *Lincoln Steffens*, p. 93.
26. Rose Pastor Stokes, *The Woman Who Wouldn't* (New York, 1916).
27. Letter from Rose Pastor Stokes to Olive Tilford Dargan, dated Feb., 1925. Rose Pastor Stokes Papers, Yale University.
28. Letter from Rose Pastor Stokes to Charles Recht (attorney) dated Nov. 5, 1925. Rose Pastor Stokes Papers.
29. *Collier's Magazine*, Feb. 13th, 1926.
30. Interview with Mrs. Betty Friedkin, August, 1972.
31. Diary, Rose Pastor Stokes Papers, Yale University Library.
32. Letter from Joanna Cooke, East Barrington, N. H. dated Sept. 24 (no year). Rose Pastor Stokes Papers, Yale University.
33. Letter from Jeannette B. Rogers, dated Jan. 1932. Rose Pastor Stokes Papers, Yale University.

Chapter Eleven

1. Esther Pohl Lovejoy, *Women Doctors of the World* (New York, 1957), p. 148.
2. I. A. Watson, *Physicians and Surgeons of America* (Concord, N. H. Republican Press Ass'n, 1896), p. 794.
3. This phrase was used by a New York newspaper in connection with a women's rights convention held in New York State.
4. *Women's Work in America*, ed. Annie Nathan Meyer (New York, 1899), p. 139.
5. Ibid., p. 144.
6. Quoted to the author by a twentieth-century refugee physician.
7. Lovejoy.
8. Marie E. Zakrzewska, *A Woman's Quest* (New York, 1924).
9. Francis R. Packard, *The History of Medicine in the United States* (New York, 1963), p. 952, II.
10. Ibid., pp. 737–821, *passim*.
11. Ishbel Ross, *Child of Destiny* (New York, 1949), p. 103.
12. Ibid., p. 99.
13. Lovejoy, p. 51.
14. Ibid., p. 79.
15. Ishbel Ross, p. 106.
16. Lovejoy, p. 86.

17. Ibid., p. 40.
18. Ibid., p. 91.
19. Ibid., p. 39.
20. Ibid., p. 75.
21. The amount is sometimes given as $500,000 and at other times as $400,000.
22. Carol Lopate, *Women in Medicine* (Baltimore, 1968), p. 21.
23. Ibid., p. 17.
24. Emily Dunning Barringer, *Bowery to Bellevue* (New York, 1950), p. 79.
25. Rhoda Truax, *The Doctors Jacobi* (Boston, 1952), pp. 157–58.
26. Ibid., p.158.
27. Lovejoy, p. 81.
28. Lopate, p. 19.
29. Ibid., p. 9.
30. Elizabeth Blackwell, *Opening the Medical Profession to Women,* printed for the Trustees of the New York Infirmary (1960), p. 28.
31. *In Memory of Dr. Elizabeth Blackwell and Dr. Emily Blackwell,* Academy of Medicine of New York (1911), pp. 11–12.
32. Geneva Historical Society Records, Geneva, New York.
33. Geneva *Gazette,* Jan. 26, 1849, p. 2. From the archives of the Geneva Historical Society, Geneva, N. Y.
34. Marie Zakrzewska, p. 197.
35. Lovejoy, p. 44.
36. Ibid., p. 52.
37. Ishbel Ross, p. 206.
38. Ibid., p. 212.
39. Elinor Rice Hays, *Those Extraordinary Blackwells* (New York, 1967), p. 149.
40. Lovejoy, p. 68.
41. Ibid., p. 70.
42. Elinor Rice Hays, p. 307.
43. Marie E. Zakrzewska, p. 129.
44. Ibid., p. 189.
45. *The Journal of the American Medical Association,* vol. 160, No. 7, p. 562.
46. During the fire of 1871 the College burned down, but was soon rebuilt. In 1891 it was renamed the Northwestern University's Women's Medical College. It closed in 1902 when the study of medicine became coeducational.
47. *Notable American Women,* pp. 529–30, II.
48. Physicians are not listed according to place of birth. Information can therefore not be ascertained except through serendipity.

49. Joy Daniels Singer, *My Mother, the Doctor* (New York, 1971).
50. Geoffrey Marks and William K. Beatty, *Women in White* (New York, 1972), p. 218.
51. Ibid.
52. Sources for Dr. Formad: Letter from Pauline Johnston, Associate Medical Librarian, the Medical College of Pennsylvania, dated Sept. 30, 1973. Also the New York *Times* Feb. 24, 1944, 15:3.
53. Source for Dr. Yarros: *Journal of Social Hygiene* (April, 1946), vol. 32, No. 4.
54. Sources for Dr. Rabinoff: *New York State Journal of Medicine,* 1957, p. 3720. Also, New York *Times,* Oct. 3, 1957, 29:2.
55. Interview with Ms. Pauline Newman, Director of the ILGWU Health Center.
56. Source for Dr. Anna Kleegman: Joy Daniels Singer, *My Mother, the Doctor.*
57. Source for Dr. Sophie Kleegman: *New York State Journal of Medicine* (Nov. 15, 1971).
58. New York *Times,* March 23, 1970, 41:4.
59. Joy Daniels Singer.
60. New York *Times,* Sept. 27, 1971, 38:2.
61. *New York State Journal of Medicine* (Nov. 15, 1971).
62. Helene Deutsch, *Confrontations With Myself* (New York, 1973), pp. 179–80.
63. Source for Dr. Karen Horney: The New York *Times,* Dec. 5, 1952, 27:2.
64. Source for Dr. Fromm-Reichman, New York *Times,* April 30, 1957, 29:2.
65. Interview with Dr. Catherine Lodyjensky, Oct. 26, 1973.
66. Sources for Dr. Lydia Rabinowitch-Kempner, *World Who's Who in Science,* p. 1387; also letter from Ms. Pauline Johnston, Associate Medical Librarian, the Medical College of Pennsylvania, dated Sept. 30, 1973.
67. Sources for Dr. Gerty Cori: *Some of the Men of Science at Washington University,* published by St. Louis *Post-Dispatch,* 1948; also the New York *Times* (Oct. 27), 86:6; *Current Biography* (1947).
68. *Some of the Men of Science.*
69. Sources for Dr. Maria Goeppert-Mayer: *Current Biography* (1964); *Newsweek* (Nov. 18, 1963); New York *Times* (Feb. 22, 1972), 40:4.
70. *Newsweek,* Nov. 18, 1963, p. 78.
71. Source for Dr. Suntzeff: Unpublished autobiography in possession of Dr. Suntzeff.
72. Source for Dr. Weiner: Ruth Weiner, "Chemist and 'Eco-

Freak' " *Annals of the New York Academy of Sciences,* vol. 208 (March 15, 1973), pp. 52–56.

Chapter Twelve

1. Giulio Gatti Casazza, manager of the Metropolitan Opera Company between 1908–1935, claimed that the salaries paid by the Metropolitan have often been considered lower than those paid by other institutions. Giulio Gatti Casazza, *Memories of the Opera* (New York, 1941), p. 303.

2. Marcia Davenport, *Too Strong for Fantasy* (New York, 1967). p. 208.

3. K. J. Kutsch and Leo Riemens, *A Concise Biographical Dictionary of Singers* (New York, 1962).

4. In 1910 Oscar Hammerstein, who built the Harlem Opera House and the Manhattan Opera House, was bought out by the Metropolitan Opera Company on the condition that he stop producing opera in the U. S.

5. Gatti Casazza.

6. Jenny Lind, clipping file, The Library of Performing Arts, Lincoln Center.

7. Ibid.

8. J. N. Burk, *Clara Schumann* (New York, 1940).

9. Lucy Poate Stebbins and Richard Poate Stebbins, *Frank Damrosch: Let the People Sing* (Durham, North Carolina, 1945), p. 288.

10. Irving Kolodin, *The Metropolitan Opera* (New York, 1930). p. 6.

11. K. J. Kutsch and Leo Riemens.

12. Kolodin, p. 17.

13. Ibid., p. 214.

14. Kutch and Riemens.

15. Kolodin, p. 212.

16. Marcia Davenport, p. 107.

17. Ibid., p. 107.

18. Clipping file, Library of Performing Arts, Lincoln Center.

19. Marcia Davenport, p. 107.

20. Clipping file, Library of the Performing Arts, Lincoln Center.

21. The source for Mme Sembrich is: An Outline of the Life and Career of Mme Marcella Sembrich, The Sembrich Memorial Association, Inc., 1940. Clipping file of the Performing Arts, Lincoln Center.

22. The source for Mme Schumann-Heink is Mary Lawton, *Ernestine Schumann-Heink, The Last of the Titans* (New York, 1928).

23. Mary Lawton.
24. Ibid.
25. Ibid.
26. Marcia Davenport, p. 255.
27. Ibid., p. 264.
28. Metropolitan Portraits, Lotte Lehmann clipping file, Library of the Performing Arts, Lincoln Center.
29. Ibid.
30. Galli-Curci clipping file, Library of the Performing Arts, Lincoln Center.
31. Clarence Edward La Massena, *Galli-Curci's Life of Song* (New York, 1945), p. 77.
32. David Ewen, *Men and Women Who Make Music* (New York, 1939), p. 45.
33. Clipping file, Library of the Performing Arts, Lincoln Center.
34. Maria Augusta Trapp and Ruth T. Murdoch, *A Family on Wheels* (Philadelphia, 1959), pp. 71, 75–77.

Chapter Thirteen

1. Walter Damrosch, *My Musical Life* (New York, 1926). Also Cecyle S. Neidle, *The New Americans* (1967), pp. 150–54.
2. Ibid.
3. Lucy & Richard Poate Stebbins, p. 211.
4. *Baker's Biographical Dictionary of Musicians* (New York, 1971).
5. David Mannes, *Music Is My Faith* (New York, 1938), p. 241.
6. Interview with Marya Mannes, Oct., 1973.
7. David Mannes, p. 241.
8. Richard Aldrich, *Concert Life in New York* (New York, 1941), p. 221.
9. Interview with Marya Mannes.
10. Ibid.
11. David Mannes, p. 267.
12. Marya Mannes, *Out of My Time* (New York, 1971), p. 162.
13. *The Mannes College of Music*, 1972–1974, p. 10.
14. *Notes from Mannes*, vol. 7, No. 1 (November, 1972).
15. Information on Mrs. Reisenberg was secured through interview, Dec. 1973.
16. This information was communicated to the author by an official of the Juilliard School of Music.
17. Catalog, Juilliard School, p. 14.
18. Interview with Suzanne Bloch, Dec., 1973.
19. Robert Jacobson, *Saturday Review*, March 28, 1970. Rosina

Lhevinne clipping files, Library of the Performing Arts, Lincoln Center, N. Y.

20. Ibid.

21. Ibid.

22. Winthrop Sergeant, *The New Yorker*, Jan. 12, 1963, p. 46. Rosina Lhevinne clipping file, Library of the Performing Arts, Lincoln Center, N. Y.

23. Told to the author by Suzanne Bloch.

24. Ibid.

25. Robert Jacobson, p. 57. Rosinna Lhevinne clipping file, Library of the performing arts, Lincoln Center, N. Y.

26. Donald Henahan, New York *Times* (1970). Rosina Lhevinne clipping file, Library of the Performing Arts, Lincoln Center, N. Y.

27. Harold C. Schonberg, New York *Times* (March 25, 1970). Rosina Lhevinne clipping file, Library of the Performing Arts, Lincoln Center, N. Y.

28. Interview with Mme Dorfman, Dec., 1973.

29. *Herald Tribune*, Nov. 2, 1957. Ania Dorfman clipping file, Library of the Performing Arts, Lincoln Center, N. Y.

30. Information suplied by an official of the Juilliard School of Music.

31. Miss Bloch's account is based on interview, Dec. 1973.

32. The facts about Miss Lachert have been ascertained through an interview in the spring of 1973.

Chapter Fourteen

1. *Notable American Women*, pp. 57–59, I.

2. Cecyle S. Neidle, *The New Americans* (New York, 1967).

3. *National Cyclopedia of American Biography*, vol. XXIV (1935), p. 149.

4. *To Doctor R, Essays Here Collected and Published in Honor of the 70th Birthday of Dr. A. S. W. Rosenbach*, July 22, 1946.

5. The term is used by Stoyan Christowe, author of the autobiography *This Is My Country* (Philadelphia, 1938). Also see Cecyle S. Neidle, *op. cit.*

6. Morris Rosenfeld, *Songs of Labor*, translated by Rose Pastor Stokes and Helen Frank (Boston, 1914).

7. Carlos Bulosan, *America Is in The Heart* (New York, 1943). Also Cecyle S. Neidle, *op. cit.*

8. Pascal d'Angelo, *Pascal d'Angelo, Son of Italy* (New York, 1924). Also C. S. Neidle, *op. cit.*

9. Ludwig Lewisohn, *Up-Stream* (New York, 1926); *Mid-Channel* (New York, 1929).

10. George Santayana, *Persons and Places* (New York, 1944); *The Middle Span* (New York, 1945).

11. Editorial Comment Mary Antin "They Who Knock at Our Gates," *The American Magazine*, May 10, 1914, p. 44.

12. Ibid., May 2, 1914, p. 65.

13. Ibid., p. 44.

14. Vicki Baum, *It Was All Quite Different* (New York, 1964), p. 290.

15. Ibid., p. 296.

16. New York *Times*, August 20, 1960, 29:1.

17. Cleveland *Plain-Dealer*, July 13, 1931.

18. Vicki Baum, p. 357. Clipping file, the Library of Performing Arts, Lincoln Center, N. Y.

19. New York *Times*, Nov. 26, 1963, 37:3.

20. Martha Ostenso, *Waters Under the Earth* (New York, 1930).

21. Anzia Yezierska, *Salome of the Tenements* (New York, 1923).

22. Anzia Yezierska, *Red Ribbon on a White Horse* (New York, 1950).

23. Anzia Yezierska, *Hungry Hearts* (New York, 1920), p. 41.

24. New York *Times*, Nov. 23, 1970, 40:2.

25. Ibid.

26. Anzia Yezierska, *Children of Loneliness* (New York, 1923), p. 12.

27. Ibid., p. 18.

28. Anzia Yezierska, *Red Ribbon on a White Horse*, p. 159.

Chapter Fifteen

1. Alice Morse Earle, *Colonial Days in Old New York* (New York, 1938), p. 156.

2. Ibid., pp. 158–60.

3. Patrick O'Higgins, *Madame* (New York, 1971).

4. *New York Times Biographical Edition*, Nov., 1972.

5. Ibid.

6. Ibid.

7. Harold Jaedeker Taub, *Waldorf in the Catskills* (New York, 1952).

8. Ibid.

9. Morris Friedman, "The Green Pastures of Grossinger's," *Commentary*, July, August, 1954.

10. Ibid.

11. Harold J. Taub, p. 207.
12. Patricia Murphy, *A Glow of Candlelight* (New York, 1961).
13. *Current Biography (1962)*, p. 314.
14. Ibid.
15. Patricia Murphy, *A Glow of Candlelight*.
16. *Current Biography (1962)*.
17. *A Glow of Candlelight*.
18. *Current Biography (1942)*.
19. *New Yorker* Profile, March 31, 1934.
20. Information secured through interview, Spring, 1974.
21. Interview.
22. Patrick O'Higgins, *Madame*.
23. Ibid., p. 45.
24. Ibid., p. 288.
25. Helena Rubinstein, *My Life for Beauty* (New York, 1965).
26. O'Higgins, p. 295.
27. Helena Rubinstein, *My Life for Beauty*.
28. *Current Biography (1943)*.
29. O'Higgins, p. 254.
30. Richard Gehman "Elizabeth Arden—The Woman," *Cosmopolitan*, June, 1956, p. 72.
31. *Current Biography (1957)*.
32. Hambla Bauer, "High Priestess of Beauty," *Saturday Evening Post*, April 24, 1948, p. 190.
33. *New Yorker* Profile, April 23, 1938, p. 24.
34. Interview.
35. *New Yorker*.
36. *Current Biography (1951)*.
37. Ibid.
38. Ibid.

Selected Bibliography

Blegen, Theodore C. *Norwegian Migration to America*. Northfield, Minn.: Norwegian-American Historical Association, 1955.

Bradford, William. *History of Plymouth Plantation*. New York: Charles Scribner's Sons, 1908.

Demos, John. *A Puritan Commonwealth*. New York: Oxford University Press, 1970.

Tocqueville, Alexis de. *Democracy in America*. New York: Henry J. Langley, 1845.

Morris, Richard B. *Encyclopedia of American History*. New York: Harper & Bros., 1953.

Handlin, Oscar. *The Uprooted*. Boston: Little, Brown & Co., 1951.

Herberg, Will. *Protestant, Catholic and Jew*. New York: Doubleday & Co., 1960.

Hudson, Winthrop S. *Religion in America*. New York: Charles Scribner's Sons, 1965.

Jones, Maldwyn Allen. *American Immigration*. Chicago: Chicago University Press, 1960.

Kraditor, Aileen S. *Up From the Pedestal*. Chicago: Quadrangle Books, 1968.

Mather, Cotton. *Magnalia Christi Americana*. Hartford, Conn.: Silus Andrus & Son, 1853.

Miller, Perry. *From Colony to Province*. Boston: Harvard University Press, 1953.

————. *The New England Mind: The Seventeenth Century*. New York: The Macmillan Co., 1937.

Morgan, Edmund S. *The Puritan Family*. Boston: The Trustees of the Public Library, 1944.

Morison, Samuel Eliot. *Builders of the Bay Colony*. Boston: Houghton Mifflin Co., 1930.

Parkes, Henry Bamford. *The American Experience*. New York: Alfred A. Knopf, 1947.

Parrington, Vernon. *Main Currents in American Thought*. New York: Harcourt, Brace & Co., 1930.

Rayback, Joseph G. *A History of American Labor*. New York: The Macmillan Co., 1959.

Solomon, Barbara Miller. *Ancestors and Immigrants.* Cambridge, Mass.: Harvard University Press, 1956.

Stein, Leon. *The Triangle Fire.* Philadelphia: J. Lippincott Company, 1962.

Trollope, Frances. *Domestic Manners of the Americans.* New York: Alfred A. Knopf, 1960.

Winthrop, John. *The History of New England.* Boston: Phelps & Farnham, 1825.

Wittke, Carl. *We Who Built America.* New York: Prentice-Hall, 1939.

Selected Biographical Sources

Casazza, Giulio Gatti. *Memories of the Opera.* New York: Charles Scribner's Sons, 1941.

Davenport, Marcia. *Too Strong for Fantasy.* New York: Charles Scribner's Sons, 1967.

Gold, Michael. *Jews Without Money.* New York: International Publishers, 1930.

Tharp, Louise Hall. *Adventurous Alliance.* Boston: Little, Brown & Co., 1959.

Kaplan, Justin. *Lincoln Steffens.* New York: Simon & Schuster, 1974.

Kolodin, Irving. *The Metropolitan Opera.* New York: Alfred A. Knopf, 1930.

Mason, Alpheus T. *Brandeis, A Free Man's Life.* New York: The Viking Press, 1946.

Ross, Ishbel. *Child of Destiny.* New York: Harper & Bros., 1949.

Sandoz, Mari. *Old Jules.* Boston: Little, Brown & Co., 1952.

Truax, Rhoda. *The Doctors Jacobi.* Boston: Little, Brown & Co., 1952.

Selected Memoirs

Adamic, Louis. *Laughing In The Jungle.* New York: Harper & Bros., 1932.

Antin, Mary. *The Promised Land.* Boston: Houghton, Mifflin Co., 1912.

Bok, Edward W. *The Americanization of Edward Bok.* New York: Charles Scribner's Sons., 1937.

Bulosan, Carlos. *America Is In the Heart.* New York: Harcourt, Brace & Co., 1946.

Cohen, Morris R. *A Dreamer's Journey.* New York: The Beacon Press, 1943.

Corsi, Edward. *In the Shadow of Liberty.* New York: The Macmillan Co., 1934.

Damrosch, Walter. *My Musical Life*. New York: Charles Scribner's Sons, 1923.

Goldman, Emma. *Living My Life*. New York: Alfred A. Knopf, 1931.

Gompers, Samuel. *Seventy Years of Life and Labor*. New York: R. P. Dutton & Co., 1925.

Hillquit, Morris. *Loose Leaves From A Busy Life*. New York: The Macmillan Co., 1934.

Jones, Mary. *The Autobiography of Mother Jones*. New York: reprinted by Arno Press, 1969.

Pupin, Michael. *From Immigrant to Inventor*. New York: Charles Scribner's Sons, 1922.

Steiner, Edward. *From Alien to Citizen*. New York: Fleming H. Revell, 1914.

Yezierska, Anzia. *Red Ribbon on a White Horse*. New York: Charles Scribner's Sons, 1950.

Index